More Parties or No Parties

More Parties or No Parties

The Politics of Electoral Reform in America

JACK SANTUCCI

OXFORD
UNIVERSITY PRESS

OXFORD
UNIVERSITY PRESS

Oxford University Press is a department of the University of Oxford. It furthers the University's objective of excellence in research, scholarship, and education by publishing worldwide. Oxford is a registered trade mark of Oxford University Press in the UK and certain other countries.

Published in the United States of America by Oxford University Press 198 Madison Avenue, New York, NY 10016, United States of America.

Library of Congress Cataloging-in-Publication Data
Names: Santucci, Jack, author.
Title: More parties or no parties : the politics of electoral reform in America / Jack Santucci.
Description: New York : Oxford University Press, 2022. | Includes bibliographical references and index.
Identifiers: LCCN 2022002582 (print) | LCCN 2022002583 (ebook) | ISBN 9780197630655 (hardback) | ISBN 9780197630679 (epub) | ISBN 9780197630662 (ebook)
Subjects: LCSH: Elections—United Statess. | Political parties—United States. | Two-party systems—United States.
Classification: LCC JK1976 .S26 2022 (print) | LCC JK1976 (ebook) | DDC 324.973—dc23/eng/20220427
LC record available at https://lccn.loc.gov/2022002582
LC ebook record available at https://lccn.loc.gov/2022002583

1 3 5 7 9 8 6 4 2

Printed by Integrated Books International, United States of America

Contents

List of Figures

List of Tables

Acknowledgments

This book began as an effort to learn "what happened" to proportional representation (PR) in American cities. Most of it was written from 2019 into 2020, alongside the ongoing pandemic. Special thanks for friendship and patience to Mike Latner, Matthew Shugart, Pedro Hernandez, Dave O'Brien, Jody Schroeder, Brett Connors, Will Dunkelberger, and Judith Todd.

The story might start with Juliet Johnson, who turned me onto academia and what was then the Center for Voting and Democracy. "Work for a year in politics," she said. "Then go to the best school you can get into." Several people mattered between that conversation and the start of my doctoral education. Rob Richie and Cynthia Terrell gave me substantive work in my first year out of college. Matthew Shugart's blog provided my early education on electoral systems, and Barak Hoffman kept it going. Steve Heydemann taught me the value of comparative-historical research. Two years in charge of IFES's ElectionGuide.org kept me in touch with electoral systems.

Much later, after I had started the dissertation, Doug Amy and Dennis Pilon shared whatever they had on the North American PR movement. Doug handed over the contents of Leon Weaver's file drawers. Dennis provided digital copy of the *Proportional Representation Review*, up to its 1932 absorption by the *National Municipal Review*. Much of this had not yet been digitized. Much of it still is not.

Each member of my committee left their mark. Hans Noel pressed that politics is, for many, about control of government. Dan Hopkins urged me to study the adoptions as well as the repeals. Kent Weaver once remarked that the reforms straddled a realignment. Josep Colomer frequently noted the role of prior multipartism. Eusebio Mujal-Leon saw reason for me to be at Georgetown in the first place.

Moving to Philadelphia crystallized my "shifting coalitions" perspective. Marcus Kreuzer introduced me to the best new work on electoral-system choice, especially that of André Walter and Patrick Emmenegger. Jack Nagel and I discussed New Zealand, the state of the modern movement, and "empirical social choice." Thanks to Richard Dilworth, Amelia Hoover-Green, and Joel Oestreich for bringing me to Drexel.

Several scholars provided data: Jessica Trounstine, André Blais, Rick Feiock, and Indridi Indridason. Not all of it appears here, but all of it shaped my thinking in some way.

Numerous people were helpful in sleuthing local-level records: Robyn Conroy, Howie Fain, Joy Henig, A. J. Pottle, David Rushford, Niko Vangjeli, (Worcester); Tim De Carlo (Waterbury); Carolyn Ford, Paulette Leeper, and Amy Searcy (Cincinnati); David MacRae and Lucia Shannon (Brockton); and Douglas Di Carlo (New York City).

Thanks go to several research assistants: Hunter Books, Benjamin Balough, Alexis Campbell, Suzanne Trivette, and Charles Wathieu (all Georgetown). Jasmine Underwood (Wright State University) photographed the Cincinnati records I could not get myself. Andrew Rosenthal's (Drexel) ongoing work has been crucial to understanding the role of majority-preferential systems.

Institutional support mattered. Georgetown University's Massive Data Institute paid for archival work in New York City and Worcester. On my second trip to Worcester, Daniel Klinghard, Father John Savard, and Pat Christensen arranged for a room in the Jesuit Community at Holy Cross.

Many institutions house the records that became facts and figures: the Hamilton County (OH) Board of Elections, Cincinnati History Museum, Silas Bronson Library (Waterbury), Worcester Historical Museum, Worcester Public Library, Worcester City Hall, Brockton Public Library, New York City Municipal Library, La Guardia and Wagner Archives at La Guardia Community College, New York Public Library, Los Angeles City Archives and Records Center, the Sterling Library at Yale University, and Robert Winters' digital collection on the single transferable vote in Cambridge (MA).

I was fortunate to check my story with people who either lived the politics or knew others who did: Bill Collins and Bill Gradison (Cincinnati); then John Anderson, Paul V. Mullaney, Al Southwick, and Joseph Zimmerman (Worcester).

Deep thanks to those who read the manuscript as it neared completion: Eitan Hersh, Jack Nagel, Ben Reilly, Henry Schlechta, and two anonymous reviewers.

Others gave feedback on early versions of chapters: Laura Bucci, Todd Donovan, Lee Drutman, Howie Fain, David Fortunato, Kevin Johnson, John Polga, and Steven White.

For thorough conversations as the argument developed, thanks to: Malcolm Baalman, Mike Bailey, Dan Bowen, David Farrell, Jacey Fortin, Erica Frazier, Alex Garlick, Matt Grossmann, Nat Herz, Chris Hughes, Alex Keena, Sarah John, Jon Ladd, Theo Landsman, Michael Maley, Jason Maloy, Jason McDaniel, Anthony McGann, Ben Raue, Charles A. "Tony" Smith, Daniel M. Smith, Michele Swers, Steven Taylor, and Colin Woodard.

Thanks also to the team at Oxford University Press, especially: Angela Chnapko, Alexcee Bechtold, and Gayathri Venkatesan.

The road has been long. Thank you, Sandra and John Santucci, Nick Santucci, Hilary Espinosa, and Mike Lavorgna.

Any errors are mine.

Preface

This book is for the next generation of electoral reformers. It aims to accomplish three things.

First, it argues that we should think about reform in terms of what it means for control of government. To this end, the book develops a "shifting coalitions" theory of electoral-system change, validates it against non-U.S. reform episodes, and uses the theory to structure a story. This story covers the rise, evolution, and failure of a movement to adopt proportional representation (PR) in the United States.

There are other ways to think about electoral reform: in terms of "voter choice" or "fair representation," for example. The former perspective is now on display in the movement for "ranked-choice voting." Hence public debate does not reflect crucial nuance: that "ranked-choice voting" can refer to a range of systems, each with different effects on representation. But even if we choose the most permissive of them—the single transferable vote—other details become crucial. What if those details make it hard to govern?

The book's second goal is to highlight pitfalls, and this is where the story comes in. It runs from 1893 into the early 1960s, showing how reform worked in practice. Several features of the old and new movements are similar: absence of pre-existing multiparty politics, temptation to compromise with anti-party reformers, and strategic silence on who will govern (so that reform can get passed).

Third, I want to suggest that the *reform coalition* may be more important than the reform itself. We dance, the saying goes, with those who bring us to the party. I argue below that those who bring us to the party define the range of possible reforms. As I write this, there is a fight over access to voting, period, which will define the range of possible reform coalitions. Already, some on either side of this fight have set it aside to proceed with election reform.

My point is not to beat on reformers. Many opinion leaders, including some political scientists, insist that reform must come before multiparty politics. This makes people apt to support anything "goes against" the two-party system. But some reforms may be better than others, and some may be worse than none at all. One bad reform is the "plurality-at-large" system, widely promoted by the old PR lobby, and now a target of voting-rights litigation. In our own time, we see a range of reforms designed to "get parties out of politics." Commentators wanting to avoid such devices may need to make peace with the idea of "more parties."

Overall, I hope this book helps people learn from last century's mistakes. In putting it together, I have tried to look at the issue from two overarching perspectives: that of the reformers, and that of those who had to govern. Some of these people were the same.

The language will be technical at times, but not more than is needed to grasp key issues at play. Changing how we choose is serious business. Overall, if we must have reform, we should build it to accommodate parties. History suggests they will emerge anyway.

December 28, 2021.

1

Forcing Reform onto a Two-Party System

The solution isn't more parties. Every party, regardless of size, searches for power. The solution is walking away from parties, expanding Ranked Choice Voting, hopefully leading to more independent legislators. The change starts when no party has majority in house or senate [sic]

Mark Cuban on Twitter, October 30, 2020[1]

We hear a lot these days about dismantling systems. Familiar ones deal with race relations and the distribution of wealth. Others are said to ship jobs overseas and erode the national character (e.g., globalization). Another target is the *electoral system*, broadly defined as rules about voting and turning those votes into winners.

Under normal circumstances, electoral systems are a niche topic.[2] But recent surveys show that up to half of Americans are open to a having new one (McCarthy and Santucci 2020). It is not hard to see why. Twice in this century has a person become president with fewer votes than their main opponent. Demand for "a third party" is at a twenty-year high (Drutman et al. 2018), and so is the share of self-identified independents. Party primaries have become crowded even though they are "winner-take-all."[3] Finally, the presidency of Donald J. Trump (R) has left important players feeling homeless in politics.

The thing about dismantling electoral systems is that they need to be replaced. This involves decisions about three components and, crucially in the United States, two auxiliary issues. First is district magnitude, otherwise known as the number of seats per district. Second is ballot type, or what

---

[1] https://twitter.com/mcuban/status/1319287043311063041.

[2] I thank John Polga for reminding me that this less true outside the United States.

[3] "Winner-take-all" is a reformer way of describing status quo elections. Typically, it refers to a system in which *one slate is likely to win every seat*, but its definition can change over time. For example, a recent report by the American Academy of Arts and Sciences described single-seat ranked voting as non-winner-take-all. Earlier writing in reform circles would have called this system winner-take-all (Cossolotto 1993).

More Parties or No Parties: The Politics of Electoral Reform in America. Jack Santucci, Oxford University Press.

appears on a ballot and how voters express choices. Third is allocation rule or what we do with votes to decide who gets seats (Rae 1967). The auxiliary issues concern assembly size and whether parties will structure nominations. Who will design the electoral system? Whose ox will get gored?

What follows will be technical, and that is by design. As I write this, there is confusion about "ranked choice voting" (RCV). Broadly, this means ranking candidates in order of preference. But RCV can refer to many electoral systems, each with different implications for representation. One version, the single transferable vote (STV), might bring more parties into legislatures. Its single-seat version, the Alternative Vote (AV), tends to keep them out. It is common to differentiate these by district magnitude, i.e., "single-winner RCV" and "multi-winner RCV." But a third RCV uses multi-seat districts with a majoritarian formula. This "block-preferential" system is explicitly designed to minimize minority representation. All of these will be explained in due course, as well as the role of assembly size. For now, note how much detail is swept under the rug.

Further, STV is one of many types of *proportional representation* (PR), now crowded out by the term "ranked choice voting." Broadly, PR refers to a class of electoral systems that make parties' seat shares more *proportional* to their vote shares. PR carries potential to "slay" the gerrymander, undo the urban geographic disadvantage, and give more votes equal weight overall.[4] I do not want to be too hard on STV. The *Fair Representation Act*, which is based on STV, may be our best hope for more democratic congressional elections. Yet STV comes with challenges that do not exist in other systems, namely PR based on party lists. One is that a vote can leave some party (or coalition) then help the opposition get elected. Another is that candidates from one side of the aisle can owe their seats to voters on the other.

Another crucial question—who nominates what?—cuts to the heart of what happens in legislatures. Many RCV proposals would not let parties choose their own nominees, simply because non-partisanship already is law. These include the variants noted above, each used in cities around the United States. Recently, however, one part of the reform community has sought to combine AV with "open primaries," properly understood as

---

[4] On the democratic character of PR elections, see Blais et al. (2005: 182): "During this period of democratization the idea that each individual should have one vote and each vote should count the same gained enormous ground. From that perspective democracy and PR appeared to dovetail perfectly." For formal treatment, see Hout and McGann (2009) and Li (2019). On gerrymandering and geography, see McGann et al. (2016) and Rodden (2019).

non-partisan two-round systems.[5] Such proposals would not remove party labels from ballots, but they would prevent a party from advancing *one slate* to the decisive round of an election. In other words, they aim to pit co-partisans against each other *within the legislative delegation.* So far, reformers in the "more parties" camp have tended to go along with this. So have some proponents of minority representation, with an eye to easing transitions to STV. Such is the price, in a two-party system, of reforms to break up the duopoly. Reformers must appeal not to parties as entities, but to disaffected factions of the major parties. But if we agree that parties organize legislatures—or that majorities should be stable between elections—we need to think about how reform affects *control of government.* Otherwise, *reform may not outlast the coalition that imposes it.*

Then, unrelated to any specific electoral system, is whether it matters where reform originates. If we care about policy, it may. Say that we have problems with an incumbent government.[6] Say we think some new rule— call it Elephant Voting—is a way to change that government, either in part or in its entirety. Why would that government ever agree to such a change? One answer is that reform will not threaten its power, or that it needs reform to stay in power. And, if we cannot get reform from an incumbent government, we have to build a coalition to get around that government. How much compromise is acceptable? On what reform details? And on what issues?

Finally, why has reform gotten so much attention in so short a period of time? Just a few years ago, not many cared: a small nonprofit in Maryland, another in California, the Green and Libertarian parties, and a handful of voting-rights activists. Now, David Brooks (2018) calls STV "one reform to save America," the *New York Times* (2018) says we should use it to elect the U.S. House, and newer donors have backed AV instead. How might we think about what some have called this "new era of political reform" (Diamond 2018)?

This book explores reform politics by way of two devices. One is a theory of reform in general, based on the idea of "shifting coalitions." The players are politicians and allied interest groups, motivated to get or keep control of government. Reform can be *coalition-insulating, coalition-realigning,* or

---

[5] All candidates, regardless of party affiliation, compete in the first round. Then some number advance to round two, where AV is used to pick the winner. Open primaries are not this. With open primaries, each party still has one nominee (or slate), but any voter can participate in its selection.

[6] I am careful here to say *incumbent government,* as some incumbents may have objections to the government that has formed.

polarizing. What differentiates these modes is where reform originates. Reform episodes in other countries have tended to be *insulating*, i.e., brought about by incumbent governments facing competitive threats. A smaller set have been *realigning*: out-of-power groups peeling off some portion of a ruling coalition. Finally, in a *polarizing* mode, opposing sides of the aisle force a "middle" to pick sides. The theory suggests why reform happens at all (coalitions are shifting), illuminates why reforms take the shape that they do (they reflect the interests of the groups that strike the deals), and shows what it might take to make a government reform itself (social-movement insurgency). A typical story at the national level involves new-party entry *in advance* (Colomer 2005), but other paths are conceivable.

The second device is a history of Americans' last big push for electoral-system reform. It centers on STV in twenty-four municipalities (Fig. 1.1): its adoption, operation, and repeal in all but one case.[7] But this is not an urban politics story. Reformers were using cities as demonstration sites because they could not win PR at higher levels. Further, reformers were promoting STV in the first place because crucial allies opposed parties *in general*. Among them were proponents of majoritarian ranked-ballot systems, adopted in at least sixty-one places from 1907–25.[8] Working with this group helped get STV passed, but the reforms were not stable, and reformers found they needed parties after all.

Several ghosts of the old movement still shape American politics: party-free ballots, small city councils, at-large elections under "winner-take-all" rules, and winners who often come from a "good government" slate. Many appeared in cities that never tried STV, and they came to be seen as voter-suppression devices.[9] I will not say much about these "unintended"

---

[7] Not included are the single-tax colonies of Arden (DE) and Halidon (ME). Arden, now a village under Maryland state law, has used STV since 1912 to elect its Board of Assessors. See the *Proportional Representation Review* for October 1915, p. 2. Thanks go to Drew Penrose for discovering this continued use. In Halidon, STV was in effect for village council elections as of 1911. See the *Proportional Representation Review*, in the *Equity Series*, for October 1911, p. 193. STV also was used for New York City school board elections, 1970–2002. See http://archive.fairvote.org/library/geog/cities/ny_school_board.htm.

[8] See Weeks (1937) on eleven states' use in primaries, then Kneier (1957: 444) on at least fifty-five more cities. These cases are addressed in Chapter 3. Maloy (2019) makes a strong argument for the expressive voting that such systems enable.

[9] On voter suppression and the "good government" slate, see Bridges (1997). On at-large elections to small city councils, the best introduction is Bridges and Kronick (1999). On non-partisan ballots, see Schaffner et al. (2001). For a unified view of effects on voter turnout, see Hajnal (2009).

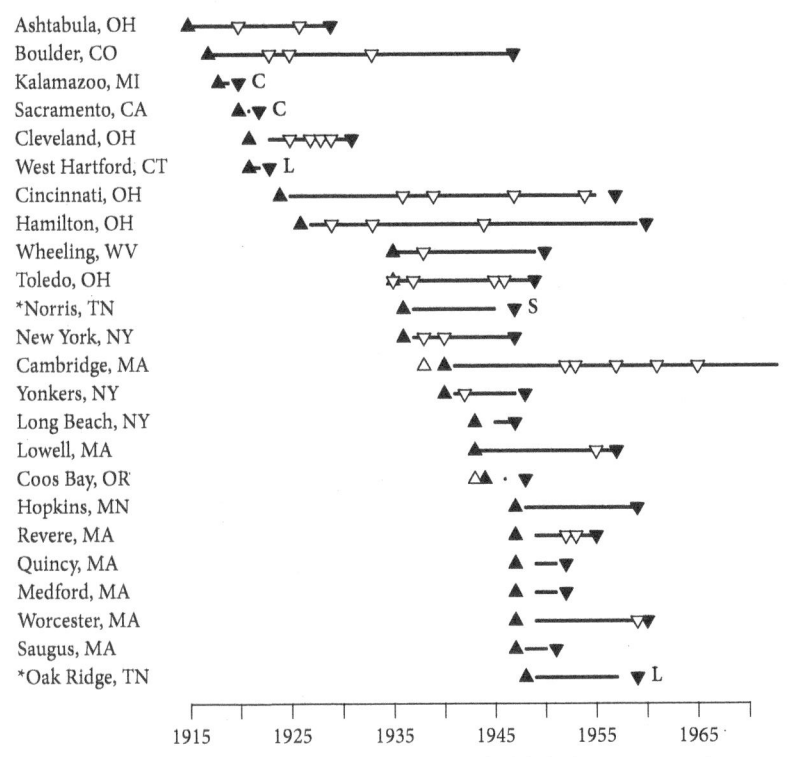

Filled triangle: adopted or repealed. Empty triangle: failed adoption or repeal.
Non-referendum repeal: court (C), state legislature (L), sale by U.S. Congress (S).
*Federally administered with advisory council.

Fig. 1.1 Spells with the single transferable vote in U.S. cities.

consequences, but readers should know that the old movement helped spread them.[10]

When we put these devices together—a general theory of reform, then American reform history—we get a clearer picture of reform in our own time. As long as there are only two serious parties, reform must cater to factions of those parties. These factions will be tempted to design reforms that do not acknowledge party organization. This is because the reform project itself goes against the overarching party system. The point is to

[10] Walter J. Millard, a key field operative, widely promoted charter reform in general, despite primary commitment to proportional representation. This was a concession to the National Municipal League, which absorbed the PR lobby in 1932. See Hallett and Woodward (1949) on his participation, then Millard (1943) for a sense of growing cynicism.

disrupt it, not to channel already-existing multiparty competition. In the short run, reformers will need some way to organize government. In the long run, *reform may not outlast the reform coalition*. Exceptions in this book prove the rule: where reform coalitions learned to ration nominations, or where fleeting new parties rallied to reform's defense. The choice between two and no parties is false. The real choice is between two and more parties.

Second, reform becomes likely where realignment is felt. By reform, I mean change of the electoral system—adoption, repeal, or to something else entirely. By realignment, I mean change in policies that opposing sides stand for, as well as the sorts of voters who tend to support either side. (I mean "side," not party, as multiparty systems also have "sides.") Without such shifting coalitions, incumbents have little reason to change the rules through which they won,[11] and out-of-power groups cannot get the votes for reform. Not all realignments bring electoral reform—there need to be reformers as well—but many reform episodes implicate realignment. Both involve decisions about ruling coalitions.[12]

1.1 On party lists and "vote leakage"

STV advocates target two constituencies. One is the fan of party proportionality. This person wants a party with, say, 10 percent of votes to get 10 percent of seats in a legislature. Or they want the party with a majority of votes to get a majority of seats. The other sort of person wants weak partisanship, e.g., for candidates to seek votes from both sides of the aisle. These goals are fundamentally in tension. A review of STV around the world—and of PR more generally—shows that the second sort usually loses out. For now, STV has the following properties:

1. Voters rank candidates in order of preference.
2. A quota is calculated, otherwise fixed in advance. The Droop quota is most common: $[V/M + 1] + 1$, where V means total valid votes cast, and M means district magnitude. Where $M = 1$, the quota is a majority, and STV becomes the Alternative Vote.

---

[11] Unless it is to shrink or grow the pool of eligible voters (T. Schwartz 1989: 14–15).

[12] I am not saying that every alternation-in-power implies a realignment has happened. However, over long periods of time, it is possible to point to "natural governing parties," both in comparative and American politics.

3. First preferences are tallied. Candidates with quotas win seats.

4. Votes in excess of a quota are *surplus*. Surplus ballots transfer to the next-ranked candidate on each. Which ballots are deemed surplus? A subset can be drawn at random, or every ballot can transfer at a fraction of its value.[13]

5. If no candidate has a quota, the last-placed candidate is *eliminated*, and ballots for that person flow to the next-ranked picks on each.

6. Seat allocation iterates between elimination and surplus transfer, until all seats in the district are awarded.[14]

In every other PR form, votes are counted at the level of the party, and seats are allocated to parties in proportion to their vote shares. Winners are drawn from *party lists* such that, e.g., if a party gets ten seats, the first ten people on its list win office. Voters may be asked to choose among parties (closed list), among the candidates of a preferred party (open list), or among the candidates of multiple parties (free list). If voters choose among candidates, these choices set the order of a party's list.[15]

Therefore, elections in list systems are fundamentally contests among parties. There may be contests within parties over list position, and there may be efforts to form cross-party alliances (e.g., under free list, or where parties have joined lists). Under no circumstances, however, can a vote pass between parties in a list system.

The seemingly technical issue of transfers has profound implications. It means that deputies from one party can owe their seats to voters whose loyalties lie with different parties. Further, if politics means choosing sides, transfers can be seen as having reversed the result of an election. If the winning side trails in terms of first-choice votes, this can be due to transfers coming from the other side. The problem is known as "vote leakage."

---

[13] Among the cities studied here, there were two main transfer methods. One, the "random" Cincinnati method, involved drawing every *Nth* ballot from a winner's pile. This is still used in Cambridge. A second, known as the Boulder method, was a "fractional" rule. This had three general steps. First, determine what *proportion* (p) of the winner's votes are surplus. Second, consult next choices on *all* the ballots in the winner's pile, noting each candidate's *next-choice total* (t). Third, add to each of these candidates' existing totals the following number, so long as a candidate has not been eliminated: $p \times t$. See Binstock (1960: II-7) for further detail.

[14] Most transfer rules do not permit votes to flow though elected candidates. Meek STV is an exception.

[15] "Flexible" lists are another option. With these, parties set the orders of their lists, and votes for candidates must exceed some threshold to change those orderings.

Parties in other STV countries have found ways to control transfers. In Malta, since 1987, the law has been that a party with a majority of first-preference votes automatically gets a seat majority. Since 1996, this has been applied to the party with a plurality of such votes (Hirczy de Miño and Lane 2000: 186), such that it is a "majority bonus" rule. Australia regularly updates rules that shape voter behavior: requiring voters to rank all candidates (until recently), making it easy to ratify a party's rank-ordering (since 1984), and, since the very beginning, grouping co-partisans on the ballot. Further, when a voter ratifies some party's rank-ordering, that ordering may reflect an *interparty coalition deal* (Farrell et al. 1996: 31; Reilly and Maley 2000: 47; Sharman et al. 2002). In Ireland, as far as we can tell, constituent service and party identification hold down split-ticket voting (Marsh 2000: 114).[16] More recently, in Scotland, the national government has imposed STV for local-council elections. To varying degrees, the national party system replicates in these races, with four main competitors: Conservative, Labour, the Liberal Democrats, and the Scottish National Party. These parties have tended to keep transfers within their slates, or at least within ideological blocs (Clark 2020: 11–13). In none of these countries has STV incurred majority opposition, at least so far.[17]

Contrast the "stable" cases with the United States and Canada, where twenty more cities also used STV (Johnston and Koene 2000). In both countries, reformers promoted a Model City Charter built on the idea of "nonpartisanship." The ballot itself did not induce party-line voting. Candidates appeared in alphabetical or random order, and there were no party designations (except in New York City). Further, there was no control of ballot access. Such systems are known as "open-endorsement" STV, notorious for letting candidates campaign against their own parties (Carey and Shugart 1995: 425; Renwick and Pilet 2016: 20). A candidate who campaigns against their own party will have to find transfers elsewhere.

The experience of Cambridge (MA), as we will see later, illustrates the need for strategies known as "vote management." STV has survived there since 1941, and it has not seen a repeal effort since the 1960s, when the local slating organization began to limit nominations. In turn, its leakage

---

[16] Further, Irish ballots have included party labels since 1965 (Farrell et al. 1996: 26). Ireland also generates the literature on "vote leakage" (Gallagher 1978), reflecting the relative "purity" of its STV rules.

[17] In Northern Ireland, where transfer patterns have been fluid (Mitchell 2014), government formation is automatic and by proportional representation, based on parties' shares of legislative seats. This ensures that the two largest parties share power (McGarry and O'Leary 2006: 61–62).

rate fell precipitously. This innovation, covered in Chapter 7, obviously can be imitated elsewhere. However, it is telling that this emerged so late, after all but one other city had repealed STV.[18]

Finally, it is worth noting that, in all other countries, the parties contesting STV elections have mass bases in the electorate. Ireland and Scotland suggest this may be sufficient for keeping transfers within a party (or coalition of parties). Neither has developed the sorts of formal modifications present in Australia and Malta. In the United States, by contrast, STV was built to defy the party system.

1.2 A shifting-coalitions theory of reform

Why do electoral systems change at all? Why does change tend to come in waves? And why do reform packages have this or that "fine print"?

Shifting-coalitions theory builds on insights from two fields. In comparative politics, the past three decades have brought numerous studies of electoral reform. Meanwhile, scholars of American politics have been building a policy-centered theory of coalition management and change. It seems like reform could be another tool for shaping coalitions—making them, breaking them, holding them together.

The tenets of Americanist coalition theory might be as follows. Political parties are internally diverse, formed because governing takes a majority at least. Each party coalition has divisions, which can be managed by "splitting the difference" or avoiding issues entirely. And voters have little control of this process, tending to vote their party identifications. Who controls each coalition? The current answer is: influential figures who coordinate with either party. This leadership can be cast as a network of interest groups, donors, journalists, "insider" politicians, and so on. And divisions that these leaders cannot manage may lead to party realignment: change in how the parties present themselves to voters, as well as the sorts of groups who tend to support either party.[19]

---

[18] That city was Hamilton (OH), repealed 1961, in the same year that the Cambridge Civic Association first seems to have limited the size of its slate. Again, this is covered more fully in Chapter 7.

[19] For a general statement of this theory, see Bawn et al. (2012). On logrolling and agenda control, see Tullock (1970), T. Schwartz (1989), Aldrich (1995), and Cox and McCubbins (2005). On control of the party, see Cohen et al. (2008), Koger et al. (2010), Dominguez (2011), and Hassell (2017). On control of subnational parties, see Masket and Shor (2014). For a cautionary note about elite

Common themes become apparent when one reads comparative literature on electoral reform. According to a review by Benoit (2004), for example, "electoral laws will change when a coalition of parties exists such that each party in the coalition expects to gain more seats under an alternative electoral institution, and that also has sufficient power to effect this alternative." And Riker (1980) once cast institutions as "congealed tastes," subject to the same instability as the majority itself.

If we take a global view, we see that electoral reform is common in periods of party-system instability. Such periods in America have been the years before the Civil War, the Progressive Era, the Civil Rights realignment, and whatever we now seem to be entering. The corresponding reforms have been single-seat districts for U.S. House elections, primaries and other mechanisms to increase choice among candidates (such as the subject of this book), single-seat districts again in the Civil Rights period, and the current wave of interest in more candidate-choice reforms.[20]

The U.S. periods line up roughly with those in Western Europe. These include the emergence of mass parties in the middle of the nineteenth century, the rise of socialist parties around the turn of the twentieth century, the need to contain Communism during the Cold War, and conflict over neoliberalism from about 1980 to present. And the corresponding reforms were: invention of and experimentation with various new electoral rules (including STV), the decision to adopt PR or not, PR modifications that restrict new-party entry (including the rare wholesale repeal), then another wave of the same with efforts to increase choice among candidates.[21]

endorsements, see Kousser et al. (2015). On the parties internal divisions and whether the Democrats manifest more of them, see Grossmann and Hopkins (2016). On the rigidity of party identification, see Green et al. (2002). On realignment, especially see Karol (2009).

[20] On prohibition of multi-seat districts for U.S. House elections, see Calabrese (2000, 2006), E. J. Engstrom (2004), Tamas (2006), and Ahmed (2012). Also in this period, Thomas Gilpin (1844) of Philadelphia gave the first known description of list PR. Gilpin was concerned with two forms of instability: pivotal third parties and, like the Whigs, the potential for small vote shifts to have massive seat-share consequences. His paper is reprinted in James (1896). On single-seat districts and equal apportionment in national and state elections, see Cox and Katz (2002). On primary and ranked-ballot reforms in both periods, see Richie (2004), Masket (2009), and McGhee and Shor (2017).

[21] On the role of globally felt realignments in electoral reform, see Pilon (2013). On invention of new electoral rules, see Colomer (2007, 2017). On working-class repression and accommodation, see Ahmed (2012). On subsequent modifications of PR, see Bol et al. (2015) and Renwick and Pilet (2016). Notably, the latter argue that candidate-centered reforms have not affected satisfaction with democracy. This is likely because those reforms have been establishment-led (i.e., *insulating*), mainly to manage voters' rejection of establishment parties. For theories of how party-system instability might lead to pressure for reform, see Nagel (1998) and Shugart (2003). Nagel's case study suggests that reform supporters effectively flirt with the idea of a new coalition structure, then that reform's passage reflects completion of the process. For Shugart, the mechanism is a widely

Finally, comparative and American reform episodes may have more in common than we previously thought. For example, Renwick (2010) shows that: (1) reform can split parties internally, (2) formally non-party actors often get involved, (3) reform is not always controlled by those who control government, (4) mass-level attitudes can matter, and (5) reformers often imitate each other rather than consider every possible electoral system. Many of these points can be found in a recent study of reform initiatives in American states (Masket 2016). Similarly, Bowler and Donovan (2013: 11–12) see reform "as a constant process," repeatedly splitting the same city into opposing coalitions of voters and interest groups.

The theory in this book aims to integrate the above insights. Policy seems to matter, and reform can pit co-partisans against each other. Change can come from "above" or "below," in decision-making processes that are boundedly rational. And discontent with an as-is party system seems like a good place to start in building a theory of reform—one that sees adoption *and replacement* as equally interesting phenomena.

1.2.1 Ideas matter

Above, I noted the role of imitation in reform-bargaining processes. Another term I used was "bounded rationality." What exactly binds the thinking of otherwise rational actors?

One possible answer is: the zeitgeist. It seems to have been unthinkable, in Progressive Era reform circles, to base reform proposals on the idea of "party." The idea gave way, as I note in Chapter 3, to a search for ways of eliciting the "will of the people."[22]

Emphasis on technical solutions chilled scholarship and cast the voter as a problem. Early on, the socialist Carl Thompson (1913: 421) found it "astonishing... that our whole host of municipal reformers... have been swept off their feet with the so called non-partisan idea." Within a few years, however, critical assessments were toned down. The first empirical

---

unexpected election outcome, given the electoral rules in place. On the substance of party-system change in comparative politics, see Stoll (2013) on fragmentation and Dalton (2018) on the familiar economics/culture dichotomy.

[22] One might say there was a durable shift in the terms of social control, paving the way for two or three generations of reform activity. See Orren and Skowronek (2004: 124–31) on the significance of such shifts. Also see T. P. R. Weaver (2021) on the interplay of ideas and interests in political development.

study of STV, by political scientist Arnold Lien (1925: 265), referred to ballot invalidity as a "purely mechanical" problem. This was in an early piece *recommending party lists instead*: "much more in accord with our voting habits and consequently much more acceptable and intelligible to the voters." Another study of invalid ballots did not even name alternatives. "The method of voting contemplated under proportional representation," wrote political scientist Rodney Mott (1926: 874), "*requires that the voters be converted* from their traditional habits of expressing preferences by cross marks... [emphasis mine]." Harold Gosnell (1930: 471) handled the new culture playfully: "Assuming that the voters of a given characteristic, such as affiliation with a party, tend to choose candidates of that party...." Even in 1949, at least one parties expert denied the existence of a party "system" (Wickham-Jones 2018: 66).

My "shifting coalitions" theory is very much interest-based. It does a good job at accounting for behavior, particularly in cities that reformed after the mid-1920s.

Yet I want to acknowledge the role that ideas may have played—in setting reform up to "win" at all, limiting the options, and, once the zeitgeist changed again, helping to discredit the entire project.[23] Today, the hunt for an algorithm is back on: ranking candidates, approving of them, scoring them, and so on. This may come with a tendency to ask too much of voters.[24]

1.2.2 How the number of parties matters

We typically think of electoral systems as "shaping" or "constraining" the number of parties. This view is often attributed to Maurice Duverger (1954). But Duverger himself acknowledged the potential for reverse causation.

This book covers what can happen when people try to reform their way out of a two-party system. The already-existing number of parties leaves its mark on the reform. It may even shape ideas about what reforms seem "winnable." Multiparty systems rarely produce movements for non-partisan elections.[25]

As for governing, the number of parties may be less important than whether coalitions have the tools to hold themselves together. This book,

---

[23] See Millard (1943) for a trace of the second change in thinking.
[24] Consider recent research on ranked-choice voting, which has cast the preference for single-mark ballots as an example of status quo bias (Blais et al. 2021).
[25] See Noel (2013) on how party systems might give structure to ideas.

I hope, invites us to ask whether a system of three or more disciplined parties is better, worse, or not really different from weakly structured factionalism.

1.3 Comparing the American reform path

One constant reality of the American reform movement was its effort to "win" PR in the midst of a two-party system. This colored many aspects of its work: twenty-two years without traction, the turn to city government, experimentation with non-partisan reforms, an ironic need to create parties, and the overall failure to "retrofit" STV as described above.

A simple model of PR adoption might run as follows. Voting experts organize reform societies. In public, they say PR is fairer than the existing electoral rules. In private, they broker reform deals, seizing on fissures in the party system. These conversations have five topics: assembly size, district magnitude, ballot structure, allocation rule, and nominations. If reformers have done their work well, and if fissures run deep, the bargain gets majority support.[26]

1.3.1 American exceptionalism shapes the movement

In other countries, reformers could exploit the rise of socialist parties.[27] The causes of electoral reform are widely debated, but there are two glaring differences between the U.S. and other wealthy democracies. One is the failure to have spawned a mass-based party of the left (Archer 2010). The closest we ever came were the years around 1912. In that presidential election, the Socialist Party polled its largest-ever share of votes. Far more numerous were the Progressives, a collection of reformers with divergent views on race, gender, public morality, and government's role in the economy (Barber 1995c: 38–39; McConnaughy 2013: 170–206; Leonard 2016).[28] The other big

---

[26] This is essentially a "policy window" model. For a general statement, see Kingdon (1984). For application to (the lack of) electoral reform, see R. K. Weaver (2003).

[27] On Western democracies, see Rokkan (1970) and Boix (1999) for key statements. On Latin America and the mobilization of new voters, see Wills-Otero (2009). Green and other parties played similar roles toward the end of the twentieth century. Greens were most clearly on display in New Zealand, which switched to PR in 1993. They also have been a key pro-PR constituency in the United States.

[28] Strictly speaking, the Progressive Party was a Republican social movement (Wolraich 2014) that morphed into the New Deal wing of the Democratic Party (Hirano and Snyder 2007). But some

difference has been relative lack of attention to systems of proportional representation (Taylor et al. 2014).

For a reformer bent on seeing wins, local government was an obvious target. Left-leaning journalists like William D. McCrackan (1893) had advocated imitating Switzerland, where PR adoption in the canton of Ticino would prefigure uptake elsewhere. Mugwumps like John R. Commons (1893) had framed PR as a way to fight corruption in general.[29]

Within a few years, reform proposals would proliferate, some under the aegis of the National Municipal League (NML). Most of them called for non-partisan ballots, nomination by petition, and citywide elections to single-digit assemblies. One of these, commission government, became a vector for ranked ballots. First tried in 1909, this combination spread to dozens of cities in the wake of the "spoiled" 1912 presidential election.

The PR League acted quickly. By 1911, it had "initiated a policy...of concentrating its efforts on the adoption of P. R. for city councils, so as to get actual demonstrations of its merits" (Hoag and Hallett 1926: 188). Then, in 1913, it proposed grafting STV onto the council-manager plan (which had been a rival to commission government).

Socialists protested the emerging non-partisan bargain. Without party labels on ballots, they argued, voters would rely on "the great daily newspapers" to make decisions for them (Thompson 1913: 422). More generally, they worried about legislative bargaining, control of nominations, and having a party platform separate from Progressivism (Lippmann 1913 [1975]: 190). Overall, they disliked STV and preferred list PR (Barber 1995c: 54).

1.3.2 The mugwumps take control

Three developments settled contestation of the model charter's features. One was the failure, in 1913, to bring list PR to Los Angeles. So far, PR historiography has not said much about this. Chapter 3 tells the story. Its core features are the left-right split in Progressivism, then the role of local newspapers, consistent with the Socialists' concerns. Second was Ashtabula's

---

Democrats also called themselves "progressive," especially as they pursued electoral reform. See, e.g., Sarasohn (1989).

[29] Gamson (1990), cited in Tilly and Wood (2013: 49), equates the PR League with the cause of municipal anti-corruption, i.e., "PR against urban political machines."

(OH) adoption of the STV charter in 1915. Scholarly legitimacy followed (Hatton 1916), but not without detractors (Lien 1925: 265). Third was movement reorganization around 1932. This included new leadership, NML's takeover of the PR League, and a scathing report by political scientist Joseph Harris (1930).

Harris's report is an astounding read. Modern readers might view it as a "lessons learned" exercise. It surveyed the STV wins to date, asking why so many had become unpopular. There were three key conclusions: "first-class candidates" not being elected, shifting council majorities, and voters' inability (or refusal) to rank very many candidates. The solution, Harris argued, was to convert future reform coalitions into "good government" slates. Ironically or not, the idea originated with "a Fabian Socialist."[30] Finally, Harris argued against the term "proportional representation," which made little sense outside the context of a list system. Instead, he suggested the "more pleasing" term "choice voting" (4).

Other than the many that removed STV on adoption, just four cities deviated from the model charter. One was Cleveland, where Socialists and ethno-racial minorities objected to the proposed district structure, i.e., an "at-large" election to a small city council. These groups were able to force a larger council, divided among four multi-seat districts that respected neighborhood lines. In turn, those districts respected settlement patterns, particularly among Blacks (due to the Great Migration), as well as Southern and Eastern European immigrants. National reform leaders came to regret this concession, and it figured prominently in Harris's report.

Another deviation was in New York City, which did not get council-manager government. "Under the city's electoral system, by which an individual must run citywide," wrote former Councilmember Adam Clayton Powell, Jr. (1971: 68), "no Negro could be elected without the complete unity of all of Harlem, plus considerable support of whites in other areas." Powell misunderstood two details—elections were at the borough level, and district magnitude changed with voter turnout (valid ballots only)—but his core point stands.[31]

---

[30] See Millard (1924) and C. V. Anderson, "Charter Trots Out Cox, Hynicka Ghosts to Scare Voters, Businessman Says; But PR Is Real Bogey for City, He Adds," *Cincinnati Enquirer*, p. 6, October 31, 1954.

[31] The election returns from New York STV elections also include numerous Latino surnames. Yet no such surnames appear in lists of winners. See *Annual Report of the Board of Elections in the City of New York*, odd years 1937–45, on file at the Municipal Library.

Two more cities deviated from the model, yet not in a way that made it easy for minorities, political or otherwise, to elect candidates of choice. One was West Hartford (CT), where fifteen seats were apportioned among four districts in proportion to voter registration (Gallup 1921). In turn, voter registration was tied to literacy testing (Keyssar 2000: A.13). A second city was Boulder (CO), which staggered elections to its nine-seat council, three seats at a time (Lien 1925).[32]

1.3.3 A new perspective on repeal

The going explanation for the failure of the movement is that STV "worked too well" in generating diverse outcomes (Amy 2002: 274). High-profile victories by Blacks and leftists tarnished the "P.R." cause. These included Benjamin Davis, a Black Communist in New York City (1943–47), and Theodore Berry in Cincinnati (1949–57), rumored as on his way to becoming the city's first "Black mayor" (Heisel 1982: 3; R. L. Engstrom 1990: 219–20). As national elites withdrew support, opponents found it easier to assemble repeal coalitions, including in cities with less exciting politics (Kolesar 1996). This is a good explanation. It can account for the tone of the Harris report, the League's reorganization in 1932, and three deviations from the model charter—all of these responses to similar outcomes in 1920s Cleveland (Barber 1995b). Movements care about optics.[33]

But from a strategic point of view, STV in American cities rested on a series of coalition deals. The object of those deals was, for some, to get and keep control of government. Nothing in the foregoing history suggests those deals had diversity at heart. Therefore, as coalitions shifted, the rules came into question.

Note how a shifting-coalitions theory unites other facts about American experience. First are the cities without "unpopular minorities" in government, and where PR outlasted the Davis-Berry years. Second, we hear frequently that STV confuses voters, is difficult to tabulate, and leads to unpredictable results. None of this is new (Gove 1893: 21; Lien 1925: 265;

---

[32] Millard (1923) writes: "Inquiry among members of the commission which framed the charter disclosed that the reason for this arrangement was to ensure continuity of experience in the council. While it of course produces this result, it has the disadvantage of leaving 25 per cent of the voters without representation."

[33] See, for example, Francis (2019) on funding of the National Association for the Advancement of Colored People in the 1910s–30s. More generally, see McCarthy and Zald (1977).

Mott 1926: 874; Gosnell 1939: 645–46). The striking fact is that these issues did not matter until, at some point, they did. Nor did they bother opinion leaders until, at some point, they did. We may take issue with STV. We may object to the people who promoted it. One thing is clear, however. In any given city, for as long as STV existed, it reflected some set of interests that controlled an electoral majority.

Further, from a comparative perspective, the repeal dynamics are not special. PR countries frequently change their electoral rules. We tend not to notice, though, because change is limited to seemingly minor details (Jacobs and Leyenaar 2011, Bol et al. 2015). One might make a similar point about "winner-take-all" systems in America. Our electoral rules are more diverse and subject to change than the "first-past-the-post" system many people have in mind (Bowler and Donovan 2008: 105).

1.3.4 Having more parties might have changed history

For those who see PR as having been worth rescue, multiparty politics might have helped: by generating commitment to proportionality as a normative standard (Banducci et al. 1999; Bol 2016; Plescia et al. 2020), giving coherence to new coalition deals (McGann and Latner 2012), and restricting change to "minor" details while leaving the larger electoral system in place. Similarly, versions of "preferential" voting have been stable in other countries, all of which began to use it in multiparty settings (Bowler and Denmark 1993; Farrell and McAllister 2005). In other words, STV might have evolved as it did in Australia, Ireland, and Malta.[34] Or we might have gone with list PR from the start.[35]

Above all, multiparty politics might have freed the PR movement from doing the work that parties do. This includes recruiting candidates, mobilizing voters, teaching them how to rank choices, and then organizing

---

[34] On Malta, often seen as a two-party outlier, see Hirczy de Miño and Lane (1996: 24): "Over the years, Malta has moved from a multiparty to a two-party system."

[35] Courts in two states ruled STV unconstitutional, on the grounds that deprived voters of the right to cast a full vote for every seat contested. Strategically, it stopped the plurality-winning slate from claiming *every seat* in an at-large district. These states were California and Michigan, reacting to events in Sacramento and Kalamazoo, respectively (McBain 1922). Had there been multiparty politics, had it been the basis for coalition in government, and had those coalitions controlled judicial appointments, these courts may have ruled differently.

legislatures. We will see that these jobs fell to the PR lobby itself, via local "good government" groups, which it found the need to create.

We cannot observe the multiparty counterfactual. But we can note that PR *writ large* has been stable in other countries. We can find independent candidates helping to defeat repeal initiatives in cities. This "third force" presence bears similarity to multiparty politics. Finally, we can note that experts did not consider modifying STV, nor switching to some other form of PR.[36] There was no incentive to do so, as the two-party system continued to supply the logical basis for coalition. "P.R." in America meant open-endorsement STV (Banfield and Wilson 1963: 96–97).[37]

1.4 Plan of book

The next chapter derives three types of electoral reform, depending on whether reform initiates with those who control government. These types are: coalition-insulating, coalition-realigning, and polarizing. An *insulating* reform originates with ruling-coalition leadership. As its name implies, it is meant to keep that coalition in power. A *realigning* episode displaces at least part of the ruling coalition. These reforms tend to occur via popular initiative (but do not have to), which leads us to ask where such avenues originate. And *polarizing* reforms are led by leaders of the ruling coalition, as well as that of its opposition, to discipline some set of players not committed to either side. Those players might be cast as "troublemakers," but another route to the same result is a party system changing around them.

Since the rest of the book is about American experience, I also show how the three-type framework accounts for other well-documented cases. Then I state expectations about the compositions of reform coalitions (single-party, multiparty, or anti-party), as well as the rules that result (hostile or hospitable to party organization). Both depend on the pre-existing number of parties. Here, bans on formal nominations appear unique to North America (and mainly the United States), at least among advanced democracies.[38] Finally,

---

[36] The exceptions were Lien (1925) and Gosnell (1939). Neither paper, even today, gets very many citations.

[37] Again, Cambridge (MA) complicates this story. Therefore, the broader argument about American exceptionalism largely depends on whether Cambridge experience, via reformer persistence and know-how, can be replicated elsewhere.

[38] With respect to North America, the PR Leagues of Canada and the United States were fused for most of the Progressive Era.

I discuss the style of coalition politics that come in reform's wake. Part of that discussion covers realigning reforms in general (which can be "messy"). Another part deals with effects on governance.

Chapter 3 asks the "fine print" question: why did the movement embrace STV with party-free ballots and nomination by petition? Why did it reject outright the party-based alternatives? In order to pursue a series of *realigning* reforms, the PR movement needed a proposal that could appeal to referendum majorities. And, because those majorities were at least partly anti-party (versus, e.g., Switzerland's multiparty-led effort), they had to appeal to general distaste of parties. Learning this lesson took a test-case referendum, held in Los Angeles in March 1913, on a form of PR that incorporated party lists.[39] This vote also taught the movement to bundle reforms into a package, rather than ask voters to approve of measures separately. Meanwhile, anti-party Progressives had been combining ranked ballots with the commission plan of local government. All of this informed the Model City Charter of the National Municipal League, which contained STV until 1964.[40]

New York City and Cleveland are the exceptions that prove the rule. Only in these cities did multiple parties *bargain* over reform's details.[41] As noted above, Cleveland had an unusually large assembly. And STV in New York City came with partisan ballots and a gatekeeping role for party committees. This coalition also rejected the template PR-manager charter (Tanzer 1936: 537). At the same time—whether due to movement-elite involvement, the role of Tammany Hall defectors, or simply falling back on imitation—other anti-party features also appeared in the Big Apple (i.e., STV, nomination by petition, prohibition of graphic party logos on ballots, and a relatively small assembly).

Chapter 4 documents how the movement built reform majorities. Although theoretically possible, no STV adoption was *insulating*, i.e., the work of a sitting government.[42] And in very few places were new parties

---

[39] Even this package included anti-party features (STV preliminary round, no control of party labels), owing to Progressives in the reform coalition.

[40] In 1916, St. Louis voted on "proportional representation and the non-partisan ballot." So far, this is not mentioned in the STV historiography, and I do not cover it here. Note, however, that this followed settlement on the Model City Charter. See *The St. Louis Post-Dispatch*, November 6, 1916, p. 2. Also, Minneapolis defeated an STV-manager charter in June 1926. Historiography has not noted this either. See "City Manager Charter Sunk," *The Minneapolis Star*, June 22, 1926, p. 1.

[41] Some very early adopters reflect Socialist involvement, as shown in Chapter 4, but the Los Angeles episode persuaded many to accept non-partisan STV.

[42] West Hartford (CT) comes closest, but the rules were imposed by a charter commission elected for that same purpose (Gallup 1921: 357; Harris 1930: 30).

present on the reform scene. Therefore, the modal outcome was an alliance of convenience between ruling-party defectors and the local minority party. A background condition for such a coalition is a locally competitive party system. This leads to a "party parity" hypothesis: that STV charters should not have appeared outsize a zone of two-party competitiveness. But in non-competitive territory, the reform faction of a ruling party might pursue rules to cement its dominance—the non-partisan, plurality-at-large election. The chapter also looks at three similar cities, each with a different reform outcome: an STV-manager charter that won, an STV-manager charter that lost, and a winning manager charter with plurality instead.[43]

Terminological note on non-STV reform charters: "Plurality-at-large" is an oversimplification. Such cities may have had "limited voting" rules, wherein the voter gets fewer votes than there are seats to fill.[44] Others may have had multi-seat runoff systems. To keep the text simple, I will refer to all of these as "plurality" or "plurality-at-large" charters. (In a system without runoffs, the technical term would be multiple non-transferable vote [MNTV], although limited voting adds a layer of complication.)

Chapter 5 documents the rediscovery of party organization. Politics were unpredictable in the earliest adopters, as one might expect of a reform that dissolves the ruling coalition (i.e., is *realigning*). Some of these councils struggled, for example, to choose mayors and city managers (Hermens 1941: 417). The national movement responded by twinning future STV wins with "good government" parties. This strategy emerged in Cincinnati, where field operatives sought solutions to problems they had found in other cities (e.g., ballot invalidity, fractious council majorities). One of them, Cleveland, went on to drop the entire manager system—a major defeat for reformers who cared more about "efficiency" than "P.R." elections.[45] I find evidence of "good government" slates in most STV adopters from the late 1920s onward.

Chapter 6 looks at the working of "good government" parties. STV opponents based their critiques on popular claims about PR in general:

---

[43] Model Charters *without* STV could appear in both types of locales. An example is when the "reformers" already controlled government, making adoption *coalition-insulating*. Kansas City offers an example of this, where "Boss" Pendergast turned council-manager government to his own "machine" ends. We also see *coalition-realigning* adoptions where one party used reform against the other (e.g., Brockton [MA], which I document). For more on such episodes, see Bridges (1997) and Trounstine (2008).

[44] See Chapter 7 for one such proposal, the "majority-minority" or "6X" system. Such rules do not appear to have caught on until the postwar period.

[45] Note, however, that non-partisan elections remained. On general use of the word "efficiency," see Thompson (1913: 416–17).

that it invites party-system fragmentation. Reformers would counter that local "P.R." tended to produce a two-party system. Neither side had it quite right. More likely is that these "good government" parties were complex logrolls, meant to isolate the locally dominant parties (cf. Laver 2000).[46] Further, STV systems in general tend to promote geographic campaigning. Therefore, the STV charter combined the logics of leading alternatives: "city-wide focus" from council-manager government, then "neighborhood issues" from mayor-council government. If true, this implies higher government spending than in cities with either alternative. Such is the price, for better or worse, of binding a coalition in which everyone can be their own boss. Chapter 6 documents that spending pattern, then reviews some accounts of campaign strategy.

Chapter 7 turns to repeal politics. The key idea here is *legislative limbo*, or when noncommittal "centrists" frustrate leaders on opposing sides. I look closely at two well-studied cases—New York City and Cincinnati—as well as Worcester (MA), which has not been analyzed extensively. These cases play several roles. First, they let us reassess conventional wisdom in the contexts that inspired it: that *election* of "unpopular minorities" explains STV abandonment. I am not saying that these outcomes played no role. Repeal forces clearly used them to mobilize public sentiment, and the optics demobilized some national PR advocates (Kolesar 1996). Hence the cases' second role: lessons learned from these very cities continually shaped movement thinking. Some focused on the sorts of people elected. Others, we will see, began to rethink STV. Beyond these reasons, the cases tap two sorts of variation: the states in which STV clustered (Ohio, New York, Massachusetts), then its use with separation-of-powers versus the fused-executive (council-manager) format in all cities but New York.

For each city, the chapter does three things. First, it shows that repeal coalitions drew support from both sides of the aisle. To the extent that data are needed for this, they appear in an appendix. Then it works backward from these outcomes, asking whether two measures of party control can account for repeal activity. One is *control of the legislature*, measured as "roll rates."[47] A legislative majority is "rolled" if a majority of that majority takes some

---

[46] Larger assembly sizes might have produced more than two parties, although without disrupting the basic logic of competition (i.e., isolating the largest party). Given an assembly of nine, elected citywide, the "seat-product" model of the effective number of parties (Shugart and Taagepera 2017) predicts almost exactly two.

[47] I use the plural here because, for New York City, the relevant metric is a "minority frustration" rate.

position on a bill, yet that position does not prevail. This is a common way to assess a legislature's degree of party organization (Cox and McCubbins 2005; Knight 2018). The second measure is *control of voters' rankings*, measured as the rate of "transfer leakage" from reform coalition to opposition and vice versa. Both of these metrics can be connected to repeal, as well as to realignment of the local party system, shown in a "spatial map" of the respective legislature. The chapter also covers signs that "limbo" obtained elsewhere.

Readers may wonder about Cambridge (MA), which never repealed STV, as well as failed repeal votes in the cities studied here. In an appendix, I give evidence that reformers replenished pro-STV coalitions with voters who had supported third-party and/or independent candidates. This is consistent with broader patterns of local-level realignment. Reform coalitions evolved, such that the new boss was *not* the same as the old boss (cf. Santucci 2018). And what about Cambridge? Transfer data show that, in the late 1950s, the reform slate here also encountered problems with vote leakage. For whatever reason, rather than repeal STV, this group began to limit nominations. That suggests a broader strategy of nominating only as many candidates as it needed to dominate the council, avoiding bargaining by vote-seeking candidates with opposition forces.

Chapter 8 summarizes the book, surveys the modern reform landscape, and suggests that history may be repeating. Part of this chapter covers single-seat reform, now the more popular cause. The rest of it covers STV. Already, old tensions color the *Fair Representation Act* (FRA), a sort of model charter for the twenty-first century. Like the reform template of the last century, the FRA is vague about nominations. Based on theory and comparative evidence, national-level adoption seems unlikely, or at least that it would come in a way we have not seen before. Even so, the FRA represents one possible consensus: minority representation, potential for party proportionality, but overall hostility to organized parties. Ways of making it (or reforms like it) stable include: having more parties, reducing voter choice, and adopting some form of list PR instead. All of these might well lead back to having more parties.

2

Party Government and Electoral Reform

The system has always recommended itself to men with a mission, but
without much visible evidence of popular support.

Herman H. Finer (1924),
The Case against Proportional Representation

People have different reasons for wanting electoral reform. Some are
attracted to normative values: majority rule, procedural fairness, equality of
voice, and so on. Others seek to ensure "a seat at the table" where decisions
are made that affect some community. Still others see reform in *realpolitik*
terms: a way to stay in power, to force one's way into office, or to get a
preferred party or candidate elected.

Whatever one's reasons for seeking reform, some efforts succeed, and
many others do not. Depending on how we define "reform effort," we might
even say that most do not succeed. Do we count just referendums? Bill
introductions? Petition drives by concerned citizens?

For these reasons and others, electoral reform can be a complicated
topic. We can look at it from the *voter's perspective*, prioritizing range-of-
choice and, by extension, features of the ballot. Or we can think in terms
of representation, i.e., *who gets seats*. This adds importance to other factors:
district magnitude, assembly size, and seat-allocation rules. Finally, we can
look at reform in terms of *who controls government*: who is in the group that
makes policy, sets the agenda, issues vetoes, and so on.

This chapter lays out a control-of-government perspective. It casts electoral reform as an extension of coalition politics—as an effort to shape the
ruling coalition by changing how people run for office, vote, and/or win.
By "ruling coalition," I mean the range of groups and players that comprise
"an organized attempt to get control of government" (Schattschneider, 2004
[1942]: 35).

My perspective is abstract and oversimplified. It does not grapple with
normative issues. It ascribes too much intentionality to people "just going
about their business."

More Parties or No Parties: The Politics of Electoral Reform in America. Jack Santucci, Oxford University Press.
© Oxford University Press 2022. DOI: 10.1093/oso/9780197630655.003.0002

But simplification has benefits. First, it draws attention to electoral systems *as packages*. Not all proportional systems are alike, for example. They vary by district magnitude and other features. Second, it draws attention to *negotiation*. Reformers may disagree on seemingly minor details. Some may not see every change as "a step in the right direction." Third, it helps account for unsuccessful reform efforts. Those who controlled government had no need for reform, and/or those who did not could not "raid" that coalition.

The central assumption of the theory that follows is that modern democracy requires a majority at least, whether to change political institutions or public policy. The players in the theory will be party leaders, broadly understood, who compete for control of government to influence policy. Its core results are three reform types, depending on whether change initiates with those who control government (either directly, as office-holders, or indirectly, as interest groups).[1] These types are: coalition-insulating, coalition-realigning, and polarizing.

Coalition-insulating reforms are led by the ruling coalition and meant to keep it in power. Coalition-realigning reforms are led by those excluded from power, some of whom may be in (or in support of) the elected opposition. And polarizing reforms come from the ruling coalition and its opposition, in order to deal with players who do not commit to either side. That can be because they are "troublemakers," because their parties have evolved, or some combination of the two.

Three more implications are derived. First, reform packages can be hostile or hospitable to party organization. This depends on the composition of the reform coalition, which itself depends on the pre-existing number of parties. That number closes off certain options, e.g., multiparty realigning coalitions.

Second, the rules that reformers choose should affect subsequent legislative politics. For example, and all else equal, reforms that make it easier to win should make future coalitions more costly to hold together.

Third, reform should become likely when coalitions are shifting. There is no reason to "insulate" unless some threat is widely perceived. There is no way to "realign" without sufficient demand for change. And there is no reason to "polarize" as long as the existing coalition structure is intact.[2]

---

[1] See Karol (2009) on the relative importance of groups and elected officials for explaining party-position change, which is one part of realignment.

[2] Again, not all realignments bring electoral reform. Sometimes there is simply a change of coalition, and this coalition has no need to change the rules (cf. Benoit 2004). At other times, there may not be reformers on the scene, or the "reformers" (and their work) go unnoticed. One largely unnoticed "reform" may be the U.S. settlement on single-seat districts as means of delivering racial-minority representation, mainly via the courts in the 1980s (see, e.g., *Thornburg v. Gingles*, 478 US 30 [1986]).

Since the rest of the book is about the American PR movement, this chapter also substantiates the model by reference to other well-studied cases, many of which come from the field of comparative politics. Special attention is paid to Western Europe, where, according to conventional wisdom, reform was about keeping some presence in parliament in the face of the "socialist threat." Recent scholarship suggests other motives, e.g., breaking emerging oppositions and preserving seat *majorities*. A related issue is whether reform can backfire, fail to do what (we think) it was intended to do, et cetera. The short answer is: yes. Several *insulating* reforms have worked to the detriment of those who imposed them (Andrews and Jackman 2005; Evci and Kaminski 2020). Also, some participants in *realigning* episodes have been excluded from power after the fact, e.g., Swiss Socialists in 1919 (Lutz 2004: 287) and Cincinnati's Black nationalists from 1924–31 (R. A. Burnham 1997: 134–44).

2.1 Definitions

2.1.1 Party leadership

What do we mean by party leaders, as well as control of government? The latter is straightforward; it is the power to enact policy. Party leaders are more ambiguous. At an abstract level, they set a party's policy direction and exert influence over nominations. In other countries, party leadership may be a formal role (Cross and Pilet 2015). In the United States, however, the important players tend to be interest groups and other well-organized "policy demanders" (Bawn et al. 2012).[3] This leadership may be so diffuse that it resembles an "extended party network" of politicians, interest groups, media outlets, and so on (Koger et al. 2010).

2.1.2 Electoral reform

What do we mean by electoral reform? At the broadest level, it is some set of changes to electoral rules. One way to think of electoral rules is as determining how votes are cast, then converted into legislative seats (or the choice of a single winner). The most common variables are: party-versus-candidate

---

[3] For comparative evidence of the role of "policy demanders," see Leyenaar and Hazan (2011), who refer to these as "pressure groups." Renwick (2010) also pays attention to actors not explicitly affiliated with political parties.

voting (Carey and Shugart 1995); whether the rule requires a plurality, majority, or PR quota to win (Powell 2000); and how big that quota must be, which often depends on the number of seats per district (Taagepera and Shugart 1989; Cox 1997). Assembly size is another crucial factor, often for the number of parties (Shugart and Taagepera 2017). We might add rules about ballot access, the number and nature of party labels on ballots, whether ballots are government-printed (Argersinger 1980), whether they permit fusion (Disch 2002), the potential for gerrymandering (McGann et al. 2016; Walter and Emmenegger 2018; Keena et al. 2021), and so on. Table 2.1 summarizes some common electoral systems according to three key variables (setting aside assembly size and rules about nominations): ballot type, district magnitude, and allocation formula. Verbal descriptions appear below, and, obviously, many other systems are conceivable.

2.1.3 Reformers

Related to electoral reform is the idea of "reformer." Here it is useful to think of a continuum, running from sincere to strategic. At the sincere end, one may be committed to reform as an idea, e.g., voter choice, fair representation. The sincere reformer may have a favorite electoral system—or some preferred feature along one of the dimensions. Examples are supporters of PR writ large, Approval Voting writ large, ranked voting writ large, and so on.

Strategic reformers, on the other hand, support some reform because it is good for them. Obviously, many reformers blend sincere and strategic considerations. The more strategic one is, the more they will care about a reform's "fine print." Also, as one becomes more strategic, the more likely they are to reverse position in response to an adverse outcome (e.g., an election or policy fight).[4]

2.1.4 More electoral systems covered in this book

Most of this book is about the single transferable vote (STV), so that is worth describing once more. The voter ranks candidates in order of preference.

---

[4] There are other views on defining "reformer." See Masket (2016: 1, 25–31), for example, who casts "reform" in opposition to "party." Our perspectives are consistent with one exception. Masket includes "more parties" in the set of anti-party reforms, notably along with "top two" elections and "open primaries." One might cast that inclusion as United States-centric—as this is where "reform" tends to oppose "party"—but we will see later that some U.S. reformers did not define their cause in that way.

Table 2.1 Some common electoral systems, by three of the five key variables.

System	Ballot type	District magnitude	Allocation rule	Typical outcome with disciplined voters
Majority runoff	Categorical (person)	One	Second election if no majority	One winner, majority-supported
Alternative Vote	Ranked	One	Transfer votes until majority	One winner, majority-supported
Single Transferable Vote	Ranked	More than one	Transfer votes until quota	Multiple winners, majority and minority
Block-preferential Voting	Ranked	More than one	Transfer votes until majority	Multiple winners, majority only
Open-list PR	Categorical (person)	More than one	One seat per party, per quota	Multiple winners, party-proportional result
Closed-list PR	Categorical (party)	More than one	One seat per party, per quota	Multiple winners, party-proportional result

To win, each candidate must have a quota. This quota is a function of total valid ballots and the number of seats in a district (i.e., district magnitude).[5] Ballots for candidates in excess of quota transfer to the next-ranked picks on each. Ballots for hopeless candidates also transfer to next-ranked picks. The transfer process continues until the requisite number of seats is filled.

The chief alternatives to STV are various forms of list PR, wherein "list" refers to some ordering of a party's candidates. If a party is entitled to five seats in some district, the top five candidates on the list get them. If votes are for parties only, such that lists are "closed," these determine seat share. If votes are for candidates only, such that lists are "open," these determine both list order and seat share. And if the list is "flexible," votes for candidates must exceed some threshold for list order to change. Another variant is "panachage" (more precisely "free list") which lets the voter select candidates from multiple parties.[6]

In contrast with STV, no list system permits votes to leave one party (or coalition of parties, i.e., a "joint" list) and contribute to another's total. STV works like list PR only if partisanship determines voters rankings. If Party A voters only rank Party A candidates, any ballot transfers will stay within Party A.

As an invention, STV is often thought to predate disciplined parties (cf. Farrell and Katz 2014: 13).[7] The usual genealogy begins with Thomas Hare (1859), an English lawyer, and Carl Andrae, a Danish mathematician and

---

[5] Formally, the Droop quota is [(total valid votes)/(district magnitude + 1)] + 1.

[6] Panachage emerged in Switzerland in the 1890s, and early American reformers were fascinated by it. The French word *panacher* means "to blend" or "to mix," which becomes "ticket-splitting" in an Anglophone context. The "ticket" that reformers had in mind was the voter's chosen set of candidates in a multi-seat district. To cast a party ballot (or ticket) would be to vote only for the party's candidates. To split a ticket would be to vote for candidates from more than one party. The next chapter covers why this rule failed to catch on.

[7] It may be that STV was invented *to break* disciplined parties. Consider that list PR and disciplined parties emerged simultaneously, both on the European continent and *even in the United States*. Thomas Gilpin (1844) of Philadelphia gave its first known description, with an eye to solving two problems. One was to secure minority-party representation in the local assembly, in which one party held all of the seats. Another was to secure seats for "a third party coming forward," whose voters otherwise would decide which "major" party that would be (page 69 in James [1896], which reprints Gilpin's pamphlet). The logic resembles a recent "party-building" account of list-PR adoption in Norway (Cox et al. 2019). Further, note that both cases had been using majority runoff, improving the bargaining position of "a third party coming forward." In contrast, STV became popular as a reaction to cabinet (i.e., party) government (cf. Cox 1987). Consider Riker (1982: 755) on cumulative voting, which British STV advocates also favored: "Clearly [John Stuart] Mill expected the proposed system would produce Tory free traders and Tory corn law supporters without upsetting the two-party system."

politician.[8] Hence it was known in the United States as the "Hare system" of proportional representation. John Stuart Mill, the British philosopher, popularized it in *Considerations on Representative Government* (1861), which spread throughout the English-speaking world. Thereafter, it underwent modification by Henry Droop, an English mathematician who modified the quota formula, and Andrew Inglis Clark, an Australian "founding father" who modified the counting rules.[9]

A few more electoral systems will appear in this chapter. One is the Alternative Vote (AV), otherwise known as "instant runoff" or what many people think of when they hear about "ranked-choice voting." Australians might call it "preferential voting in a single-seat district." Articulated by William Ware (1873: 351–55) for internal elections at what was then Harvard College, AV applies the STV allocation formula to the choice of a single winner.[10] James W. Bucklin (1911) of Grand Junction (CO) gave his name to yet another single-seat, ranked-ballot rule, common in many cities from 1909 onward. This "Bucklin system" involved the addition of lower preferences to first-choice votes, until some majority winner was found.

Majoritarian ranked-ballot systems also can be made to work in multi-seat districts. There are at least two variants of this and, in the presence of strong coordination, each results in the minority winning no representation.

One such variant, block-preferential voting, was used for Australian Senate elections from 1918–48, typically in three-seat districts. Of sixty such elections, fifty-five produced single-party delegations (Reilly and Maley 2000: 42). This variant, recently mandated in Utah, involves transferring votes for winning candidates to next-ranked candidates at full value. That

---

[8] Denmark used STV for parliamentary elections in 1856, then for indirect elections to parliament's upper chamber until 1915. According to Homeshaw (2001: 97), Andrae's system was used for lower-chamber elections from 1855–63, and "continued to be used after [the chamber's] reformation in 1863." According to Humphreys (1911: 112, 131), the 1867 constitution abandoned STV for lower-chamber elections, yet applied it to indirect upper-chamber elections. Then, in 1915, a new constitution abandoned STV while implementing other reforms (woman suffrage, a larger upper chamber, abolition of the right of the monarch to appoint members, but creating the right of the outgoing majority to choose part of the new membership).

[9] Droop added a "1" to district magnitude, in the denominator, to minimize the chance that a party with a majority of votes might not win a majority of seats. Clark developed rules so that *all* votes for a winner transfer to next-ranked candidates at a fraction of their value.

[10] Ware was not alone in developing ranked-ballot, single-seat electoral systems. Another variant, named for Edward J. Nanson (1882), contains modifications for handling (a) incomplete rankings and (b) the use of the same ranking for more than one candidate. This was the American PR League's preferred single-winner system—probably because it minimized disenfranchisement due to voter error—but the League did not support single-seat reform of legislative elections (Hoag 1914c: 50; 1914b: 5).

means ballots cast for winners count twice, thrice, and so on, until all seats are filled.[11]

In a similar vein, the Bucklin system was used with the commission form of government, which divides a multi-seat district into a series of "numbered posts" (see Chapter 3 for more information). Although still technically a single-seat election, the combination of such elections in one district meant that the majority in said district could win every seat.

The chapter also refers to runoff systems, which are straightforward. Typically, these elections proceed in two rounds. If no candidate garners a majority in the first round, there is a second election between the top two vote-getters. Runoffs also can be used in multi-seat races. An example of this is the "preliminary election," now used in some cities with non-partisan at-large systems. Both types were popular in Europe prior to the introduction of PR, as noted in some vignettes below. Runoffs also have seen use for presidential elections in multiparty settings, as in France or many South American countries (McClintock 2018). Finally, they have been common in American subnational elections, adopted to manage factionalism in the Southern "white primary" (Fain 2021). U.S. primaries often are (wrongly) seen as runoff rules with varying eligibility restrictions.

Finally, the chapter refers to mixed-member proportional representation (MMP). MMP systems broadly comprise two sets of seats (or tiers): one from single-seat districts, then a second allocated from party lists. The basic idea is that the list tier will be used to reduce disproportionality arising from the district-based elections. There are other details, and an edited volume by Shugart and Wattenberg (2003) gives the best introduction. Two crucial issues are: whether the voter gets to cast one vote (in their district) or two (in both their district and for the list-tier allocation), then whether the size of an assembly may fluctuate (as in Germany).

2.2 The logic of party government

One way to model democracy is as factional competition for control of government. Control then confers the power to enact policy. My account

---

[11] See Santucci (2021) for a catalogue of use as of January 2021. More recently, the system was used to elect part of the Portland (ME) Charter Commission. The first election resulted in a sweep by the Democratic Socialists of America.

Table 2.2 Noel's "game of politics," with coalition of A and B.

	Leader A	Leader B	Leader C
Issue 1	~~Favor~~	Oppose	Indifferent
Issue 2	Oppose	~~Favor~~	Indifferent
Issue 3	Oppose	Indifferent	~~Favor~~
Issue 4	**Favor**	Indifferent	**Oppose**
Issue 5	Indifferent	**Favor**	**Oppose**
Issue 6	Indifferent	Oppose	~~Favor~~

of reform follows in this tradition (cf. Aldrich 1995, Schwartz 2021). It begins with three party leaders (see above) who have positions on six issues (Table 2.2). Again, these party leaders may be legislators, formal "bosses," or key interest groups. The important thing is that they command votes both in and out of government, i.e., those of legislators and voters, respectively.

For each of the six issues, one leader opposes it, one supports it, and one is indifferent. There are six issues because this lets us represent all possible combinations of positions. This "game of politics" is identical to one that Noel (2013: 19–20) uses in his account of ideology. The only change is using party leaders instead of generic people (or legislators, pundits, and so on).

Typically, this setup is used to explain why coalitions form. Any proposal needs two votes to become policy. If leaders only support proposals that they favor, each gets only one vote, and none becomes law. If they also support proposals on which they are indifferent, every proposal becomes law. But this leaves every leader with two policies they oppose. Any two leaders can shed those policies by forming a coalition with each other.

Say that leaders A and B have made a coalition deal. Maybe they co-lead a single party, or maybe their separate parties have agreed to work together. The terms of this deal are: support proposals where one leader is indifferent and the other is in favor. This leaves our A-B coalition with policies on issues 4 and 5. The price of that coalition is inaction on issues 1 and 2, where A and B favor action, respectively. As long as they weight all policies equally, each now gets more policies they want than policies they seek to avoid. The A-B deal is stable because the alternative for each player would be netting zero in a world where every policy passes.[12]

---

[12] Do multiparty coalitions set aside disagreement in this way? Comparative evidence suggests they do. Minor-party voters often punish their parties for making policy concessions to larger coalition partners (Strøm 1990; Klüver and Spoon 2019; Fortunato 2019). Hence it can be rational for "minor" parties to *not oppose* minority cabinets (Thürk and Klüver 2021).

The immediate issue is that any of three coalitions are possible. One is the A-C deal in favor of issues 1 and 6, at costs of issues 3 and 4, respectively. The other is a B-C deal on issues 2 and 3.

Real-world party realignments can be cast as movement among such states,[13] and such realignments have tended to come with waves of electoral reform. One was with the rise of workers' parties around the turn of the twentieth century. A second came with the postwar social-democratic consensus. A third wave since the 1980s has come with what some might call the neoliberal consensus (Pilon 2013).[14]

2.3 Shifting coalitions, three kinds of reform

Returning to our A-B example, rank-and-file may be unhappy with the terms of coalition. For A, the price of majority status is agreeing with B not to act on issue 1. B is in the same position with respect to issue 2. And note that C is indifferent on both issues, which makes them a potential partner in some new coalition. C also has reasons to help the A-B deal fail: changing the existing policies on issues 4 and 5. Further, note that C has been cast as a *party leader*. Maybe there are problems with some of their rank-and-file, such that C's indifference on issues 1 and 2 actually reflects disagreement within an overall C grouping. Depending on how the instability shakes out, there are three modes of electoral reform.

2.3.1 Coalition insulation

The first mode corresponds to cases in which the ruling coalition pursues reform unilaterally. A core puzzle in electoral systems research has been why politicians change the rules under which they get elected. The game of politics in Table 2.2 suggests one possible explanation: the A-B deal is

[13] Aldrich (1995) and Poole and Rosenthal (1997) show this clearly for Southern Democrats, whose type became Republican over the second half of the twentieth century. Dalton (2018) shows for advanced democracies that emphasis on the "cultural" cleavage has produced new parties and coalition alignments. On abandonment of mainstream parties (i.e., dealignment), also see Stoll (2013) and Spoon and Klüver (2019).

[14] On policy consensus and new-party containment in recent reform episodes, see Shugart and Wattenberg (2003) and chapters therein, Colomer (2011), Bol et al. (2015), and Renwick and Pilet (2016).

breaking down, and some mechanism becomes attractive for holding it together. Looking at it from a different perspective, A and B fear that some other deal will take shape (i.e., A-C or B-C).

Examples

Many national-level reform episodes can be recast as coalition-insulating, *depending on whether reform initiates with the ruling coalition*. In 1899, for example, Belgium was the first country in Europe to turn to list PR. Emmenegger and Walter (2019) show convincingly that the Catholic majority used PR to break an emerging coalition between younger Liberals and the upstart Socialists. District committees of both groups had been forming joint tickets under the previous runoff system, presumably on the basis of some policy agreement that defied the status quo.[15] By restoring the Liberals as an independent player, PR freed them of the need to run joint tickets with Socialists.

Another example comes from Australia, where a Nationalist government imposed the Alternative Vote in 1918. AV had been a well-developed proposal since 1902, and states had been free to experiment with it. But in 1918, in a special election, AV suggested is capacity to isolate the Labor Party. In the Division of Swan (Western Australia), Labor won a seat on 34 percent of votes, against the Nationalist and Country parties.[16] A second by-election, in Corangamite, threatened to produce the same result. Federally, the Nationalists introduced AV (along with compulsory ranking), and the Farmers Party (a cousin of the Country Party) won the seat on transfers from the Nationalist candidate (thereby defeating Labor). As long as the Nationals and upstart rural parties could cooperate in this way, the transfer process would keep Labor out of power.[17] And not only did the Nationals impose AV for the House of Representatives. They also forced it to work for the Senate, elected in multi-seat districts. Only in 1948 did a Labor government undo this block-preferential system, replacing it with STV for Senate races (Graham

---

[15] Although the Catholics did not need their votes in parliament, five old-guard Liberals joined them in voting for PR (Emmenegger and Walter 2019: 446). Recall Renwick's (2010: 52) observation that reform can split parties internally, even in multiparty systems.

[16] The Country Party was an agrarian offshoot of the Nationalist Party, which had resulted from the merger of the Liberal Party with a pro-conscription wing of the pre-World War I Labor Party.

[17] Critical to achieving this was requiring voters to rank all choices for a ballot to be valid ("compulsory preferencing"). Otherwise, there was no guarantee that ballots would flow among the right-leaning parties. Another right-leaning government added this rule for Senate elections in 1934 (Farrell and McAllister 2006: 42).

1962: 173–74; Farrell and McAllister 2006: 36–43)—yet another instance of insulation.

New Zealand shows that coalition insulation can happen on the "left" as well. As in Australia, the 1890s–1900s evinced popular fascination with various ranked-ballot rules. But in 1908, a Liberal-led government introduced two-round elections in order to contain Labour "spoilers," and to isolate the right-wing Reform Party. When Reform won power in 1912, it summarily replaced two-round elections with single-seat plurality. That was yet another instance of coalition insulation (Lipson 1948; Nagel 1993).

A fourth well-studied case is Norway, where a closed-list PR system with single-digit district magnitudes replaced runoffs in 1919. The coalition for this package included literal leaders from the Liberal and Conservative party groupings, as well as canadiates that had faced strong Labor challengers in first-round elections. Initially, Labor had supported PR, due to concentration of its voters in cities. But subsequent negotiation led to districts favoring smaller towns and rural areas. Overall, the reform was meant to ease coalition formation among the anti-Labor parties (Cox et al. 2019).

One might continue finding examples, since most countries with unconventional electoral systems (from an American perspective) got those institutions from sitting governments. Rather than do that, I want to make a general point. Then I will come back to a few more cases from American politics.

Accelerated change in a party system tends to precede the turn to proportional representation (cf. Nohlen [1984] on "extraordinary historical circumstances"). Combined with the fact that most PR adoptions have been by incumbent governments, this suggests that most reforms have been meant to insulate. Consider the old critique of proportional systems—that they invite instability and situations of "ungovernability" (Hermens 1936, 1941; Quade 1991). Given that this is widely believed, and has been since 1901 at least (Riker 1982: 756), why would a sitting government ever bring that on itself? Is it not more plausible that reform is meant to preserve some status quo, even if it fails to achieve that effect in the long run?[18]

Insulating logic probably is not limited to electoral systems (understood narrowly), nor to countries outside the United States. The secret ballot had

---

[18] Reforms often fail to achieve what we think their designers have in mind (e.g., keeping them in power). See Andrews and Jackman (2005) on both post-Communist Eastern Europe and the field-defining interwar cases. See Evci and Kaminski (2020) for a more recent example. Again, this suggests that incumbents use reform to manage situations that seem out of their control. One such situation can involve a rising number of political parties (Colomer 2005; Calvo 2009).

insulating properties as well. What we call the "secret" or "Australian" ballot may be better understood as a government-printed ballot.[19] Prior to such ballots, voters either supplied their own or obtained them from preferred candidates. The secret ballot therefore amounted to new state power over voters' preference expression. Once such power exists, incumbents can use it to their ends.

Scholars have identified several ways in which the secret ballot propped up incumbent coalitions. First, it could be used to depress turnout among illiterate voters. Previously, those voters got their ballots directly from parties or candidates, otherwise by tearing them directly from newspapers. Second, by removing parties' ability to monitor voter behavior, it frustrated their efforts to traffic in patronage. Heckelman (1995, 2004) argues that these effects tended to benefit incumbents. One recent study of the secret ballot finds no effects on legislator behavior (Moskowitz and Rogowski 2019). This makes sense, as the secret ballot came from incumbent legislators. Another effect of the secret ballot was to break fusion coalitions, which is partly why the People's Party disappeared so rapidly (Argersinger 1980).[20] Finally, the secret ballot had little effect on voter fraud, even though this was how it tended to be sold to the public. One recent study of U.S. Congressional elections, 1860–1930, finds that fraud reappeared as both ballot-stuffing and padding of voter registries (Kuo and Teorell 2017).

Two more examples will reinforce the point. Anzia (2012, 2014) shows that subnational governments during the nineteenth century manipulated election timing to depress opposition turnout. This is one reason why some state and local elections do not coincide with national ones. More generally, Trounstine (2008) argues that "political monopolies" in cities use a range of election policies to keep themselves in power, confer benefits on supporters, and avoid needing to broaden their coalitions.

2.3.2 Coalition realignment

So far, we have considered cases in which the A-B coalition runs into cohesion problems, leading some part of its leadership to pursue reform "from

---

[19] It is telling that the secret ballot carries the name of a country (Australia) where, early on, politicians would have worried about directing voters' rankings. For evidence of a direct link, see L. J. Johnson (1914) on the United States (emphasis mine): "It looks as if preferential voting were about to sweep the country as did its *logical forerunner and basis*, the Australian ballot."

[20] For more on fusion in American history, see Disch (2002). On the contemporary effects of fusion, see Michelson and Susin (2004).

above."[21] A smaller set of cases concerns reform "from below," highlighted as such by Georg Lutz (2004) because they seem to throw a wrench into the standard model of reform. PR reforms in American cities all were of this type, as I show in the next chapter.

A coalition-realigning reform is an end-run around the ruling coalition. In terms of the game of politics above, Leader C (who leads the opposition) has cut a reform deal with either A or B, in order to bring about some new ruling coalition. To gain the power to do so, C must find some way to get control of the reform process from A-B.

C and the A-B defector might not say that they plan to share power. They may say they want more independent leverage, "a seat at the table," to press new issues, etc. They may couch their appeals in such terms, to the point of believing them, especially if such appeals are needed to win votes at referendum. Jack Lucas (2019: 10) calls this "ideational glue," focusing on STV adoptions in twenty Canadian cities during the Progressive Era. In a content analysis of newspaper arguments for and against PR, he finds two clusters of ideas: one related to municipal efficiency (e.g., getting rid of wards), then a second "built on a commitment to inclusion in the changing postwar city."[22]

Nevertheless, it will be rational to form a new coalition, as the only other option is the status quo ante. To borrow from Lucas (2019: 4) again on Canada, "As local actors learned more about the actual operation of the P.R. system, filling in their 'local' strategic knowledge, I show that more strategic considerations became prominent in each city." Evidence in Chapter 5 is consistent with such learning in America—especially the late decision to create "good government" parties. It is not enough to change the electoral system. There needs to be some plan for governing.

How do disadvantaged groups get the power to pursue realigning reforms? One answer is over the long haul, by extracting influence over potential reform processes from incumbent-coalition leadership.[23] This

---

[21] Many of the examples I gave involved the emergence of new parties. An obvious question to ask, therefore, is the extent to which an expanding electorate drove the emergence of such parties. If it did, some may say that the A-B analogy is strained; rather than coalition breakdown, the important factor is enfranchisement, which leads to more parties. Dewan et al. (2019) give some evidence on this point. They show that, in Victorian England, the *enfranchised* working class tended to vote for Liberals. Therefore, the emergence of the Labour Party implicated coalition breakdown (i.e., dealignment) to a nontrivial extent. Calvo (2009) remarks on similar developments in Belgium, and Wills-Otero (2009) gives evidence from Latin America.

[22] For signs of this "ideational glue" in at least one U.S. case, see R. A. Burnham (1990).

[23] This is why, for Renwick (2010), some reforms are cases of "elite-mass interaction."

typically involves building alliances with sympathetic legislators and/or helping third-party candidates get elected. These players then can demand concessions if they end up being pivotal to ruling-coalition initiatives. Call this a "wedge strategy."

"Wedge" strategies have been common across realigning reform episodes. American reformers used them to win woman suffrage (McConnaughy 2013) and power of initiative (Smith and Fridkin 2008), both at the state level.[24] Canadian reformers used them to get recalcitrant governments to send PR to referendum—first at the provincial level (Johnston and Koene 2000; Pilon 2006), and then within cities without power of initiative (Lucas 2019).[25] In Switzerland, reformers first won the national-level initiative in 1891, which they then used to impose PR in 1918 (Lutz 2004). Before that, the ruling Radical Party relied on gerrymandering to dilute the power of opposing-party voters (Walter and Emmenegger 2018). Nearly a century later, in New Zealand, a coalition of minor parties formed the core of a lobby for the MMP reforms: NewLabour [sic], a group of Labour defectors; the Green Party (which had emerged earlier as the Values Party), and the Democratic Party (once known as Social Credit). Vowles (1995: 105) gives the best overview of these players, who pressured government for several years to hold a plebiscite on PR. When Labour reneged on a promise to do so, reformers worked with the opposing National Party for a vote in 1993. More generally, New Zealand's two-party system had been breaking down for two decades (Nagel 1998), culminating in a series of "anomalous" election results (Vowles 2008).[26]

Realigning reforms can be "messy"

With realigning reforms, it may not be clear who *plans* to "come out on top." Contrast the logic with that of *insulation*. The incumbent coalition either succeeds or miscalculates, but the plan all along was to keep itself intact. Rather, with *realignment*, groups are maneuvering around the incumbent

---

[24] See Bridges and Kousser (2011) for a complementary account of the initiative based on "anti-machine progressivism" (i.e., non-party and major-party reformers). Crucially, they invoke reformers' desire to bring policy into line with the (not-always-benign) preferences of the "median voter." The key "disadvantage" these groups faced was malapportionment.

[25] Within government, pro-reform forces typically included labor, women, young people, farmers, military veterans, and middle-class professionals. In Winnipeg, however, business took the place of labor because labor had been strong there, following a general strike in 1919 (Lucas 2019: 7, 10).

[26] In the run-up to 1993, third-party voting deprived both major parties of seat majorities—twice for Labour and once for the Nationals.

coalition. Maybe they have a plan, and maybe they do not. If they do not have a plan, the realignment must shake out.

There are several examples of "messy" realigning episodes. At the start of this chapter, I noted the Swiss Socialists (1918) and Cincinnati's Black nationalists (1924), neither of which entered the respective post-reform government. In Switzerland, the Catholic-bloc parties forced a coalition deal with the formerly hegemonic Radicals, immediately after the first PR election (Lutz 2004: 280). This was not the same coalition that pursued "reform from below," but it did differ from the one that had been in power. In the Canadian cases, declining candidate entry was one factor in STV's repeal, such that all but Calgary and Winnipeg were back to plurality voting by the start of the Great Depression (Johnston and Koene 2000: 222–23). These repeals themselves suggest completion of some reshuffling process. Finally, since New Zealand turned to MMP in 1993, nearly all governments have been multiparty—sometimes anchored by the Nationals, sometimes anchored by Labour.

Not all realignments lead to reform

Again, not all realignments bring about or implicate electoral reform. Nor do "boilerplate" changes of coalition composition. If boilerplate change happens exclusively within government, we can refer simply to a coalition change. There is no need to change the rules because the current ones already produce sufficient seats for the coalition partners.[27]

Not all referendums are realigning

Many *realigning* reforms involve referendums, but the fact of a referendum does not mean the episode is *realigning*. Incumbent party leaders frequently use plebiscites to gain legitimacy for reforms they support (Leduc 2002), fulfill campaign promises while campaigning against change (Vowles 2013), and/or get around legislators who owe their seats to current rules (Katz 2003).

---

[27] The German centrist bloc (Christian Democratic Union/Christian Social Union) attempted such a change in 1953. Namely, it sought to eliminate compensation under MMP (such that the system would become mixed-member-majoritarian, MMM). Its junior partner, the Free Democratic Party (FDP) blocked the change, then shored up its own position (by demanding two-vote MMP) with help from the Social Democrats (SPD, who favored proportionality in general). Kreuzer (2004: 231–33) describes the episode, and Bawn (1993) summarizes it neatly: "The system did change in 1953, but it changed in a way to offset changes in the environment."

2.3.3 Polarizing reforms

Some episodes involve leaders of opposing parties working together. These are not leaders of separate parties (as in a multiparty system) but leaders of the coalitions that compete for control of government. Why would they do this? Presumably, a change of rules would benefit one side more than the other. To answer the question, we have to go beyond the "seat-maximizing" model of electoral reform. Other things matter, namely, policy and party brand.

Voters refer to a party's brand to help them make decisions. The brand communicates expectations about what policies a party would pursue, were it to control the governing institutions. Commitment to this brand can be so stable that some researchers cast it as a "psychological attachment" (Campbell et al. 1960). But another view of party identification holds that voters keep a "running tally." If voters perceive policy to stop meeting expectations, given the brands in their minds, they may begin to switch sides (Fiorina 1977, 1981).[28]

Party leaders therefore police the brand as well as fulfillment of it. They build it in the public mind, then seek to keep officials working broadly in service of it. According to Cox and McCubbins (1993, 2005), this policing falls to legislative leadership. But others have shown that interest groups can play a similar role–often leading legislators to do things that hurt their individual re-election prospects (Bawn et al. 2012: 572 and sources therein).

To see where the brand originates, we can return to the example in Table 2.2. Recall that A and B have agreed to go forward on Issues 4 and 5 (which both favor), then set aside Issues 1 and 2 (which one of each favors) as the price of coalition. And C gets none of what they want, suffering the costs of Issues 4 and 5, both of which they oppose. When politics are "normal," voters do not see this negotiation. They see the party platform or a simplified version of it—in the media, from friends, from trusted politicians, etc.

And C has an incentive to find ways to split the A-B coalition, then draw one of those players to its side. If C can bring about a B-C coalition, it can gain on Issue 3 (which it favors) in return for acting on Issue 2 (which B favors). But the costs of this deal are: B must agree to give up Issue 5, and C must agree to put aside Issue 6.

---

[28] Note that the "running tally" model emerged in the midst of the Civil Rights *realignment*.

In a normal multiparty system, the terms of the B-C deal are enforceable. This can be for many reasons. Maybe a parliamentary cabinet can set the legislative agenda (Cox 1987). Maybe a presidential cabinet works closely with legislative parties, such that it has agenda power in a separately elected legislature (Amorim Neto et al. 2003; Taylor et al. 2014). And legislators in the B-C coalition want that coalition returned to office, so they respect its terms (Fortunato 2019). Another possibility is that certain types of bargains get more buy-in from civil society (e.g., social democracy), possibly because memory of crisis (war, economic depression) moderates radicalism (Bermeo 1992; Velde 2013: 142).

Voters may get used to seeing certain policies from certain kinds of governments. In other words, the "party brand" in U.S. Congressional politics has its multiparty analogue in expectations about cabinet. (Consider frequent references in German politics to "Jamaica" and "traffic light" coalitions, etc.) And voters have some sense of what the opposition would do, were they to vote it into office.

But players who refuse to pick a side create problems for both brands. For example, B may vote with C on Issue 3, yet refuse to give on Issue 5. Other such scenarios can be derived from Table 2.2.

Polarizing reform is a mutual agreement to protect opposing-coalition brands. It is meant to rein in (or remove) legislators who do not commit to either side of the aisle. That can be due to those legislators' own recalcitrance. Or it can be due to further party evolution, e.g., "I didn't leave my party; my party left me." Whatever the cause, if one needs an image of negotiation behind such reforms, it might sound like this: "They are making both of us look foolish."

Examples

Aside from the cases covered later in this book, there are two clear examples of *polarizing* reform: France's turn to majority runoff in 1958, then the United States' 1967 single-seat district mandate.

The French Fourth Republic ran from 1946–58, and was notorious for "one of the highest levels of cabinet instability known to modern democracies (an average six-month duration)" (Alexander 2004: 212). Therefore, in 1958, the change of electoral system coincided with strengthening of the executive over the legislature. Rosenthal and Voeten (2004: 621, 626) report that, over the course of the entire Republic, discipline varied substantially by party. It was strongest among Communists, Socialists, Gaullists, and

Poujadists; then weak among parties of the "center" and pro-regime right.[29] Impetus for revision of the electoral system came in 1958, as the Gaullists gained seats in the National Assembly. Prior to that, in 1947, the centrist parties had imposed a hybrid PR system: pure party-list in Paris, where they were weak, then an allowance to combine lists in the rest of the country, presumably aggregating votes over large geographic areas. Note the provision for combined lists; this allowed center parties to run as separate entities, rather than combine into a single party.[30] After 1956, the Gaullists began a campaign to switch to plurality-at-large. Needing support from center-left parties, however, they instead agreed to runoffs. According to Michel Debré, who brokered the deal, the point was to "bipolarize" the party system (Alexander 2004: 211, 216).

A second example of polarizing reform occurred in 1967, when the U.S. Congress and President Lyndon Johnson mandated single-seat districts (SSD) for all federal House elections. By 1967, all but two states already had settled on SSD. Yet the passage of the *Voting Rights Act* (VRA), with court decisions mandating districts of equal population, threw the existing regime into question. The new law targeted Southern Democrats, and it also may have targeted Black members of Congress. The coalition politics were as follows.

Congress depolarized rapidly during the Jim Crow years. Stopping people from voting gave "Bourbon" Democrats control of politics in formerly Confederate states. With the onset of the Great Depression, this allowed legislators to write segregation into much of the New Deal (Katznelson and Mulroy 2012; Katznelson 2013). Gradually, Southern Democratic members formed a habit of teaming up with Republicans to defeat left-liberal legislation, as well as early civil rights measures (Brady and Bullock 1980). But as civil rights "burst" onto the national agenda, both parties' leaderships came to see segregation as a brand liability.

The VRA and related court decisions shifted calculations about electoral rules. There was a threat from Southern states of switching to at-large elections—both to mute the voting strength of newly enfranchised persons, and to satisfy requirements that districts be of equal population. Some states

---

[29] Note, however, that these data cover legislative voting over the entire period. Relative discipline on the left and among Gaullists only becomes important in 1956, with relative decline of the centrist group in the National Assembly.

[30] Although Rosenthal and Voeten (2004) show that it is hard to talk of a "center," as legislative voting reflects at least two dimensions.

began adopting multi-seat plurality for state legislative races,[31] and Trebbi et al. (2008) document similar changes at the municipal level.[32] Multi-seat districts, in other words, might have been a lifeline for segregationist elements of the Conservative Coalition. And the 1967 law was a bipartisan deal to cut off that lifeline.[33]

There is a second perspective on the single-seat district requirement. Some scholars have insisted that single-seat districts make minority politicians uncomfortably dependent on the Democratic establishment. Non-plurality rules in multi-seat districts would let them win office without "benevolent gerrymandering," i.e., the drawing of majority-minority and minority-influence districts (Guinier 1992; Guinier and Torres 2003). Whatever the value of this perspective, there is historical basis for it.

In the same year that Congress mandated single-seat districts, the House of Representatives censured Rep. Adam Clayton Powell, Jr. (D-NY). Powell is famous for having destabilized the Democratic Party in the House, via a strategy of sponsoring "killer amendments" on the floor.[34] In other words, he made the party look bad, which the Harvard Crimson (1956; 1963) twice noted. A lesser-known fact about Powell is that, in 1941, he entered politics in New York City, demonstrating the ability of Blacks to win under such systems (Powell, Jr. 1971: 68).[35] PR was gaining popularity among some civil rights activists, as a way to gain leverage in the changing party system.[36] PR also would have obviated the work of drawing equal-population districts, now also legally required, and Flores (1993: chap. 4) suggests that some worried about judicial imposition of it.

Single-seat districts therefore dealt with two "brand" problems at once. The first of these affected both parties: Southern Democratic segregationists in the Conservative Coalition, seeking a lifeline via multi-seat plurality. The second was more clearly a Democratic problem: civil rights activists on the left flank, who might have pressed for PR, and possibly via the courts.

---

[31] See Flores (1993: chap. 4) and items cited therein.

[32] They argue that single-seat districts were more attractive than at-large if enfranchised persons constituted a majority. If so, single-seat districts could be used to "pack" that majority.

[33] Calabrese (2006: 38) emphasizes the Democrats' motive, but all relevant votes had support from both parties.

[34] See Jenkins and Munger (2003) for Reconstruction Era examples.

[35] On this, see Hermens (1943: 55-56, n. 44): "About [Powell's] personal qualifications there seems to be some doubt and future developments will have to show whether or not his election will result in the formation of something amounting to a negro party. If this should be the case, another unwelcome chapter in the history of P.R. in New York City would have been opened."

[36] According to Banfield and Wilson (1963: 307): "In Cincinnati, PR produced a Negro councilman as militant as Congressman Powell (although neither as flamboyant nor as unpredictable)."

It may be that polarizing reforms only happen in contexts where agenda control is weak, due to either formal institutions or the natures of parties themselves. If party leaders can discipline legislators, the need for polarization does not arise, and there is no need to change the electoral rules. Contexts with weak agenda control might include: local and state politics,[37] systems where executive and legislative powers "answer" to different electorates (Samuels and Shugart 2010), parliamentary assemblies without internal hierarchy (Cox 1987), small assemblies generally (cf. A. J. Taylor 2006, Kirkland 2014), and two-party systems with nomination-by-primary (Taylor et al. 2014: 181).

2.4 The reform coalition shapes the rules

It follows from the logic of reform adoption that "fine print" will reflect the reform coalition's structure and interests. Namely, it will be some blend of four (and sometimes five) manipulable features. These will be configured in a way that protects the reform coalition, yet minimizes opportunities for challengers to emerge.[38] Most would say that there are four such features: district magnitude, ballot type, allocation formula, and assembly size. The fifth concerns rules about nominations.

2.4.1 Manipulating district magnitude

District magnitude is a technical term for the number of seats in a legislative district. Taagepera and Shugart (1989) showed systematically that countries' average district magnitudes are highly correlated with their effective numbers of parties.[39] One possible conclusion is that, all else being equal, larger district magnitudes permit more parties to survive. A related tool is the formal threshold, which is the minimum share of votes needed for a party to earn seats.

---

[37] See Bucchianeri (2020) and Shor and McCarty (2011), respectively, on how party government may vary.
[38] Again, reformers can miscalculate and/or discount future elections. This may be how Europe got social democracy, in spite of a series of socialist-containing PR adoptions.
[39] The effective number of parties is a weighted index of party vote or seat shares. It is the inverse of a Hirschman-Herfindahl index, which measures market concentration in the analysis of economic firms.

Reform coalitions take district magnitude seriously. Many of the insulating PR adoptions just above came with district magnitudes in the low single digits. In a recent study of PR adoptions in Swiss cantons, Walter and Emmenegger (2019) find that average district magnitude was lower when the reform coalition included the ruling party. And the current proposal for the United States House of Representatives would implement districts of three to five seats each, resulting in thresholds of 18–25 percent (assuming straight-ticket ranking behavior).[40] This is in order to make the proposal palatable to Democrats and Republicans, who are being asked to pass it. In practice, some higher threshold may be needed, and possibly even set-aside seats for racial-minority representation.[41]

2.4.2 Manipulating assembly size

Although not usually thought of as part of an electoral system, the size of an assembly sets an upper limit on the number of parties that can be sustained, taking account of other factors (Shugart and Taagepera 2017: 119). As such, assembly size is a close cousin of district magnitude. In most cities covered later, the two were the same.

Unsurprisingly, disputes over how many parties (or factions) should be represented often turn up in assembly-size talks. With respect to the Model City Charter in this book, Frederickson et al. (2004) show how the recommended upper bound declined from fifty in 1900, to twenty-five in 1916, and then to nine in 1941.[42] When New Zealand abandoned its first-past-the-post system in 1993, reformers disagreed about how big the new assembly should be. Going by Vowles (1995: 107–108), including right-wing parties in the reform coalition meant that other parties had to agree to a smaller number of seats (but still an increase over what had been in place). More generally, Jacobs and Otjes (2015) find that increases are associated with

---

[40] These figures are derived from the Droop quota formula, with a numerator of one hundred valid votes.

[41] On building set-asides into reform packages, see New Zealand's 1993 reforms, and how accommodating the Maori was necessary for reform to go forward (Vowles 1995; Nagel 1996). For a sense of the U.S. conversation, see Clyburn (2020).

[42] Harris (1930) recommended a smaller number much earlier, based on experience in early STV adopters, all of which but Cleveland and West Hartford had assemblies of seven or nine. Childs (1949) says that five was the original vision for reform charters in general, as this was "about as many candidates as a voter will select for himself without becoming blindly dependent on ready made tickets prepared for him by interested leaders."

increased numbers of parties, while decreases are associated with economic contractions.

2.4.3 Manipulating ballot type

Ballot type refers to what information the voter sees, what entities they choose among, how many choices they can make, and how they make those choices. For example, a ballot can be ranked or not. If it is ranked, the voter may be required to rank all options for the ballot to be valid. Or the voter may be restricted to some number of rankings less than the number of candidates. If the ballot is "categorical" (i.e., not "ordinal" or ranked), the voter can be permitted to mark one or many options (e.g., an Approval ballot). These options can be parties, candidates, either, or both. I already have reviewed the basic types of list PR. These reflect different combinations of ballot type and allocation rule.

If voters only see candidates, or many candidates from one party, non-party information becomes more important to their choices. This can be race, ethnicity, gender, incumbency status (if supplied), occupation (if supplied), residential address (if supplied), or anything else.

2.4.4 Manipulating allocation rule

Allocation rule refers to how we translate votes into seats. If district magnitude is large, for example, but other features of the electoral environment induce polarized voting, it is possible for one group or party to win every seat in the district.[43] This is why "proportional" (and single-seat) systems were invented in the first place—as ways to ensure that the minority grouping gets at least some legislative seats (Colomer 2007). There are many possible allocation rules: divisor-proportional, quota-proportional, majority, plurality, and so on.

As with district magnitude, reform coalitions manipulate the allocation rule. Parties in Western European countries frequently fight over the method

---

[43] Polarized voting exists where groups A and B are both cohesive in their voting behavior, and they tend to vote for different entities. When I say "features of the electoral environment," I mean incentives built into the rules, as well as the tendency of majority-seeking factions to emerge in democracies (Riker 1962).

for allocating seats in list PR. More recently, in the United States, reformers have rediscovered a way to apply the majoritarian logic of the Alternative Vote to multi-seat districts. Other reformers would prefer that they use the single transferable vote instead.

2.4.5 Decisions about nominations

Nominations have not been prominent in comparative literature, but they are central to the American reform debate (see, e.g., Alvarez and Sinclair 2011).[44] It is temping to view nominations as related to ballot type—or to ballot type in tandem with district magnitude. For example, Renwick and Pilet (2016: 17–41) identify five dimensions of electoral-system "personalization."[45] One of these is the upper limit on the number of candidates, which they code as district magnitude in the absence of formal rules (25). But no such limit can exist in a system without nominations, nor in a system of nominating primaries (unless a party committee must grant access to the primary). More work needs to be done on nominating rules and how they matter. For now, what seems important is whether a party controls use of its label.

2.4.6 Multi- versus anti-party reform coalitions

Each key feature of an electoral system can be more or less hospitable to party organization. District magnitude and the size of an assembly jointly determine how many parties the overall system can support. Larger legislatures may develop more party discipline.[46] Ballot type determines whether voters choose among parties or candidates, and nomination rules

---

[44] See Cross and Pilet (2015) for a survey of European democracies.

[45] These are defined in terms of "preference expression" and include: number of preferences that can be expressed, level of differentiation (e.g., ranking or not), within versus across parties, potential for intra-party choice, and district magnitude (which constrains choice if it is low).

[46] See A. J. Taylor (2006) for a cross-national test, then Kirkland (2014) for indirect evidence from American legislatures. I thank Mike Crespin for alerting me to these papers. Jacobs and Otjes (2015: 283) also suggest this point in passing, based on Martin's (2014) study of competition for Irish "mega-seats." It is telling that business Progressivism targeted large assemblies as part of its attack on "bossism." Also telling is that decennial U.S. House enlargement stopped in 1913, just after the "revolt" against Speaker Joseph Cannon (R-IL). Since then, there has been no serious effort to enlarge the House.

determine the extent to which parties may structure those choices. Finally, seat allocation may or may not be based on party grouping, e.g., list systems versus "pure" STV.

Whether a reform is party-hostile or -hospitable depends on the composition of the reform coalition. It can comprise a single party, multiple parties working together, or a coalition that defies party lines (i.e., is cross-party). The pre-existing number of parties limits which of these are possible. In a two-party system, a cross-party coalition *must* be anti-party, unless it is a polarizing one. Consider recent data on public views of reform.

In 2018, the Democracy Fund Voter Study Group polled several items on electoral reform. One of these pit party-based PR against candidate-based plurality. The survey also asked if people want "a third party," and just under 70 percent said yes—the highest rate since 1994, when Pew Research first polled the item. Additional items suggested demand for roughly five parties: one in the "center," one to the Democrats' "left," and one to the Republicans' "right." Turning to the items on electoral reform, only 17 percent supported a party-based PR system. By contrast, 52 percent supported "voting for individuals" even if the overall result would not be party-proportional. The remaining 31 percent said "don't know" (Drutman et al. 2018). There is a striking contradiction in these data: Americans want more parties (whose ideological "locations" are knowable, no less), yet they do not want the appropriate electoral system.[47]

Contrast the U.S. results with data from other countries, where party cues generate rational electoral-system preferences (Banducci and Karp 1999; Vowles 2013). One might say that Americans do not really understand proportional representation, but that would be consistent with the point about cues. Or one might point to general status quo bias,[48] except that the comparative data came from in-progress reform campaigns. One key difference may be the pre-existing number of parties.

If party structures thinking on electoral reform, and if there are only two parties, there are just are two ways to induce a reform coalition. One is to appeal to a single party, which is what we have seen recently in two key AV

---

[47] Also, predictors of support for STV and AV are not substantively different (McCarthy and Santucci 2020: 9, n. 5). Both are candidate-based. The former at least makes party-proportional results possible. Yet most of the public either does not see this difference or has other goals in mind. We argued that one of those goals was "disruption."

[48] Heller (2021) argues that prior experience shapes preferences in the absence of cues, consistent with recent work by Blais et al. (2021). But the party system shapes the electoral system, which people then experience.

adoptions: Maine (2016–18) and New York City (2019).[49] The other is to propose a cross-party coalition by priming opposition to parties writ large, which is what we recently saw in Alaska (2020).[50]

The Swiss "from below" case is important here, as a contrast to what happened—and still happens—in the United States. Its free-list PR system is unusual, allowing voters to "split their tickets" by voting for candidates on multiple lists. Yet the system is still based on party lists (not transferable votes). This reflects the structure of the coalition that imposed the system: multiparty, not anti-party. Critically, *Swiss parties had separate media outlets*, which helped build support for the free-list package (Lutz 2004: 285-87).[51] In the next chapter, we will see that at least one major U.S. newspaper opposed list PR because it "provides for a government by parties."

Note on single-party realigning coalitions

The logical goal of a single-party realigning coalition must be one or both of two: long-term damage to the opposition, or to dislodge lingering sources of obstruction (cf. Bridges and Kousser 2011, especially on malapportionment). If such a coalition has the votes for reform, it also has the votes to win control of government—unless some other rule gets in the way (e.g., malapportionment, staggered elections, or both). We will see examples in Chapter 3, when cities removed STV from the Model Charter on adoption. In those cases, the Model Charter's other features were attractive: non-partisan elections, small assemblies, etc.

2.5 The rules affect how you govern

In the short run, rules reflect the institutional preferences of the coalitions that impose them. In the long run, they can change. But they also structure

---

[49] Also, in a failed 2020 referendum on AV in primaries, Massachusetts reformers argued that it "strengthens party unity." See https://www.yeson2rcv.com/about/.

[50] Maine's AV adoption was an overwhelmingly Democratic action (Santucci 2018b; Anthony et al. 2021), originally meant to apply to gubernatorial primaries and generals. In New York City, the Democratic Party imposed AV for primaries, possibly seeking to prevent a split. But in Alaska, AV comes with two-round elections and a ban on nominations. The system is designed to insulate a bipartisan coalition, currently in control of state government (Herz 2020).

[51] It is tempting to invoke concepts like "segmented society" and "subculture" and how these generated multiparty systems. Key works might be Lipset and Rokkan (1967) and Lijphart (1977). For reformers, the bad news is that the United States is not likely to spawn mass-based third parties any time soon. The good news is that PR—should it ever be adopted—might not totally fragment the party system.

governance in the medium term, as many have suggested with respect to policy output (e.g., Lijphart 1999). The logic begins with legislative leaders and is fleshed out in Chapter 6. For now, I revisit the distinction between list systems and STV (particularly its "open-endorsement" variant).

Legislative leaders can be understood as "peak bargaining units" or, as Cox and McCubbins (2005) prefer, "senior partners" in a firm. When there are fewer such units (or partners) to satisfy, and when these units (or partners) can control their rank-and-file, majority-supported bargains are easier to strike.

One way to think of peak bargaining units is as the number of parties in government. By government, I mean a parliamentary cabinet, but possibly also the cabinet of a separate executive who wants a good relationship with the legislature (Amorim Neto et al. 2003).

But the number of units does not have to correspond to the number of parties in government. In a small, non-partisan assembly, for example, it may just be the legislative majority. And if that majority is controlled by something outside (e.g., a non-partisan slating group with ties to the local Chamber of Commerce), that entity is the only bargaining unit.

Research has shown that the number of parties in government (not just parliament) is related to government spending (Bawn and Rosenbluth 2006). The core distinction here is between "coalition parties" and "coalitions of parties." In a coalition party, there is less credible threat that a government will lose its legislative majority. Therefore, the party can impose costs on its own rank-and-file; it can refuse to do things that some of them want. Coalitions of parties do not have this luxury. Partners can threaten to bolt because they answer to separate electorates. In a multiparty system, each party has its own brand (possibly in addition to being known for regularly choosing the same coalition partners). But in a two-party system, all share the same brand.

Electoral rules matter for rank-and-file control. I have noted in several places the differences among list systems: closed empowers party leaders, open empowers voters (at least formally), and flexible lists are a middle position. Carey and Shugart (1995) extend this logic to a range of electoral rules. They argue that candidate-based ballots give candidates incentives to campaign independently of party brand. We can look at this dynamic from the party perspective as well. Party-based ballots *discourage* candidates from cultivating their own brands. Vote pooling also reinforces brand loyalty. When candidate votes contribute to party totals (as in Switzerland, for example), candidates' fortunes are tied to those of the party, especially those candidates with less popularity.

But to reinforce a point made earlier, only STV permits votes for Party A's candidate to leave Party A, then contribute to the election of someone from Party B. Party B may find these vote transfers attractive. So may Party A, under certain conditions. After all, any vote helps to increase the seat total. But candidates can use transfers to form their own coalitions. Less popular candidates may find this strategy attractive. They can breach party brand, yet still get elected, thanks to transfers from other parties.

In other words, in STV, every candidate can be their own brand. And if they get elected, they become their own bargaining unit. It follows that, all else equal, STV makes it costly (literally) to keep a coalition together— especially where parties cannot keep people off the ballot (e.g., where nomination is wholly by petition).[52]

Many Progressives do not seem to have been thinking about downstream issues: legislative organization, cost implications, and so on. Some may have expected to "keep things under control," owing to experience with small councils elsewhere. Yet there were dissenters who issued reasoned warnings, as we will see in the next chapter.

2.6 Recap

Coalition government is a fact of political life, and any coalition has tensions. This chapter has cast reform as an effort to get or keep control of government. It derived three reform types: insulating, realigning, and polarizing. Each involves some "shock" to the existing coalition structure, which activates its internal tensions. Insulation aims to keep the coalition intact, realignment aims to change it, and polarizing reform targets noncommittal "centrists."

Realigning episodes require control of the reform process, which may need to be gotten via "wedging." Further, they may may be "messy," such that nobody really knows who will get control of government. In the simple model here, however, the reform coalition's only option is to become a

---

[52] Note that literature on PR and government spending has been inconclusive. See, for example, Aidt et al. (2006). The preceding discussion suggests some reasons why. Many PR adoptions have been insulating, with low district magnitudes, and designed to contain socialists.

governing one. Not all real-life scenarios are this simple (see, e.g., the short-run fate of the Swiss Socialists above).

I also argued that reform can be more or less hospitable to organized parties, depending largely on the pre-existing number of parties. Namely, coalitions can be single-, multi-, or cross-party. In a two-party system, a cross-party coalition also must be anti-party—unless it is polarizing. Finally, I introduced the idea that electoral rules shape governance in the medium-term, mainly through their effect on the number of "bargaining units."

3
From More Parties to No Parties

> It is a grotesque scheme of the Socialists to secure control of the city. . . . It provides for a government by parties. . . .
>
> *Los Angeles Times*, March 23, 1913

Writing in 1939 for the *American Political Science Review*, Harold Gosnell had a reasonable idea. Cities with "proportional representation," he argued, would be better off under his "list system with single candidate preference." The ballot would contain party-written lists of candidates. The voter would vote by marking an "X" next to their most preferred candidate. These votes would count for people as well as their parties, delivering proportionality and voter choice at the same time. According to Gosnell, this open-list system would be easy on voters and election officials. And it would acknowledge a reality that had emerged in the reformed cities: "non-partisanship is a fiction" (647).[1]

What we got instead was cognitively challenging, costly to tabulate, and completely blind to parties: the single transferable vote with non-partisan ballots and nomination by petition. Several cities used this rule at the time of Gosnell's writing: Boulder, Cincinnati, Hamilton (OH), Toledo, Wheeling (WV), New York City, and Norris (TN). Five had just repealed it, and twelve more would adopt it.

Why did STV become the preferred PR system in America? Why was its design so hostile to party organization? Gosnell's proposal had been known to reformers. Between 1893, with the founding of the PR League, and 1915, with the first STV adoption for public elections in America, there was vigorous debate over types of PR and how they might combine with other reforms.[2] Then, around 1912, many reform-minded Americans became

---

[1] Lien (1925: 265) had made a similar argument, calling for free-list, after observing four STV elections in Boulder (CO).

[2] This does not include the single-tax colonies of Arden (DE) and Halidon (ME). Arden adopted STV in 1912. Halidon adopted it in or before 1911. Again, I thank Drew Penrose for alerting me to Arden's continued use.

More Parties or No Parties: The Politics of Electoral Reform in America. Jack Santucci, Oxford University Press.
© Oxford University Press 2022. DOI: 10.1093/oso/9780197630655.003.0003

enthralled with single-seat majority systems. Several in this community also supported removing parties from electoral politics. This conversation appears to have stopped in 1914, with the National Municipal League's endorsement of STV, soon to be included in the Model City Charter. A reform victory in 1915 vindicated that new charter.

This chapter tells the story of the early PR movement in America. The decision to promote non-partisan STV was closely linked to two developments. One was the rapid spread of ranked-ballot reforms in the years on either side of 1912. Some of these reforms were used in state-level primaries, likely to manage tensions within the major parties. Far more popular, however, was an urban reform template built on a functional equivalent to AV. Proponents of this template opposed parties at all levels: on the ballot, in nominations, and in legislatures. PR fans saw an opening to promote STV.

The second development was in Los Angeles, where, in 1913, PR of any type faced its first referendum test. In this case, the proposal was a hybrid system: STV for primaries, then open lists in the general. The result laid bare a major cleavage in the movement: between Progressivism's own left and right wings. Related to this, however, was a theory of parties. Socialists preferred reforms to strengthen parties (especially their own). Progressives wanted reforms that could "work" without them. Expediency led the movement to side with Progressives.

The chapter proceeds as follows. First, I characterize the actors in the reform movement, 1893–1914, and their stances on parties' role in politics. The core point here is that Socialist Party leaders understood party government, and that their preference for list PR was consistent with this understanding. Meanwhile, Progressives supported "preferential voting" in its majoritarian form. Pressure to remove party labels from ballots, as well as parties from the nominating process, seem to have originated with this group. Section 3.2 sketches the early PR movement's most popular reform options, showing that at least some reformers were aware of pitfalls. Section 3.3 turns to Los Angeles, noting its importance to the movement, and exploring patterns in the referendum outcome. These new data, which are precinct-level results from nineteen simultaneous ballot measures, offer one glaring case of the cleavage in Progressivism. Section 3.4 reflects on the STV compromise as it played out in Ashtabula (OH), which introduced that system in 1915.

3.1 Mugwumps versus left parties, 1893–1913

The PR League was born over the weekend of August 10–12, in the waning days of the Gilded Age, amidst the economic Panic of 1893. It was born, in other words, on the eve of a major realignment. Racial polarization had eclipsed economics, such that elections often were about which side one had been on during the Civil War. For other voters, less concerned about the old "bloody shirt," voting was a matter of where one stood on immigration, or on the role of Catholics in public life. Polarization in Congress approached modern-day levels, and both parties were beset by third-party insurgencies: Greenbacks, Prohibitionists, Populists, and others.[3] Such was the context, in some ways like our own (Azari and Hetherington 2016), that generated competing reform strategies: one for more parties, another to have none.

Held alongside the World Columbian Exposition in Chicago, the Proportional Representation Congress brought together professors, reformers, and international dignitaries to share ideas and set direction. Today's foundation officers might call it a "convening." Professor John R. Commons (1893, 1896) railed against congressional gridlock, party discipline, and the subjection of local parties to "great corporations and syndicates." Journalist William D. McCrackan (1893) spoke of Ticino in Switzerland, where, in 1890, the national government had imposed PR to quell labor unrest. Traveling from South Australia, Miss Catherine Spence (1893) of Adelaide introduced the single transferable vote.[4] On Saturday morning, just before a resolution on the League's formation, McCrackan again took the podium, this time to make the case for initiative and referendum (Cooley 1893).

One month later, abridged versions of the speeches appeared in the inaugural issue of the *Proportional Representation Review*. Also in that issue

---

[3] See DeCanio (2007) on voting behavior in the late nineteenth century. He concludes that Republicans were more motivated by race and religion, whereas Democrats were more motivated by economic redistribution. For Barreyre (2011: 421), this two-dimensional structure made national elections competitive for most of the post-Reconstruction era. After 1888, however, Republicans could set the national agenda, due to to Speaker Thomas B. Reed's (R) centralization of power in the House of Representatives (Lodge 1891). On the attendant polarization of Congress, see Lee (2016). Reed's centralization of authority, and the development of party government more generally, is a frequent target in the classic text by Commons (1896), *Proportional Representation*. On page 43, for example, he writes: "The American speaker, unlike the English and Canadian, is a man of dictatorial power. In the national government he is ranked next to the President. He appoints the committees, lays down the rules, and controls legislation." However, it should be noted that Speaker Reed sought such power, at least partly, to advance voting-rights legislation (Valelly 2009).

[4] Spence had been a leading developer and promoter of STV in colonial Australia.

were two pieces of model legislation. Each would have imposed a form of list PR for elections to the House of Representatives. Figure 3.1 reproduces a sample ballot from the second issue of the *Review*, published in December (Foulke 1893: 50). In this version, the voter gets ten votes. If they choose only a party, the party gets all ten votes. Or they can vote for up to ten candidates. If they vote for fewer than ten candidates, and they choose a party, that party gets whatever votes they did not use. Votes would help candidates achieve quotas, a full one of which would be needed to win.

As the ballot suggests, the early PR League had some Populist roots. Beginning in January 1896 and continuing through October 1914, the *Review* was published under the auspices of the initiative-and-recall movement. Its earliest issues appeared in the *Direct Legislation Record*, and one of the *Record*'s repeat columnists was William Simon U'Ren, early advocate of direct presidential primaries, direct election of Senators, and the "single tax." U'Ren had been Oregon lobbyist for several left-wing groups: the Knights of Labor, Federated Trades, Farmers' Alliance, and the Grange (U'Ren 1896). In

THE APPLICATION.

Form of Ballot for the Free List System.

FOR MEMBERS OF CONGRESS.

☐ DEMOCRATIC.	☐ REPUBLICAN.
☐ C. F. Crisp.	☐ Thos. B. Reed.
☐ W. L. Wilson.	☐ J. S. Morrill.
☐ W. D. Bynum.	☐ W. B. Allison.
☐ Wm. M. Springer.	☐ G. F. Hoar.
☐ Tom L. Johnson.	☐ N. W. Aldrich.
☐ J. G. Maguire.	☐ H. C. Lodge.
☐ W. B. Cockran.	☐ Eugene Hale.
☐ R. Q. Mills.	☐ M. S. Quay.
☐ D. W. Voorhees.	☐ W. B. Washburn.
☐ D. B. Hill.	☐ C. A. Boutelle.

☐ POPULIST.	☐ PROHIBITION.
☐ J. F. Weaver.	☐ John Bidwell.
☐ J. G. Field.	☐ J. P. St. John.
☐ Jesse Cox.	☐ J. B. Hobbs.
☐ Wm. A. Peffer.	☐ T. R. Carskadon.
☐ J. Simpson.	☐ T. M. Conpropst.
☐ J. Donnelly.	☐ S. W. Small.
☐ Lafe Pence.	☐ E. C. Moeller.
☐ J. H. Kyle.	☐ E. P. Auger.
☐ J. W. Allen.	☐ Walcott Hamlin.
☐ A. J. Streeter.	☐ John Russell.

Fig. 3.1 Example ballot, "free list" system, 1893.

1914, he would lead an unsuccessful referendum effort to adopt a statewide "one vote" system in Oregon.[5]

3.1.1 Progressivism reshapes the movement

Around 1914, though, movement strategy showed signs of change. This was detectable in its public communication, as well its relationship to old reform partners. The first people to go were old proponents of initiative-and-recall. With this came a split from *Equity*, a catch-all magazine for reformers of the left, and where the League had printed its *Review* since 1906. All of that ended in October 1914. Here is what Clarence G. Hoag, the *Review*'s editor, had to say about the divorce:

> The reasons for issuing the *Review* separately again, as it was issued from its founding in 1893 until 1896, are chiefly two. In the first place those members of the League who do not favor the Initiative, the Referendum, and the Recall, or any one of the three, do not like to have the official organ of the League published in such a way as to suggest that the League as a body, or proportionalists as such, necessarily support also the three political devices mentioned. (Hoag 1914d: 1)

A simultaneous move was going on with respect to the League position on electoral systems. Consider its founding mission statement (Cooley 1893: 117):

> The object of the society is to promote the reform of legislative assemblies by abandoning the present system of electing single representatives from limited territorial districts by a majority or plurality vote, and by substituting the following:

---

[5] This system is known technically as the single non-transferable vote (SNTV). The entire state would have been one legislative district. All candidates would be present on the ballot, and every voter would get just one vote. The top sixty vote-getters—that is, the size of the lower chamber—would have won the seats. Today's reformers might call SNTV a "semi-proportional system."

U'Ren's original proposal was for some candidate-based form of list PR, not SNTV, and certainly not statewide SNTV. Rather, this was the culmination of a multi-year effort to find something consistent with other state laws. One seems to have related to candidates' district residencies. Future researchers might consult the *PR Review* for the first half of the 1910s. Somewhere along the line, U'Ren came up with "nomination districts," which were re-invented in early 2021.

1. All representatives shall be elected at large, on a general ticket, either without district divisions or in districts as large as practicable.
2. The election shall be in such form that the respective **parties, or political groups,** shall secure representation in proportion to the number of votes cast by them, respectively.

That statement remained unchanged through late 1913, when the following proposed replacement circulated among League members:

Its object shall be to secure the adoption of proportional representation for state legislatures, city councils, and other deliberative or policy-determining bodies. The plan of proportional representation to be recommended by either of the League's secretaries in any particular case shall be **that which seems to him most suitable for the case,** provided always that it embodies the principle of a single vote in a multiple-membered district.

This proposal led to immediate protest from one Carl D. Thompson of Chicago:

... the old article is much clearer and more consistent. Your amended article cuts the heart out of the idea of proportional representation and makes your League *absurd.* [Emphasis in original.] Proportional representation presupposes political parties and party grouping as provided by article II, section 2, of your original constitution. . . .

To which Hoag, now Secretary-Treasurer of the PR League, replied:

I am aware that you, as a Socialist, believe that party lines, such as have hitherto prevailed in this country, are the only reasonable basis for a system of representation. Though you may be right in that view, there is no question, I think, but that proportional representation is entirely feasible without such party lines as we have been accustomed to.   (Hoag 1914a)

Thompson, it turns out, was Director of the Bureau of Information for the Socialist Party. Formerly a city clerk under Milwaukee's Socialist mayor, Emil Seidel, Thompson had led the party's study of the commission form of local government.

3.1.2 The party-government dissent

Late in 1913, Thompson published a critique of Hoag's "representative council plan," which the latter had been promoting as a compromise reform package (Hoag 1913a). While Thompson agreed with many of its features, he had two objections to the Hoag plan. First, it called for ballots "without insignia, emblem, or designation [...] of the source of candidacy." Without such markers, Thompson argued, voters' choices would reflect "the power and influence of the [...] banks, railroads, and great daily newspapers" (Thompson 1913: 421–22). If recall must be an option, he preferred that all council members be subject at the same time. Otherwise, he argued, ad hoc majorities might single out individual members for removal (419).

More generally, the Socialists seem to have understood party government. Then still his co-partisan, Walter Lippmann (1913 [1975]) sent a letter to Thompson, expressing several concerns about cooperating with Progressives. The immediate subject of this letter was a local election in Schenectady (NY), where many Progressives had rallied behind a Socialist slate. These Progressives wanted parks and public dental clinics but refused to increase taxes on non-wage income.

For Lippmann, the "Schenectady problem" tapped a broader question: should Socialists simply adopt the Progressive program? Or should they run on their own platform, then work with Progressives only on points of agreement? Lippmann advised the latter: "Of course this means that we shall win less elections and come into power more slowly" (193).

Lippmann and Thompson also seem to have understood a party's brand reputation, its maintenance through candidate recruitment, and how the media might shape voter preferences. In his letter to Thompson, for example, Lippmann called for attention to "the quality of propaganda, the kind of nominations, the nature of the platform, and the issues that are raised" (190). Note that Lippmann would go on to write *Public Opinion* (1922), the classic text on media effects.[6] For now, his immediate focus was party-building in local politics.

---

[6] Years later, he would decline to comment on the 1950 report of the American Political Science Association's Committee on Political Parties (Wickham-Jones 2018: 64).

3.1.3 The majoritarian dissent

Around the same time that Hoag was sparring with the Socialists, he also needed a way to neutralize single-seat reform. For Hoag, with his "representative council plan," the challenge was to find a way to bridge several divides at once: between proponents and opponents of initiative-and-recall, of executives responsible to council majorities, of partisanship generally, and, now in 1913, a new thing known as "the preferential ballot for insuring [sic] election by a majority"—similar to today's "single-winner ranked-choice voting" (C. F. Taylor 1913).[7]

The conversation about preferential-majority voting was a world unto itself. Just as today's reformers vigorously debate instant-runoff, Condorcet, Approval Voting, etc., there were partisans of myriad single-seat systems—all working independently of the PR movement. Hoag (1914b: 6–9) names three such proposals in written testimony to Congress. One was the Ware (1873) system, which is STV for one seat, then known to the British as "alternative vote" and to Australians as "preferential voting." A second was the Nanson (1882) system, largely designed to deal with "ballot exhaustion." A ballot becomes "exhausted" (or "inactive") when it does not continue to a subsequent round of counting, either because the voter has skipped a ranking (under more restrictive rules), or because they have ranked too few candidates. A technical description can be found in Hoag's testimony, but the basic idea is as follows: candidates would earn "credits" rather than votes, and higher rankings would contribute more credits. A third system, named for James W. Bucklin (1911), would find majority winners through simple addition. If no candidate had a majority in the first-round count, their second-choice votes would be added to their first-choice totals. Then, if there still was no majority winner, third-choice votes would be added to the second-round totals. Among majority-preferential systems in the United States, Bucklin was most common, via the commission form of local government (see below). Hoag (1914b) is worth quoting on competition among these methods. Although he preferred the Nanson allocation, he suggests that the distinctions were without difference in practice:

---

[7] Also see Hull (1912) for an early pitch.

Each of the three systems of majority preferential voting just described has its enthusiastic supporters in this country, and I am inclined to think that for a time each of them may have a place in the broad and varied field of our political life; but it is unnecessary that any blind struggle for supremacy should arise among them, for there can be no question in regard to the true nature of each in the mind of anybody who is willing to look at the facts and to give the matter a little thought. (9)

And:

And nothing short of experience can prove just what harm, if any, will result from any such effect that may be produced from any one of the sets of rules. (13)

One event clearly propelled majoritarian reforms into the spotlight: the 1912 presidential election, a classic case of the "spoiler effect." In splitting the Republican Party and running on his own, Theodore Roosevelt handed the White House to Woodrow Wilson, ushering in the first and only Democratic presidency between 1896 and 1932. Educated readers across the land discovered electoral systems. Those who dug deeper could find precedent for use. Estimates vary, but according to Porter (1914: 582), twenty-four cities around this time were using majoritarian forms of "preferential voting" for general elections. L. J. Johnson (1914) records use in several others, almost exclusively under the commission form of government. Before November 1912, there were just four such cities. After the election, fifty-six more cities would join them. Figure 3.2 gives their geographic incidence.[8] The adoption wave ended in 1918, one year after Hoag's STV plan gained scholarly legitimacy (see below).[9]

 Commission government was a natural target for fans of majoritarian reform. Invented in 1900 by the Galveston (TX) business community, it essentially set up what is known today as the "numbered post" system.[10] Under it, five or seven commissioners would be elected citywide, but in separate races through plurality or runoff voting. Each commissioner then

---

[8] Kneier (1957) reports fifty-five cities in total, which are reflected in Figure 3.2, along with six more recently discovered.
[9] Historical research with Andrew Rosenthal is ongoing. I thank him for compiling these data.
[10] Later generations noted how this became a device for minority vote dilution (Ball 1986).

Fig. 3.2 Incidence of majority-preferential systems, local level, 1909 to about 1940.

would be responsible for some executive function (e.g., parks, water). While commissioners could not dictate each other's work, they would set budgets collectively—an obvious invitation to party-like coordination (Rice 1977).

The Bucklin-commission system was problematic in two ways. Given slate voting, the numbered-post election would deliver every seat to the citywide majority. To this, the Bucklin rule added unpredictability. Given a race with three or more cohesive factions, a preference-swapping deal (à la ranked-choice) could deprive the largest faction entirely of representation. (Note that this also holds for majority runoff.) For Hoag (1914c: 54), the design was "clearly unjust to all voters who do not happen to belong to the largest group in the city." Speaking for the Socialists, Carl Thompson (1913: 420) agreed, also taking aim at majority runoff (the leading alternative to Bucklin under commission) and multi-seat plurality (under council-manager): "the fatal defect in all these systems is that they do not provide for minority representation. All of them eliminate all minorities from the governing body, council or commission."

As far as we can tell, there was little concern for minority representation in the reform community. It is not clear why. Some majority-voting pro-ponents may not have thought about the issue. As we will see below, many thought that parties could be gotten rid of, suggesting a sort of blindness to strategic coordination. Others may have thought that proportional rules would threaten a monopoly on power. Either way, Hoag took to educating reformers on "two objects of voting." He writes (1914: 4–5):

> One of the objects to be carried out by voting is to make decisions, either between policies (measures) or between candidates for administrative positions....
>
> The other object to be carried out by voting is to *make up a body fit to make decisions... on behalf of all the voters*, in other words, to make up a deliberative or representative body... [emphasis in original].

Further:

> When, however, the object of voting is not to make a decision at all, but to make up a body fit to make them on behalf of all the voters—in other words, a representative or deliberative body—then majority voting, even by an infallible system, is only one degree less absurd and less disastrous to democracy than plurality voting itself.   (16)

There was one virtue in majority-preferential voting, at least from the perspective of PR movement leadership: "In spite of its imperfections, however, the system is serving a very useful purpose in introducing the preferential or adequate ballot" (Hoag 1914c: 50). Modern reformers may recognize a familiar theme: getting voters used to the task of ranking candidates, with an eye to future STV adoption (Hoag 1914b).

3.1.4 The push to eliminate party nominations

The majority-voting community supplied new energy for "getting parties out of politics." Commons (1893) had argued years before that STV might be used to fight "corruption." Now, with the spread of majority systems, the impulse reemerged, and Hoag would need to manage it.

One part of the reform community sought to use majority systems to manage tensions in major-party primaries. Porter (1914: 582) records such use in Houston (TX) local elections as of 1913. For state-level primaries, this was in Washington (1907–17), Idaho (1909–19), North Dakota (1911–13), Wisconsin (1911–15), Florida (1912–29), Maryland (1912–unknown), Minnesota (1912–15), Alabama (1915–31), Indiana (1915–17),

Louisiana (1916–22), and Oklahoma (1925–26).[11] Modern observers will recall similar developments, with several state parties applying AV recently to nominating primaries. Some even adopted a "bottoms-up" version for selecting delegates to the 2020 Democratic National Convention.[12] The "RCV" systems now in Maine in New York City also apply AV in primaries.[13]

A larger part of the community, however, sought to eliminate nomination barriers entirely. For Porter (1914: 581), successful use of a majority system meant "voters' freedom of choice," which required ballot access "independent of boss or party." L. J. Johnson (1914: 91–92) agreed, criticizing an "excessive number of signatures sometimes required upon nominating petitions." On the "chief advantages of preferential voting," Johnson is worth quoting, as many of his claims appear in present-day advocacy:

1. "It permits the abolition of primaries without interference with the democratic method of nomination by a merely nominal number of petitioners." In modern terms, it eliminates the "low-turnout" primary.
2. "It permits the nomination of a large number of candidates with practical elimination of the danger of split tickets." In modern terms, it eliminates the "spoiler effect" in an election with more than two candidates.
3. "It fosters campaign methods which greatly reduce the difficulty of getting high grade men to stand for office. It minimizes the unattractiveness of the campaign and effectively discourages 'mud-slinging. . . .'"

---

[11] Bucklin users were Washington, Idaho, North Dakota, Florida, Alabama, Louisiana, and Oklahoma. In Alabama, North Dakota, and Florida, only the top two candidates proceeded to the second-round count. In Florida, second-choice votes were *not* added to first-choice votes for ballots already counted toward the top vote-getter. Wisconsin used conventional AV. Minnesota used STV to arrive at two frontrunners, then picked the one with more final-round votes. Both states limited voters to expressing two rankings. However, in Alabama and Oklahoma, a ballot was invalid unless the voter ranked at least two candidates. See Hoag (1914b: 6), Weeks (1937), and FairVote, "An Early 20th Century American Use of an Alternative Voting Method," http://archive.fairvote.org/index.php?page=2077, accessed November 2020. Rules used in Maryland and Indiana are unknown.

[12] The "bottoms-up" system is used for some local elections in Australia (Sanders 2011: 703). It involves eliminating trailing candidates, then reallocating their ballots to the next-ranked pick on each, until all seats have been filled. In this, it is similar to STV. However, in STV, the quota determines who wins, and ballots in excess of quota are surplus (see Chapter 1). In contrast to both the block-preferential system and to at-large elections with numbered posts, "bottoms-up" does not count the same ballot multiple times, letting the same majority of voters fill every seat. With respect to modern presidential primaries, "bottoms-up" is used with a 15 percent threshold, in accordance with national party rules (Santucci 2021: 346).

[13] Maine uniquely uses AV to structure *choice among parties* in Congressional general elections. This means that each party may nominate one candidate each.

In modern terms, it stimulates candidate entry by reducing incentives to campaign negatively.

4. "It is believed to be the safest known means of election for protecting the majority interest against machine or special interests." In modern terms, it eliminates distortion of the "public interest" (Gehl and Porter 2020: 4).

5. "It greatly simplifies the supremely important problem of securing high-grade, non-place hunting and competent elective officials." In modern terms, it elects "better people."[14]

Whereas Johnson spoke abstractly, Bucklin (1911: 100) was explicit about policy effects: "The commission government has as yet made but one tax levy, by which it reduced the tax four mills from the previous rate."

By 1913–14, then, Hoag was managing a fractious coalition of anti-party Progressives, lingering Populists, and party-government Socialists. In the end, his "representative council plan" won out. It called for STV elections to a council of seven or nine members, who then would choose a city manager. Ballots would not carry party affiliations, and candidates would self-nominate by petition.[15] In contrast to the commission form of government, all executive departments would be responsible to a council majority. Further, there would not be provision for elected figures' recall. Hoag and Thompson agreed on these last two points.

3.2 The menu of proportional systems

The PR League had been aware of at least three proportional systems (Gove 1894), as well as potential issues with the single transferable vote. At the heart of each system was election via quota: number of votes cast, divided by the number of seats to fill (i.e., district magnitude). Also at the heart of each was a preferential list. This list would determine the order in which *ineffective* votes would flow to other candidates. A vote becomes ineffective if (a) a candidate

---

[14] The term "better people" comes from a conversation, dated September 2019, with a federal campaign-finance regulator.
[15] Just before describing the "two objects of voting," Hoag (1914b: 4) writes as follows on parties: "In connection with all our voting, then, the ballots should be adequate or preferential ballots; nominations should be made by petition; party names and emblems should be excluded from the ballot; party conventions, though freely permitted, should not be officially supervised or recognized; and primary elections should be discontinued."

does not need it because they already have a quota or (b) mathematically, that candidate cannot win.

In developing PR systems, early reformers' reference point had been the "general ticket" or *scrutin de liste*, not the single-member plurality district. Other terms for this might be "at-large" election, "block vote," or multiple non-transferable vote. Colomer (2007) has shown, in fact, that many early innovations in electoral-system design were reactions to evolving strategies in this general-ticket system (i.e., slate coordination). Therefore, when early reformers were using the word "list," it was not in the way that we would use it (e.g., the only conceivable list system is one in which the party makes the list).

The first of the available PR systems was STV, then known as the "Hare system," named for its British inventor Thomas Hare (1859).[16] As advocates pointed out, this would give the voter full control, via their rank-ordering of candidates, of whom their vote would help elect. The voter would make their own list.

A second, known as the Gove system, would let each candidate make their own list. A vote cast for that candidate would flow in the order specified by the candidate.[17] There could be as many lists as there were candidates. If a party so chose, and if it were able to discipline its candidates, it could cause there to be just one list for all its candidates—dictating the order of their election.

Finally there was the ironically named (to us) "free list," which would let parties set the order of preference flow. One version of this would have come close to what we call closed-list PR. From the voter's perspective, a vote for Party X would amount to saying, "give my vote to your top candidate. If he or she does not need it, give it to your next-preferred candidate."

A second version of the free list was Gosnell's system, which we know as open-list PR with a single vote. A vote for Candidate Y in Party X would amount to saying, "I want my vote to count for Candidate Y. Use it to raise their position on your list."

If these system descriptions sound confusing, they should. We usually describe PR as a method for apportioning seats among parties. Within a

---

[16] James (1896) writes that Hare makes no reference to Gilpin, who invented free-list in 1844. Hence it is fair to call STV "first available."

[17] Alternatively, the order of flow could be determined by number of votes cast for each candidate. For example, a ballot cast for me counts first toward my election. But, if I do not need that vote, it flows to the candidate who got the most overall votes. And if they do not need it, it flows to the candidate who got the second-most overall votes, and so on.

party, list type then determines who gets to decide who gets those seats: the party or the voter. In the late 1800s, however, many people seem not to have thought in those terms. The central issue was who controlled the fate of a vote if (a) a candidate did not need it to win or (b) the most-preferred candidate ended up being hopeless (cf. Spence 1893 and possibly Commons 1896).

The PR League was aware of several potential defects in STV, all of which appear today in the reform debate. Gove (1894: 47) lists three:

1. "The one which appears to strike its advocates most forcibly is the necessity of transporting the ballots to one place to be counted, with the inconvenience and risk attendant thereon." In modern language, this is precinct non-summability. You cannot find the winners by aggregating precinct totals. Every ballot needs to go downtown. This objection appears today in modern Approval Voting advocacy, as well as in some critiques of the Alternative Vote.

2. "Another serious objection is that a heavy additional burden is imposed on the voter by requiring him to indicate several names in the order of his preference instead of indicating but one choice, as in the other systems. This burden the voter would be very loth to assume, since it is with difficulty that voters are induced to discharge the duties already imposed upon them." In other words, the voter would be overwhelmed with choice.

3. "Finally the system admits of manipulation of the ballots in the process of counting, which may affect the result. This may occur not merely in the transfer of the surplus votes of those candidates who receive more than quota"—i.e., which ballots are selected as surplus—"but in the transfer of votes cast for those who receive too few votes to be elected"—i.e., the order of candidate elimination. Later reformers developed varied solutions to these problems, e.g., fractional surplus-transfer methods such as Weighted Inclusive Gregory (now used in Minneapolis for park board elections) and another named for Boulder (CO). In Cambridge (MA), a "random draw of precincts" ensures that ballots are sufficiently shuffled so that, e.g., every Nth ballot selected for transfer is not from the same part of the city. If it were, the transfer process might benefit (or penalize) that part of the city disproportionately.

3.3   Party lists get their test

In 1913, PR faced its first referendum test in Los Angeles. Lessons learned here would set movement direction for years—with respect to reform-coalition construction and the type of PR to promote.

L.A. was important to early-1910s reformers. It had been seat of the direct-democracy movement since 1895, led by John Randolph Haynes's Direct Legislation League. The National Municipal League selected Los Angeles as the site of its 1912 conference, the primary job of which would be to rewrite that group's charter. One year later, on the heels of the NML convening, came the country's first binding referendum on PR of any type (Stevens 2003).

Schiesl (1975: 46) notes the split within the city's reform faction: "To prominent reformers who felt that political progressivism was capable of blunting the cutting edge of lower-class radicalism, the defeat of the Social-ists [in the 1911 mayoral election] was a vindication of the new politics." Even Theodore Roosevelt weighed in: "true progressives must stand against brutal wrongdoing on the part of labor." Labor had been implicated in a 1910 bombing of the *Los Angeles Times*. On the political front, Eugene Debs's old running mate, Job Harriman, nearly became mayor in 1911. Going into the reform process, the optics were not good.

From one perspective, the reform process was indeed a big-tent effort. L.A.'s PR initiative came from what might be called a coalition of the left and center. Included were: the Socialist Party, affiliated clubs, the Southern California Civic League, the local Good Government Organization, the Central Labor Council, at least two woman activists, and one Black man. Haynes of the Direct Legislation League led this group, known formally as the People's Charter Conference (PCC).

Yet there were some key omissions. Not invited to the late-1912 deliber-ations were the Merchants' and Manufacturers' Association, local Chamber of Commerce, and local Realty Board. These groups joined with the *Los Angeles Times* and *Los Angeles Examiner* to oppose the PCC, branded as the "Goo-Goo–Socialist Coalition." This right-wing reform caucus called itself the Citizens' Committee of One Thousand (CC) (Sitton 1995: 352–57).

An authoritative description of the PCC's PR amendment is hard to find, but all accounts agree on the prominence of party labels. According to Sitton (1995: 355), there were to be two stages: a primary and a general. Nomination was to be by petition, and the candidate could declare a party label. The voter would vote for a party, then rank candidates regardless of party lines. In the primary round, party-level quotas would determine how many of a party's candidates proceeded to the general (two per quota). Rankings would determine which of a party's candidates those would be (via an STV counting procedure). In the general election, party votes would determine seat shares, and rankings would determine which people got those seats. In the simplest possible terms, this was to be like open-list PR—fundamentally a contest among parties, with chance for the voter to affect who represents a party. From a party-organization perspective, it was not far from Gosnell's plan: party list, candidate vote. The one clear exception concerned ballot access. In the primary, candidates could declare whatever party label they wanted, so a party could not stop some candidate from seeking a place on its list. But, again, in the general election, the system would be based on party lists.

To counter the PCC proposal, the CC offered up a system similar to one now used in many cities: fifteen single-seat districts, six seats citywide, all filled by plurality. Either proposal would have replaced the "ward" system in use.

Beyond the election-related proposals, each side presented a raft of competing amendments. Depending on the source one consults, either the first eight or ten proposals came from the PCC, while the final eight came from the CC (Sitton 1995: 355; Stevens 2003: 35). Two more proposals from the sitting administration would have (a) fixed bonds of city officers and (b) provided for independent regulation of the city's harbor and adjacent lands, with salaries of the board members set by city council (The Editors 1913b). Also on the ballot was an ordinance to regulate "dance halls," apparently originating with a group of woman activists (The Editors 1913c).

How did the newspapers line up in this fight? On Sunday, March 23, two days before the referendum, the *Los Angeles Times* published the CC's full-page "sample ballot," instructing voters to oppose all but the eight CC amendments, including the dance-hall ordinance (The Editors 1913a). The *Times* itself endorsed all eight CC proposals, urged "no" votes on the eight obvious PCC proposals, opposed the PCC/administration harbor proposal, and gave no clear instruction on the administration bonding proposal. It did not mention the the dance-hall ordinance at all (The Editors 1913b).

Table 3.1 "Yes" vote for each amendment, Los Angeles, 1913. PCC = People's Charter Conference (reformers). CC = Citizens' Committee of One Thousand (anti-reformers).

Proposal (initiating party)	Yes %
Sale of land along aqueduct (CC)	81.9
Pension and insurance—firemen (CC)	76.3
Pension and insurance—police (CC)	73.5
Remove incumbent government (PCC)	64.3
LA River bed—regulate use and condemnatons in (PCC)	62.6
Regulate private utilities (PCC)	62.1
Municipal ownership of utilities (PCC)	61.8
Apply state home-rule law to LA (PCC)	61.6
Prohibit municipally—owned newspaper (CC)	60.5
Exec. agencies responsible to council (PCC)	59.5
Set city-council salaries (PCC)	57.4
Fix bonds of city officers (Admin)	52.2
Appointed harbor commission, council sets salaries (Admin)	51.9
Proportional representation (PCC)	**48.2**
Private biz in city parks, commission fixes salaries (CC)	46.8
Elected harbor commission, railroad, fixed salaries (CC)	39.9
Districts plus at-large (CC)	39.9
Raise electeds' salaries (CC)	37.3
Regulate the dance halls (Other)	26.3

Table 3.1 shows how each amendment fared.[18] While both election provisions failed, several features of what would become the Model Charter passed. These included powers to regulate public utilities, many of which were privately owned at the time (e.g., water, gas); municipal home rule; and executive responsibility to city council. Each of these had been a point of agreement between L.A.'s reform coalition *and* Thompson's 1913 comment on Hoag's emerging "representative council plan."[19] Finally, while the right-wing election reforms had failed, PR had lost by less than two points.

[18] The vote in favor is calculated as (yes vote)/[(yes vote)+(no vote)]. There were 455 precincts. The official results include "yes" and "no" votes for each initiative. The data are available from the Los Angeles City Archives, Erwin C. Piper Technical Center, *Records of Election Returns*, December 5, 1904, to December 9, 1920, Vol. 1, pp. 166–81.

[19] The executive-responsibility provision had been a reaction to "corruption" under the commission form of government—the main plan of municipal reform before Hoag would popularize the council-manager system. In theory, each member of a city commission would be exclusively responsible for decisions in some policy domain. In practice, however, there would be distributive logrolling, and this had been one reason for the pre-1912 turn to single-winner Bucklin voting (Bucklin 1911: 89).

The most popular PCC proposal was a measure to recall the sitting government. One might view it as the main point of consensus in the PCC coalition. Later on, when other cities' voters successfully reformed their charters, measures like this one would be built in de facto. That is because, after Ashtabula, every PR system came as part of an entirely new form of city government: the council-manager charter. At this early stage in L.A., however, reformers were considering issues in one-by-one fashion, not as a package.

Notably, PR was the least popular PCC amendment. Each of the others passed. Why did PR fail?

It is tempting to say that the *Los Angeles Times* did all it could to split the reform coalition. Working with the CC faction, it had framed the PCC amendments as a series of "Socialist designs" (The Editors 1913b). But the paper was especially critical of the PR proposal:

Amendment No. 8 seeks to set up a theoretical form of government under a proportional representation[20] which does away with majority rule upon which the very foundation of our government is based. It is a grotesque scheme of the Socialists to secure control of the city. It is un-American and un-representative. Its adoption will destroy the credit of the city, and plunge it into debt and endless litigation. It provides for a government by parties....

How effective was this strategy in defeating the PR charter amendment? One way to get a sense is to examine the returns. Treating the recall proposal as a point of reference, and comparing the PR outcome to outcomes on the other measures, we can see how the PCC had split on PR elections.

Figure 3.3 gives scatter plots for each PCC proposal. In each case, precinct-level "yes" shares for the recall proposal are on the *y* axis, and "yes" shares for the other proposal are on the *x* axis. In each plot, the diagonal line segment represents a one-to-one relationship. If people who approved of the recall proposal (the most popular PCC proposal) also tended to approve of the other proposal, dots would cluster around the one-to-one line. That is true in five of seven cases. The PCC proposal on city-council salaries was somewhat

---

[20] Note how the editors refer to "a proportional representation." In our own time, reform opponents routinely refer to "rank" (rather than "ranked") choice voting.

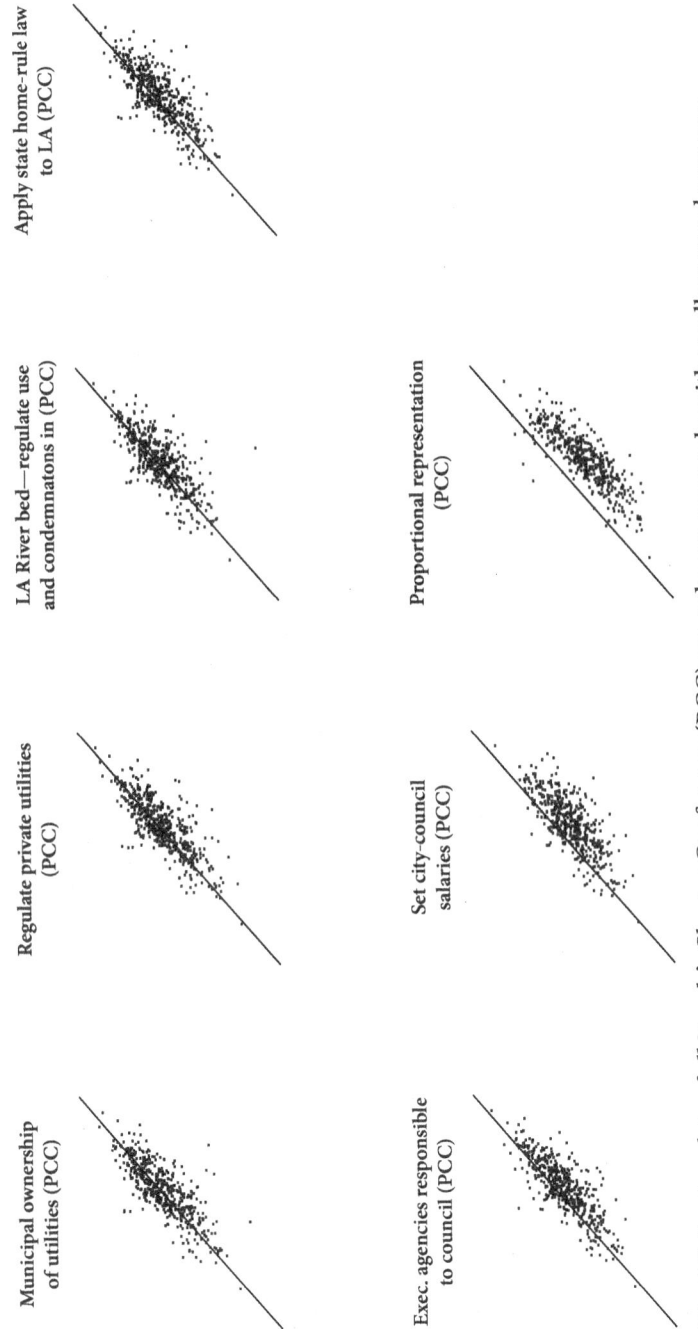

Fig. 3.3 Scatter plots of all People's Charter Conference (PCC) amendment proposals, with recall proposal on *y* axes, Los Angeles, 1913 (precincts).

Municipal ownership of utilities (PCC)

Regulate private utilities (PCC)

LA River bed—regulate use and condemnatons in (PCC)

Apply state home-rule law to LA (PCC)

Exec. agencies responsible to council (PCC)

Set city-council salaries (PCC)

Proportional representation (PCC)

unpopular, with many dots below the line. By far the least popular with pro-recall voters, however, was PR.

Hoag wasted no time in framing the outcome. Writing for *Equity* in April 1913, he published a series of "excerpts from letters from Mr. Fred Wheeler, leading Socialist the city and an active worker for proportional representation there." Wheeler emphasized the politics of navigating the newspapers (Hoag 1913b). But he also suggested a generally favorable view of the PR idea: while the CC's districts-plus-at-large proposal had lost in a landslide, PR had lost by only two points. And the very next column described Hoag's efforts to promote the "representative council plan" in Ohio, where a 1912 constitution had just established municipal home rule. Finally, he wrote:

> The information bureau of the National Socialist Party is commending the Hare plan [i.e., STV] to the attention of all Socialists seeking information on the revision of city charters. (Hoag 1913c)

It was time to take the parties out of proportional representation. The first place that would happen was Ashtabula (OH).

3.4 The Model City Charter emerges

In January 1916, a political scientist from the Case Western Reserve University announced "the latest step in municipal organization"—a city-manager charter with STV elections (Hatton 1916). This new "Ashtabula plan" got full expression in August 1915, when STV was added to a charter passed one year earlier. Reformers could identify two ways in which this plan improved on the alternatives.

Versus the commission form of government, the Ashtabula plan lodged all executive authority in a single city manager, responsible to a city council majority. The popularity of this reform had been one lesson from Los Angeles. It also made STV possible in the first place, as voters would choose an assembly, not an executive. In other words, the Ashtabula plan called for something like *parliamentary* government: the council chooses a manager, and the manager runs city government at council's pleasure.

But the Ashtabula plan also aimed for *coalition* government. On August 12, 1913, Dayton (OH) became the first major city to adopt a manager charter. Its council was to be small, elections citywide, ballots without party labels, and winners by plurality. Dayton gave Hoag a frame for pitching his representative-council plan: "a council elected at large in the usual way," writes Hatton (1916: 58), "would probably represent only one party, and that this was not desirable if the council was to choose the manager." This point Hoag had made to Asthabula's charter commission.

Ashtabula initially went with Dayton's plan. Sometime between that decision and the switch to STV, the National Municipal League wrote STV into its model charter (Childs 1965: 65). Hoag's "representative council plan" had become the national template.

Why did Ashtabula end up adopting STV? Several possibilities come to mind. First, it may have been the national consensus on the new model charter. Developments in the city make it difficult to say. Efforts to add PR to the local council-manager system appear to have been going on at the same time that the National Municipal League was deliberating STV. It is worth noting that, in the same year that the L.A. business community beat back the "Goo-Goo–Socialist coalition," a similar coalition faced similar opposition in proposing STV for Dayton (Barber 1995c: 50). One year later, in August 1914, the Municipal League had come out unambiguously for STV.

A second possibility is that reformers did not *alienate* the business community. Although the Socialists did want PR in Ashtabula, Hoag had worked primarily with one William Boynton, a former city council president and railroad engineer (Hatton 1916: 58). Boynton had secured endorsement from the local Chamber of Commerce (Busch 1995: 92). While that had not been sufficient to secure STV in the first round of charter talks, it did pass one year later in what the *Akron Beacon Journal* called "the smallest vote ever cast in the city" (The Editors 1915). Further, our best account of the newspapers suggests much less vociferous opposition than there had been in Los Angeles. According to Hatton (1916: 62), "the two daily papers were inclined to look askance at the new system." This hardly sounds like an endorsement, but it also does not sound like a full-page "sample ballot" that calls the plan a radical plot.

Finally, notes Busch (1995: 90–94), the local party system had been fractious. According to one contemporary observer, the incumbent Republican government faced criticism for its inaction on the prohibition issue (Bloomfield 1926). In the end, according to Busch, three groups put STV over the top: Ashtabula's out-of-power Socialist and Democratic Parties, then a group of "disgruntled Republicans." A reform strategy had taken shape.

3.5 Recap

Anti-party reform coalitions choose anti-party institutions. Ranked ballots became hegemonic because they "work" with non-partisan elections. Under-sized assemblies also became hegemonic. Reformers had been using all three devices already, which accelerated in the wake of the 1912 Republican schism. Socialists preferred list systems, consistent with their party-centered view of politics, but they lacked the influence to press their demand. Party-list's defeat in Los Angeles made that clear, and STV's victory in Ashtabula reinforced it. Yet an anti-party current had been present from the start, as one might expect in a two-party system.

4
Spreading the Reform Template

> The tide of sentiment in favor of change is fully as strong as it was in Cleveland and the work of organizing that sentiment is much more thoroughgoing and systematic.
>
> Walter J. Millard (1924), Field Secretary, PR League

By 1916, reformers had settled on a consensus template: council-manager government, single-digit assemblies, citywide districts, nomination by petition, non-partisan ballots, and STV elections. Most of these features can be found today in many cities—except STV. Only twenty-four cities went on to include that feature. What explains the divergence?

Despite anti-party features baked into the charter, this chapter argues that parties made the difference—in particular, the presence of a non-negligible minority party. This at least opened a path to an STV charter. As I argued earlier, electoral reforms bear the imprints of the coalitions that impose them. Already in 1914, experts knew that multi-seat plurality could cut off minority representation (Hoag 1914d). And the Socialists had warned that non-partisan elections might empower moneyed interests by depriving voters of cues (Thompson 1913; Lippmann 1913 [1975]). But STV still held out promise for minority representation, and that minority often turned out to be a party.

Just because a party joins a reform coalition does not make that coalition *pro-party*. Recall Chapter 2 on the number of parties and what kinds of coalition are possible. If there are just two parties, we get four: single-party realigners (whose goal is to damage the opposition), single-party insulators, anti-party realigners, and anti-party insulators (because the incumbent coalition is already cross-party).

The empirical trend in STV cities, as we will see below, was anti-party realignment.[1] Broadly, these are cases where one party's reformers needed

---

[1] Theoretically, an incumbent government might use STV to insulate, especially if the coalition is cross-party. No city followed such a path, at least based on evidence consulted for this chapter. We will see some examples in Chapter 8, all of which are modern cases.

More Parties or No Parties: The Politics of Electoral Reform in America. Jack Santucci, Oxford University Press.
© Oxford University Press 2022. DOI: 10.1093/oso/9780197630655.003.0004

Reproduced by Permission of The Cincinnati Post

Fig. 4.1 Newspaper advertisement for a new city charter, Cincinnati, 1924, issued to reformers in other cities via the *National Municipal Review*.

help from the local minority party (or parties). Or they are cases where the minority party needed help from the opposition "reform" faction. Figure 4.1 shows how reformers marketed such charters (Millard 1924: 602).[2] The emphasis is on getting rid of "party responsibility," with literally no mention of the electoral system.

[2] Also reprinted in Kolesar (1995).

If there is just one party to begin with, as is common in local politics, competition plays out within the party. All reform coalitions are necessarily *anti-party*. In the context of the Model Charter, there is no need for "proportional" rules. The citywide district on its own will aggregate votes over a large geographic area. Out-groups can use such rules against the incumbents, and incumbents might use such rules against their opponents. Here, it is useful to have in mind Progressive Republicans and, later, "amateur Democrats" (Wilson 1962). So, plurality charters might come through insulation or realignment. Since the focus is on STV, I do not document that extensively. The point is that one-party systems, regardless of reform mode, should lead to plurality charters.

What about two-party systems that led to plurality charters? Some of these were single-party-realigning episodes—opportunistic attacks on an opposing party. One of these is described in detail below (Brockton, MA). Another (Springfield, OH) adopted council-manager government before STV was widely promoted. Ideas matter.

Finally, there were cities with pre-existing multiparty politics.[3] In one of these (Ashtabula, OH), Socialists were responding directly to the defeat in Los Angeles. In the others, reform coalitions came close to being *multiparty realigning*. New York and Cleveland stand out, respectively, for partisan ballots and a (relatively) large council. Still, the important basics were constant, owing to the role of anti-party defectors: small city councils, nomination by petition, and non-partisan STV elections.

The chapter proceeds in four sections. First I document the STV reform coalitions. In all cases with available information, reform was realigning. No incumbent government imposed STV on its own. And the modal coalition comprised ruling-party defectors working with one or more minority parties. The sizes of winning and losing reform coalitions are consistent with this observation, partly because STV adoptions were in competitive territory (see just below).

A second section turns to plurality charters. Using county-level voting in gubernatorial elections as a proxy for partisan balance, with charter-change episodes in America's one hundred largest cities, I show that such charters tended to cluster in counties without inter-party competition. A small group of them does appear in competitive territory. This suggests that some fights over plurality charters were between-party affairs. (Recall from Chapter 2

---

[3] Kalamazoo (MI) does not appear to have had multiparty politics. Rather, Socialists were the lone opposition party.

that single-party realigning episodes can be about long-term damage to the opposition.) But no STV adoption was outside of competitive territory.

A third section tells the story of charter reform in three industrial New England cities: Worcester (MA), which adopted a PR charter in 1947; Waterbury (CT), which rejected one in 1939; and Brockton (MA), which adopted a plurality charter in 1955. Precinct-level data from Worcester are consistent with narrative evidence: ruling-party defectors (Democrats) working with the minority party (Republicans in this case). Further data show that these defectors tended to be in precincts with sharply contested primaries under the previous "partisan" charter. Waterbury shows what happened when the ruling party did not split; a minority-party-led reform campaign failed. And Brockton is an example of plurality adoption in competitive territory; Republicans used reform to displace a Democratic administration.

A final section covers "big picture" factors. One of these is known today is "identity politics." The other is organized labor. Most early STV adoptions were in Republican territory, and most late ones displaced Democratic Party organizations. This reform wave straddled one of the century's two great realignments: labor's movement into the Democratic tent. (The other was racial, and it appears later.) There are signs of labor's role throughout the PR historiography, as well as in primary sources consulted for this chapter. But the point about labor is still just a hunch and should be treated as such.

4.1 Coalition-realigning STV adoption

This section documents the STV adoption coalitions, given evidence available at the time of writing.[4] The core point is that no city got STV from its ruling coalition, on its own. In some cases, voters could impose a PR-manager charter directly, with less advance organizing. Often, such charters were written into state law, such as the Plan E charter in the Massachusetts Code. This removed the need for local-level bargaining over details. Bargaining became necessary if reformers first needed to go through a charter review commission (e.g., apparently in California, Colorado, Connecticut, Ohio, and Michigan). In cases like these, reformers first had to force the authorization of such commissions (i.e., they "wedged").

---

[4] For some cities, I have been able to update the information in Santucci (2017).

Studying the composition of adoption coalitions is not easy. This is because reformers wrote much of their own history, possibly concealing partisan motives among reform partners.[5] A good example is Harris (1930), who wrote a forty-eight-page redux of adoptions-to-date for the National Municipal League, just before its absorption of the original PR League. The article gives details on charter review processes, early STV elections, rates of voter error, advances in vote-counting, and so on. But it is mostly silent on the coalition politics of adoption.

Academic studies do exist for a few cases. But many of these are implicit (at best) about reform leaders' partisan ties. One reason is that the "extended party network" is not what authors were looking for; the city committee of Party X either endorsed reform or not.[6] Often, only people's names are given, or the names of formal pressure groups. One can search newspapers, but contemporary papers tended to not report partisanship—especially if they backed the reform project. The best one can do is to read between the lines and, if needed, search the Internet vigorously.

Nevertheless, summary statistics can be extracted from the record. For five cities, I could not find any history. Histories for two more identify ruling parties but not change agitators (Boulder and West Hartford). In two of the remaining seventeen cases documents identify only ruling-party defectors (Saugus and Revere, MA). In thirteen more cases, reform elites came exclusively from the ruling party and its main opposition. Three final cases involved elites from the ruling party and more than one former out-party (Ashtabula, Cleveland, and New York City). Overall, in fifteen of nineteen documented cases, incumbent-party defectors cooperated with the leaders of minority parties in efforts to pass STV charters. And no case involved an incumbent government acting alone, at least as far as we can tell. The data are summarized in Table 4.1.

---

[5] Consider what it took to document Maine's Democratic-led adoption of the Alternative Vote in 2016. The campaign website scrubbed endorsers' party affiliations from its website, such that these had to be recovered from archived copies on the Wayback Machine. On the Republican side, one can no longer find a video of old-line party leaders endorsing AV, which they did three weeks before the referendum. When one studies the returns, though, the coalition is obvious: four-fifths of Democrats, and one-fifth of Republicans (Santucci 2018b).

[6] Consider Weaver and Blount (1995: 213–14) on Hamilton (OH), who write that "neither party organization took a position on this issue." Closer reading of their work points to Republican support (the minority party), in tandem with support from Democratic defectors (the incumbent party). On the same page, they write, "A surprisingly broad segment of the city's political leadership, including Mayor Koehler [D], endorsed the charter. However, nine of the ten council members [seven Democrats, three Republicans] opposed it." Similarly, Barber (1995b: 123) writes on Cleveland: "PR/STV triggered the opposition of . . . both political parties." Yet Maxey (1922) suggests an alliance between Progressive Republicans and the Democratic establishment.

Table 4.1 Party affiliations of pro-reform elites for the twenty-four cities that adopted STV.

City	State	Year	Incumbent party	Elite STV supporters	Source(s)
Ashtabula	OH	1915	Rep	some Rep, Dem, Socialist	Busch (1995: 90)
Kalamazoo	MI	1918	Rep	some Rep, Socialist	Hatton (1918: 343–45)
Boulder	CO	1917	Rep	None named	Winter (1982)
West Hartford	CT	1920	Rep	None named	Gallup (1921)
Sacramento	CA	1920	None named	None named	Engler (1921)
Cleveland	OH	1921	Rep	some Rep, some Dem, Socialist	Barber (1995b: 118–122) and Maxey (1922)
Cincinnati	OH	1924	Rep	some Rep, Dem	Seasongood (1933) and Reed et al. (1957)
Hamilton	OH	1926	Dem	some Dem, Rep	Weaver and Blount (1995: 213)
Toledo	OH	1934	Rep	some Rep, Dem	Anderson (1995: 242)
Wheeling	WV	1935	Rep	some Rep, Dem	Hallett (1935)
New York	NY	1936	Dem	some Dem, Rep, Fusion, Am. Labor	Prosterman (2013)
Norris	TN	1936	None named	None named	
Yonkers	NY	1938	Rep	some Rep, Dem	Haynes (2001: 35, 162–168)
Cambridge	MA	1940	Dem	some Dem, Rep	Spalding (1987a, 1987b)
Lowell	MA	1942	Dem	some Dem, Rep	Dobrusin (1955: 62–63)
Long Beach	NY	1943	Dem	some Dem, Rep	Miller (2007)
Marshfield	OR	1944	None named	None named	
Saugus	MA	1947	Rep	some Rep	Saugus adopts (1947), Saugus elects (1948)
Worcester	MA	1947	Dem	some Dem, Rep	Binstock (1960) and Edwards (1972)
Quincy	MA	1947	Rep	some Rep, Dem	Dobrusin (1955: 160)
Medford	MA	1947	Rep	some Rep, Dem	Dobrusin (1955: 139–141)
Revere	MA	1947	Rep	some Rep	Dobrusin (1955: 118–119)
Hopkins	MN	1947	None named	None named	Vesely (1970)
Oak Ridge	TN	1948	None named	None named	

4.1.1 STV wins and oversized reform coalitions

In the next section, I will show that STV cities tended to be divided in their partisanship, at least at the gubernatorial level. If this is true, and if successful coalitions for STV charters usually included most of one party and some faction of the other, we would expect lopsided outcomes when it won at referendum. Figure 4.2 gives the distribution of referendum "yes" shares. There were fifty-nine such referendums from 1900 to 1956, with vote shares available for fifty.[7] The average vote for a winning STV charter was 69.1 percent, versus 38.6 percent for losing charters (difference significant with 99 percent confidence). Coalitions were larger when these referendums won.

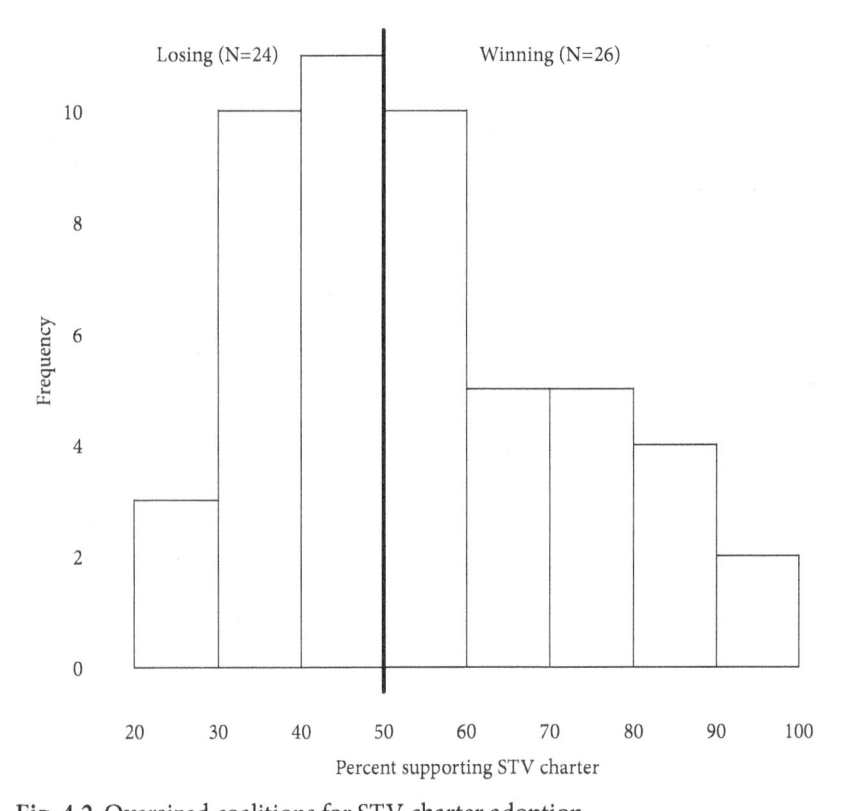

Fig. 4.2 Oversized coalitions for STV charter adoption.

---

[7] Data come from quarterly issues of the *Proportional Representation Review*, 1893–1932, then from monthly issues of the *National Municipal Review*, 1933–57. There are 26 winning referendums, not 24, because Saugus (MA) and Marshfield/Coos Bay (OR) each held two.

4.1.2 Note on near-multiparty adoption coalitions

What about cases in which the adoption coalition included minor parties? Should not these charters have been different from the reform template? In particular, should they not have provided for partisan ballots, at least? There are three clear cases of multiparty involvement: Ashtabula, Cleveland, and New York City. As noted in the previous chapter, Ashtabula Socialists went with the national template, persuaded by Clarence Hoag, PR League field staff, and the defeat in Los Angeles. Cleveland had a twenty-five-seat assembly, apportioned among four districts (magnitudes of five, six, seven, and seven). By contrast, most other councils were of seven or nine members.

New York City's reform coalition went with something different entirely, explicitly rejecting the PR-manager template (Tanzer 1936: 536). Partly, this was designed to reward party organization. Party labels (but not logos) would appear on the ballot. Candidates could not use such labels without county-committee permission. But these pro-party features should not be overstated. District magnitude would fluctuate with voter turnout, itself a function of restricted registration and disenfranchisement due to ballot invalidity: one seat to each borough for every 75,000 valid votes cast therein. As elsewhere, nomination would be by petition (2,000 signatures). Multiple parties could endorse the same candidate, and PR would be via STV.[8]

Further, the New York charter was an instrument of minority veto. Contemporary reformers played this down. Writing in the *National Municipal Review*, for example, Tanzer (1936: 537) emphasized the charter's unicameral spirit. By abolishing the old Board of Aldermen, he argued, "the council is given greater importance." But a new Board of Estimate would need to concur on "local laws" that affected "administration of the city government" (read: hiring) or amending the charter. Further, the separately elected mayor could veto any local law, and two-thirds of council were required to override this. Finally, the charter distinguished a second class of legislative action: deleting items from the capital budget. Three-fourths of council were needed to do this. These provisions ensured that the core of the reform

---

[8] See Tanzer (1937) for the actual charter.

coalition—either American Labor or the Republican Party—would be able to extract policy concessions.[9]

But most STV cities simply went with the Model Charter. And far more cities did so, while removing STV. The next section gives a sense of why that happened.

4.2 Plurality charter adoption

When Cincinnati's Progressive Republicans began their 1924 reform campaign, the goal was familiar: council-manager government, non-partisan ballots, and plurality-at-large elections. The core of the movement was a "Birdless Ballot League," dedicated to removing party logos from ballots: an eagle for Republicans, a rooster for Democrats. In return for supporting the "Birdless Ballot" campaign, Democrats insisted on the STV provision (Kolesar 1995: 163).

Contrast Cincinnati with a standard account of plurality charters. Focusing on the Southwest, Bridges (1997) argues these were built for one-party regimes. The parties in those cases were "good-government" committees, which she terms non-partisan slating groups (NPSG).[10] NPSG seized on a familiar property of at-large plurality: single factions find it easy to dominate these contests by presenting common slates (Calabrese 2000).

Others suggest that NPSG were the regular parties, just going by different names. An early analysis of precinct-level voting in three cities (1949–57) found that support for Republican gubernatorial candidates was correlated with support for slate candidates at 0.77 or greater (Williams and Adrian 1959). More recently, an event-history analysis of 191 big cities finds that county-level unemployment and Republican presidential voting are the strongest predictors of manager charter adoption, 1930–65 (Choi et al. 2013).

Existing understanding of plurality charters is consistent with three possibilities. First, they were just ways to dislodge ruling parties, then rely on non-partisanship to keep power.[11] A second possibility is that, in

---

[9] In a later article, McCaffrey (1939: 843) lists members of the charter commission: woman civic leaders, judges, lawyers, federal civil servants, Socialists, Fusionists, insurance brokers, employees of the Consolidated Edison Company, president of the Chamber of Commerce, and "a far-seeing real estate developer."

[10] Also see Schaffner et al. (2001).

[11] See Schaffner et al. (2007) on how this works for either major party.

hegemonic-party systems, reformers and/or regulars sought to dislodge each other. Finally, plurality charters may have allowed incumbents to insulate, be they party regulars or reformers.

All three possibilities suggest a "party parity" hypothesis: no STV charters where inter-party competition is low. By contrast, plurality charters can appear at any level of competitiveness.

To explore the party parity hypothesis, I analyze all council-manager adoption episodes, 1900–50, in cities ever among the one hundred largest during the twentieth century.[12] The sample comprises sixty-one charter-reform episodes, eight of which led to STV charters.[13]

I measure partisanship from county-level gubernatorial returns because results from a large number of cities' historic elections are prohibitively difficult to collect (Marschall et al. 2011). The same is true of city-level results to state and national elections. Readily available are county-level returns to presidential and gubernatorial elections. I assume that city partisanship roughly tracks gubernatorial partisanship. This assumption rests on Gimpel (1996), plus the frequent observation that state and local parties are linked.[14]

---

[12] This follows the approach of Trounstine (2008). The list of episodes comes from annual editions of the *Municipal Year Book*, 1934–50, by way of Choi et al. (2013). Cities that repealed council-manager charters prior to 1934 do not appear in those volumes. To identify these cases, I consult the *City Manager Yearbook* (1921 and 1922) and quarterly *Proportional Representation Review* (1893–1932). The *Municipal Year Book* and its predecessors document the dates that new charters took effect, but these were often a year or more after adoption. To determine adoption dates, I searched newspapers, case histories, and trade journals on Google Scholar, Google Books, and Google News. I could not find dates for nine episodes. For these cases, I subtracted two years from the charter effective date to construct a plausible adoption year.

[13] The STV charters (and dates they went into operation) are: Sacramento, CA (1921); Cleveland, OH (1924); Cincinnati, OH (1924); Wheeling, WV (1935); Toledo, OH (1936); Yonkers, NY (1940); Cambridge, MA (1942); Lowell, MA (1944); and Worcester, MA (1950). The non-STV charters (and dates they went into operation) are: Amarillo, TX (1913); Dayton, OH (1914); Springfield, OH (1914); Phoenix, AZ (1914); Bakersfield, CA (1915); Newburgh, NY (1916); San Jose, CA (1916); Grand Rapids, MI (1917); Wichita, KS (1917); Portsmouth, VA (1917); Lubbock, TX (1917); Wheeling, WV (1917); Norfolk, VA (1918); Albuquerque, NM (1918); Anaheim, CA (1919); Watervliet, NY (1920); Auburn, NY (1920); Akron, OH (1920); Dubuque, IA (1920); Lynchburg, VA (1920); Petersburg, VA (1920); Bay City, MI (1921); Middleborough, MA (1921); Tampa, FL (1921); Greensboro, NC (1921); Nashville, TN (1921); Colorado Springs, CO (1921); Glendale, CA (1921); Long Beach, CA (1921); Alexandria, VA (1922); Columbus, GA (1922); Berkeley, CA (1923); Kansas City, MO (1926); Indianapolis, IN (1927); Flint, MI (1930); Dallas, TX (1931); Oakland, CA (1931); Binghamton, NY (1932); Covington, KY (1932); Lexington, KY (1932); San Diego, CA (1932); Elmira, NY (1934); Trenton, NJ (1935); Schenectady, NY (1936); Saginaw, MI (1936); Wilmington, NC (1941); Houston, TX (1943); Raleigh, NC (1947); Hartford, CT (1948); Richmond, VA (1948); Columbia, SC (1949); and Des Moines, IA (1950). Going "into operation" means that the first government elected under said charter took office.

[14] See, e.g., Erie (1988) for an "intergovernmental" view of city politics.

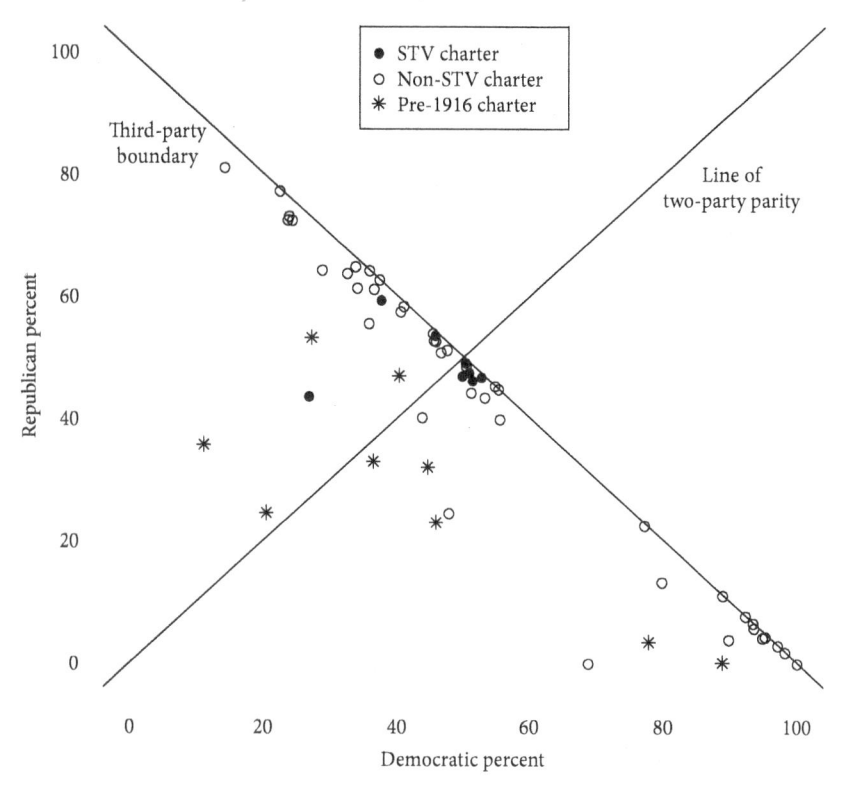

Fig. 4.3 Electoral-rule outcomes for all sixty-one big-city charter reform episodes, 1900–50, by county gubernatorial partisanship.

Figure 4.3 gives the distance from gubernatorial two-party parity for all episodes in the sample. The axes represent the Republican and Democratic proportions, respectively, of the county-level gubernatorial vote immediately preceding an episode. The data come from W. D. Burnham (1999). I lag gubernatorial partisanship in order to reduce concerns about reverse causation. Selecting an appropriate lag required determining exactly when each charter referendum occurred. When I could not find this date, I subtracted two years from the charter effective date.[15]

The northeast-southwest diagonal represents the expected relationship between these vote shares were the major parties at parity. The

[15] For the California gubernatorial election of 1918, I manually recoded one independent and one fusion candidacy as Democratic and Republican, respectively. The independent was Theodore Arlington Bell, a Democratic candidate in 1906, 1910, and 1918. The fusion candidacy appeared on the ballot as Republican, Prohibition, and Progressive. No other Democratic, Republican, Prohibition, or Progressive lines appeared on that ballot.

northwest-southeast diagonal is where a city would appear if no minor party polled votes. Filled points reflect STV charters, empty points represent plurality charters, and blown-up asterisks represent manager charters adopted before 1916 (or, if the adoption year is not available, that went into effect before 1916).[16] Recall that the National Municipal League warmed to STV during the Ashtabula effort, culminating in Hatton's (1916) paper. Before then, STV was not widely promoted.

Patterns in the plot are consistent with the parity hypothesis. No city adopts an STV charter with a two-party division more lopsided than 60–40. The glaring outlier is Sacramento, with a strong third-party presence. Second, no city adopts an STV charter where one party is hegemonic (top-left and bottom-right). Hegemonic-party jurisdictions could not supply the contestation needed for a pro-STV coalition. Third, competitiveness does not guarantee STV charter adoption. We see both STV and non-STV cases in the center of the plot, where Republicans and Democrats are evenly matched. Going by most to least competitive, the top three non-STV outcomes are: Kansas City, MO (adopted 1925); Binghamton, NY (adopted 1931); and Springfield, OH (adopted 1913). The Kansas City charter is a famous example of a party "machine" turning "reform" on its head: Democratic boss Tom Pendergast in this case (Frederickson et al. 2004: 79). In Binghamton, Democrats used the council-manager charter to oust a Republican administration, in power since 1920.[17] Finally, the Springfield charter, adopted 1913, might have contained STV if adopted later. Trounstine (2008: 242) reports "no evidence of machine or reform monopoly in the twentieth century."[18]

4.3 Different reforms in three New England cities

This section looks closely at three different reform outcomes: a non-STV charter win, an STV charter loss, and an STV charter win. One goal is to validate the "mechanisms" that underly patterns above, including by looking at a "negative" case (cf. Geddes 1990, Lieberman 2005). Another is just

---

[16] These are (with effective dates): Amarillo, TX (1913); Dayton, OH (1914); Springfield, OH (1914); Phoenix, AZ (1914); Bakersfield, CA (1915); Newburgh, NY (1916); San Jose, CA (1916); Portsmouth, VA (1917); and Wheeling, WV (1917).

[17] Compare the Political Graveyard's list of mayors (http://politicalgraveyard.com/geo/NY/ofc/binghamton.html, accessed December 1, 2020) with partisanship data from local historian Steve Litwin (http://sites.rootsweb.com/~nybroome/brpoltab.htm, accessed December 1, 2020).

[18] This also suggests that the plurality elections *alone* might not preclude responsiveness. Possible outcomes include alternation between slates (cf. Calabrese 2006), bipartisan slates, and/or multiparty slates (cf. Colomer 2007).

to look more closely at Massachusetts, where the "reform wave" has been understudied. To do these things, we go to southern New England.[19]

Sampling follows a most-similar logic. I chose three cities with common structural traits: Brockton (MA), which adopted at-large plurality in 1955; Waterbury (CT), which rejected PR in 1939; and Worcester (MA), which adopted PR in 1947. All are within 150 miles' drive, witnessed reform attempts at mid-century, were among the one hundred largest U.S. cities at the time, had similar demographic profiles, had similar economic bases, and underwent industrial decline at mid-century. Each involved an attempted departure from the mayor-council form of government. Each had direct primaries at the time of its referendum, and each had a Democratic administration. Table 4.2 presents all available characteristics of each city at the time of its referendum. Measures are from the *City Data Book* (U.S. Dept. of Commerce, Bureau of the Census 1978).[20]

Table 4.2 Background characteristics of three southern New England cities with mid-century charter referendums.

Variable	Brockton (MA)	Worcester (MA)	Waterbury (CT)
Reform outcome	At-large plurality	STV win	STV defeat
Referendum year	1955	1947	1939
Prior partisan control	Democratic	Democratic	Democratic
Had direct primaries at time of referendum	Yes	Yes	Yes
Population	62,860	203,486	99,314
Percent Black	1.5%	1.1%	2.1%
Percent of population employed	40.6%	38.8%	41.6%
Percent manufacturing production workers	32.6%	48.0%	47.1%
Percent retail workers	16.7%	17.4%	11.5%
Manufacturing establishments per capita	0.035	0.03	0.002
Occupied housing units per capita	0.304	0.270	0.256
Average monthly rent	$26.82	$30.97	$28.31

---

[19] It will be clear from the vignettes below that they were part of the same "reform project," even if the New England wave came later.

[20] Data are from the *City Data Books* (CDB) for 1942, 1948, 1950, and 1955. All variables except reform outcome, referendum year, prior partisan control, and presence of direct primaries come from the most proximate CDB. "Percent Black" for Waterbury is percent non-white, following the 1942 CDB, which uses a 1940 U.S. Census estimate.

If STV adoption typically involved a defector-minority party alliance, we expect to see most out-parties and a substantial part of the outgoing majority party supporting it at referendum. Our confidence increases if we can connect these trends to the presence or absence, in descriptive records, of party leaders' posture toward reform. Contrasting STV wins with failures and non-events (i.e., plurality charter adoptions) will draw out these differences.

On the quantitative side, I interpret the correlation of precinct-level support for charter reform with some indication of voters' partisanship. Precinct-level party registration rates are obvious candidates, but many cities have discarded them, and registration may not capture turnout. Instead I use the vote in partisan mayoral races. In two of three cities, mayoral voting was on the same day as the charter referendum.

On the descriptive side, I consult narrative sources for evidence of ruling-party disunity on the question of charter reform. The sources are secondary if available and helpful, local newspapers if not. I also consulted archives for one case. When consulting newspapers, I identified the dates of relevant elections, then read each issue for the week in advance of the relevant date. Newspapers are a good source of early century political information. Many printed precinct-level election returns for primaries and caucuses, and politicians used them to communicate with voters.

4.3.1 Plurality charter in Brockton

Brockton (MA) adopted a seven-seat council-manager charter with plurality elections in 1955.[21] The preceding mayor-council system had been in place since 1888. Change was a largely Republican effort to dislodge a Democratic administration.

Republicans consolidated control of city government following a move to biennial elections in 1921. The party thereafter built a precinct-based organization robust enough to help it survive five corruption indictments in 1925, then a series of divisive primaries in 1935. Every mayor during the period was Republican. Then the tide turned.[22]

---

[21] Gildea v. Ellershaw, 363 Mass. 800.
[22] See the Brockton Enterprise, late October and early November issues, on microfilm at the Brockton Public Library. I thank David MacRae for research assistance on Brockton.

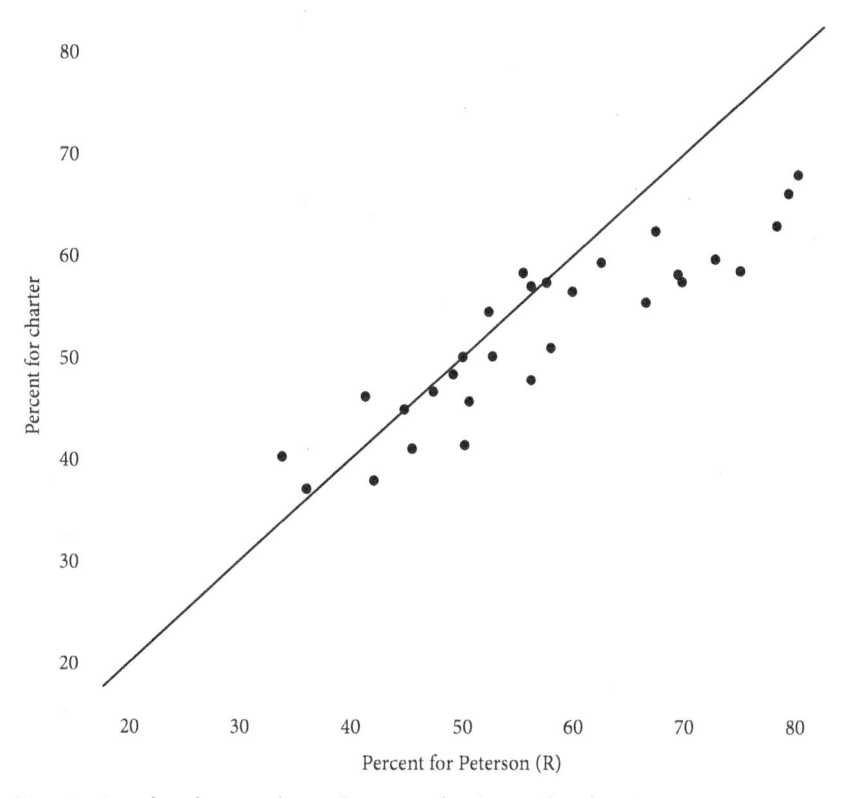

Fig. 4.4 Brockton's party-line adoption of at-large plurality (precincts).

Consistent with partisan trends in wider New England, Democrats won eight of eleven mayoral elections from 1935–55, but rising Republican strength in the late 1940s and early 1950s meant an opportunity to retake control.

Brockton's 1955 reform episode had overwhelmingly Republican support (Fig. 4.4). Graph tokens reflect the actual data, and the diagonal line segment is where they would fall if mayoral voting and charter support were perfectly correlated. All but a few wards are on or near this y = x line.

4.3.2 "No" to the STV charter in Waterbury

Whereas Brockton chose a plurality charter along party lines, Waterbury (CT) rejected an STV charter along party lines. Reform failed in 1939 because Democrats restored internal unity in advance of the referendum.

Waterbury entered the 1920s under Democratic control, direct mayoral elections, and a fifteen-member council elected from five three-seat plurality districts. The 1929–39 reign of Democratic Mayor T. Frank Hayes remains a a local legend. Leading Hayes's opposition was William J. Pape, owner of two of three local newspapers. Hayes and Pape sparred throughout the 1930s, with Pape typically backing Republican mayoral challengers (Monti 2011).

Division in Democratic ranks gave Pape and Republicans an opportunity to pursue charter reform. The first internal challenge came in 1937, when Democratic State Senator George T. Culhane ran against Hayes on a Republican-Independent Democratic fusion ticket. Then, in 1939, the Democrats verged on collapse after several Hayes associates were convicted of fraud. Hayes resigned office, and a power struggle ensued. While Culhane organized his 1939 Democratic primary campaign, party regulars searched for a nominee.[23]

Republicans and anti-organization Democrats made overtures to Democratic rank-and-file. They courted Southern and Eastern European immigrants, relative latecomers to the city, arguing that the Democratic Party was an Irish-run, Irish-serving machine (p. 53).[24] The "no" campaign featured appearances by Mayor Fiorello La Guardia, who had won on a GOP-led fusion ticket before backing the 1936 reforms in New York City (Prosterman 2013).[25]

Days before the charter vote on October 3, 1939, Democrats averted a split, uniting in public opposition to STV. The front page of the October 2 *Democrat* carried two letters-to-the-editor opposing charter reform. (Front pages are not typical places to print readers' letters.) That page also featured the following headlines: "Culhane Predicts Defeat of Charter" and "Culhane Leads Valiant Fight—State Senator Opposed Plan from Start; Organized Wide Opposition." On the morning of the referendum, the *Democrat* ran a front-page photograph of Culhane voting. The headline read, "Registering his 'No.'"

Figure 4.5 gives precinct-level charter support on October 3 by support for the Republican mayoral candidate a month later. Unfortunately there are

---

[23] The *Waterbury Democrat*, late October and early November issues, on microfilm at Silas Bronson Library. See also Monti (2011).
[24] Tensions between immigrants from Southern and Eastern Europe and Irish-dominated party organizations were common in Northeastern cities. See Erie (1988), especially Ch. 4, and Gamm (1989) generally.
[25] The *Waterbury Republican* and *Waterbury American*, late October and early November issues, on microfilm at the Silas Bronson Library.

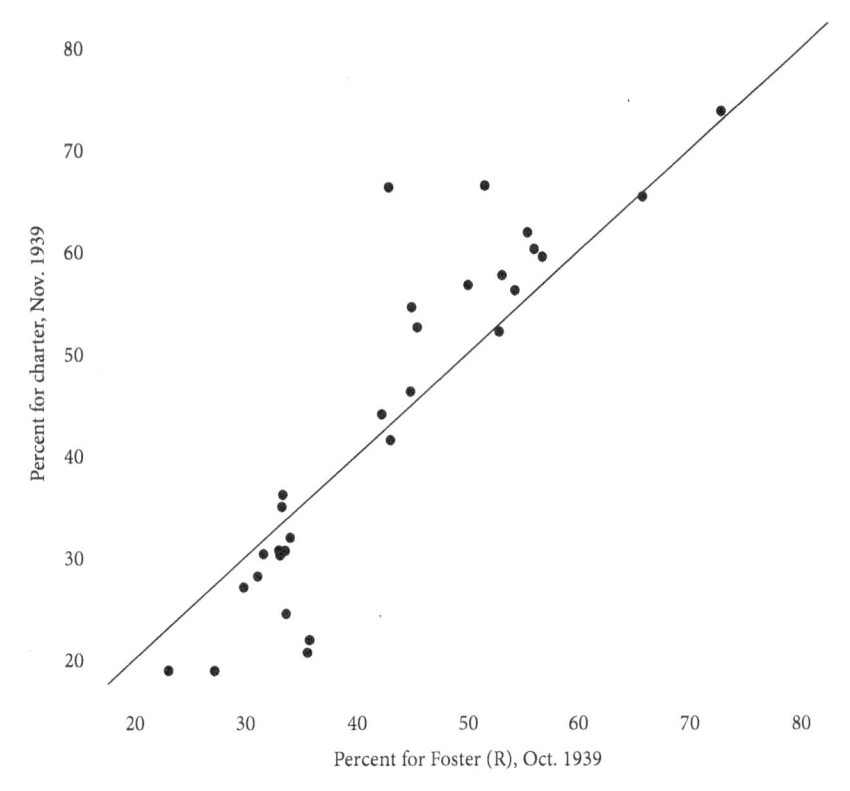

Fig. 4.5 Waterbury's party-line rejection of STV (precincts).

no proximate, pre-referendum indicators of precinct-level city partisanship. A 2005 flood at city hall destroyed most of the Hayes-era records.[26] Yet it is reasonable to assume the October 3 electorate was similar to that of the mayoral election. Waterbury then held local elections a week after the November general. The off-cycle character of both elections means turnout would have been limited to the most attentive voters (cf. Anzia 2014).

The fit between Republican vote share and referendum support is striking. Again, tokens reflect the actual data, and the diagonal is the $y = x$ line. In maintaining the allegiance of the Culhane faction, Waterbury Democrats averted a split, defeating the STV charter.

---

[26] "Records from Corrupt Waterbury Mayors in City's Hands," *Waterbury Republican-American*, April 5, 2010.

4.3.3 "Yes" to the STV charter in Worcester

No such last-minute coordination prevented the 1947 STV charter win in Worcester (MA).

In the mid-1940s, Republicans and defecting Democrats formed a neighborhood group opposing Democratic Mayor Charles F. Jeff Sullivan (Binstock 1960: II-1). This group later became the Citizens' Plan E Association (CEA), which led the reform effort.[27] Though members claimed that "there is no Democratic or Republican way to pave a street," partisan concerns were not far off. Some in the CEA complained that Republican voters were too dispersed among the city's ten three-seat wards to win office in proportion to their numbers (Edwards 1972: 3). The group also used GOP cars and headquarters in its 1947 referendum campaign.[28] Worcester's charter passed with bipartisan support by nearly two-to-one.

Figure 4.6 gives support for Worcester's new charter by support for the Republican mayoral candidate at the same election. The line again represents the fit we would observe if the Republican vote predicted the referendum vote in one-to-one fashion. The data suggest that a substantial number of voters supported both charter change and the Democratic mayoral candidate. Data points are labeled by ward so that results can be compared to the ward descriptions from Binstock (1960) below.

The ward-by-ward results are consistent with typical patterns of ethnic and socioeconomic strain on machine-style party organization. Binstock's (1960: I-23) descriptions of Worcester's wards contextualize the data. Wards 3, 4, 6, 7, and 9 were ethnically diverse but usually represented by Irish-Americans. Non-Irish immigrants were frequent machine opponents, especially as patronage dried up in cities like New York and Boston (Shefter 1986; Erie 1988). Ward 5 was Worcester's manufacturing core, so its support for reform is worth note (more on organized labor below). Wards 1 and 10 were Republican strongholds, so their interest in ousting the Democratic administration is predictable.

Ward 8 had a special role in the STV fight. This was the seat of Clark University. Jones-D'Agostino (2004) reports that Clark and Worcester Polytechnic administrators were leaders in the campaign. The CEA Board's

---

[27] Plan E was the STV-manager charter under Massachusetts home-rule legislation.
[28] See clippings titled "Daley Resignation Leaves Plan E Group Undisturbed" and "Plan E Committee Votes Expansion; Two Break Away," circa 1948, in the Plan E/CEA Collection, unsorted, at the Worcester Historical Museum.

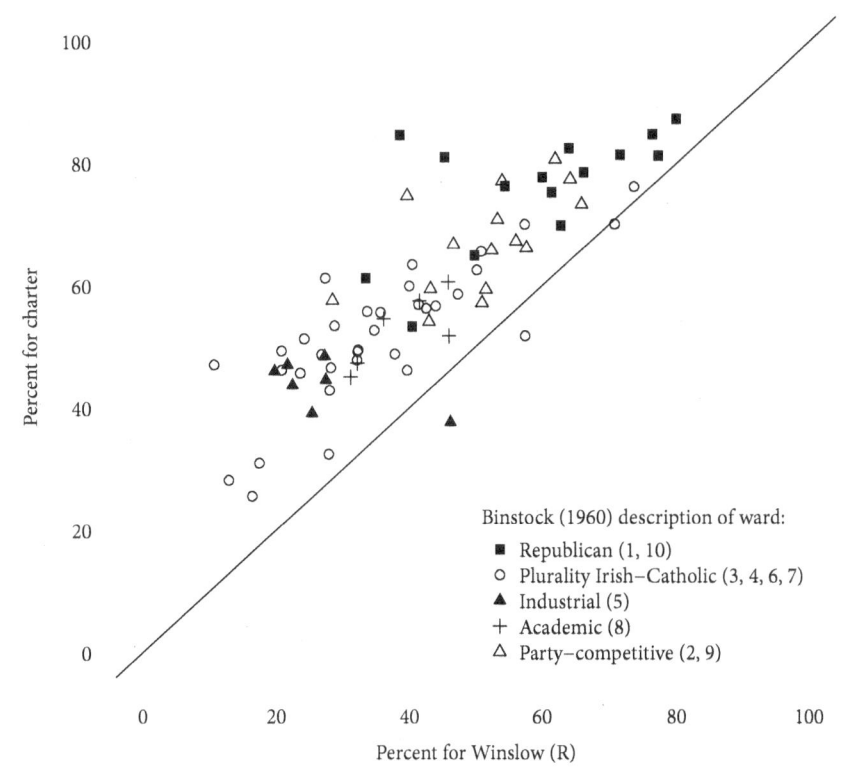

Fig. 4.6 Worcester's Republican/defecting Democratic STV adoption
(precincts).

minutes for 1947 also refer to presentations by Morris Cohen, a Clark
University political scientist who advised the group on its messaging.[29]
Overall, the locations of each precinct-by-ward in Figure 4.6 are consistent
with the general pattern above: most of the out-party (Republican) joins
forces with a faction of the ruling party (Democratic).

4.3.4 Ecological inference (EI)

As a robustness check on the preceding vignettes, Table 4.3 presents EI
estimates of party support for charter change in each of the three New

---

[29] See handwritten minutes of the CEA Board of Directors for 1947 in the Plan E/Proportional
Representation Collection (unsorted), Worcester Historical Museum.

Table 4.3 Ecological-inference estimates of charter support by voting partisanship.

Outcome	Case	Incumbent party	Est. support	Out-party(ies)	Est. support
STV win	Worcester, MA (1947)	Democratic	0.40 (0.04)	Republican	0.94 (0.04)
Plurality win	Brockton, MA (1955)	Democratic	0.14 (0.06)	Republican	0.79 (0.04)
STV loss	Waterbury, CT (1939)	Democratic	0.08 (0.04)	Republican	0.80 (0.09)
				Socialist	0.31 (0.14)

England cases. The data include actual row and column frequencies, not proportions, and I include votes for "none" when available.[30] What to look for in the table is as follows. First, we should see the least incumbent-party support when STV fails (Waterbury). When the charter is based on a plurality rule, we should see just enough to buffer the out-party's majority (Brockton).[31] We should see much more incumbent-party support for winning STV charters (Worcester). Finally, we should see high rates of out-party support in all three cases. Estimates in Table 4.3 meet these expectations. Table entries are means and standard deviations from posterior distributions. Out-party voters overwhelmingly supported charter change in each city. Yet only in Worcester, which actually adopted STV, did a large share of formerly majority-party voters support change: right around 40 percent.

4.3.5 Additional evidence on nomination conflict

Why did Worcester's Democratic Party factionalize while Waterbury's did not? One possibility is that a cohesive opposition existed within the party, which failed to make inroads at the 1947 elections. Results from the 1947 Democratic primary elections in Worcester support this conjecture.

Intra-party opposition can be more or less serious, more or less threatening. When opposition is not organized, we might expect many candidates to enter a primary race. When opposition is weak, the party's favorite wins

[30] I use a Bayesian multinomial-Dirichlet model (Lau et al. 2007). For each model, I use default priors, 250,000 iterations, a burn-in of 100,000 iterations, and a thinning interval of 10.

[31] Recall that electoral rules were not part of the messaging. As noted in the beginning of this chapter, campaigns centered on "corruption."

handily. A third possibility is that opposition concentrates geographically, so that the party's favorite dominates some contests while the opposition dominates others. One way to capture these possibilities is to use Rae's (1968) fractionalization index. Fractionalization (F) equals one minus the sum of squared candidate vote shares. It represents the probability that two randomly chosen primary voters from the same precinct voted for different Democratic candidates.[32]

When two factions are evenly matched in a primary, F will be right around 0.5. Values much less than 0.5 indicate that more than two candidates have divided the primary vote more or less evenly. This suggests disorganization. Values much greater than 0.5 suggest one faction was dominant. Finally, values of zero are only possible with uncontested primaries.

Figure 4.7 gives precinct-level support for Worcester's PR charter in November, by fractionalization of the Democratic aldermanic primary vote one month earlier. Again, data points are given by corresponding ward numbers so that results can be compared to the ward descriptions in Binstock (1960). The line of best fit is based on a polynomial regression including only those precincts that saw contested primaries. Charter support is highest in two kinds of precincts: uncontested, then those with the most evenly contested primaries. Wards 1, 2, 8, and 10 saw uncontested aldermanic primaries. According to Binstock (1960), 1 and 10 were the wealthiest wards, traditionally represented by Republicans. Ward 9 also stands out. This is where the incumbent Democratic faction faced its most serious challenge. Wards 1, 9, and 10 were unsurprisingly supportive of the PR charter one month later.

Waterbury may have turned out differently because would-be defectors retained hope of influence within the Democratic Party. By the time of the mid-October referendum, the Culhane faction had not yet been routed. This may have been due to the timing of primaries. Worcester's defectors knew the nominees before going into the November referendum. In Waterbury, by contrast, the primary campaign was still ongoing. Second, Worcester's primaries re-nominated Sullivan, an unpopular incumbent mayor. In Waterbury, the Hayes administration was on its way to jail, and there was no question that the new personnel would be different.

---

[32] F might also be called the "effective number of candidates," based on the "effective number of parties." For the pathbreaking application to party competition, see Laakso and Taagepera (1979).

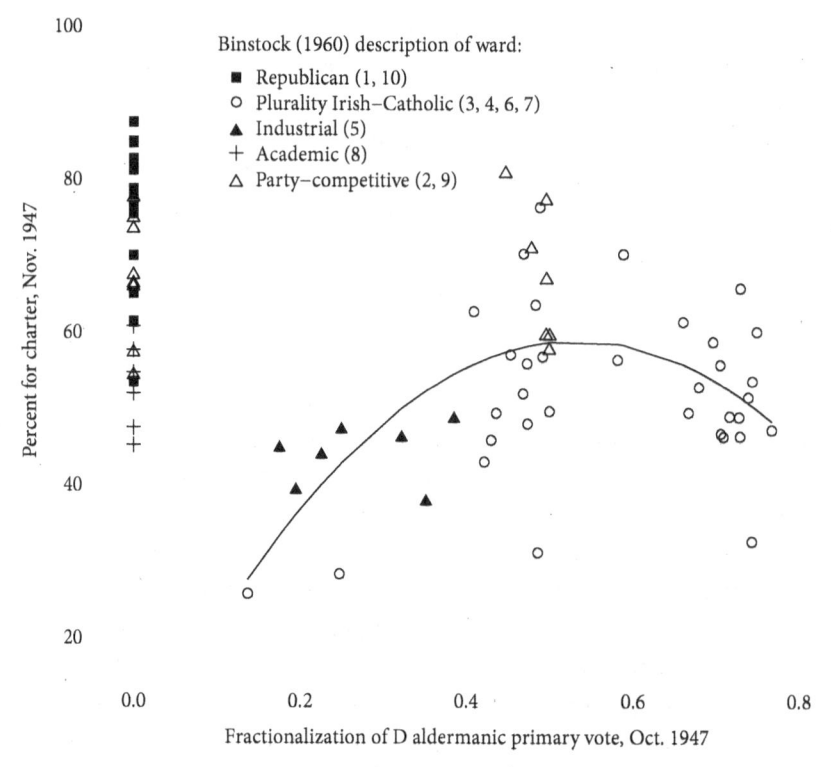

Fig. 4.7 Referendum support in Worcester by fractionalization of Democratic aldermanic primary vote (precincts).

What about Brockton? Its journal of record, the *Enterprise*, contains no evidence of Republican disunity on the question of charter reform. Nor was there evidence of nomination conflict. The paper did report primary and caucus results in earlier cycles, but it included no such coverage in advance of this cycle. All this suggests there were not any prominent nomination conflicts nor any detectable intra-party opposition to Brockton's new charter.

4.4 Sources of party disunity

Given the policy focus of this book's motivating model, a natural question is: . what split ruling parties? The PR historiography suggests two big categories: labor concerns and what modern readers might call "identity politics."

4.4.1 Some evidence on organized labor

Not all left parties supported PR in the first half of the twentieth century. Whether one did depended on whether the unions could control it, and, by extension, the levers of government (Penadés 2008). British Labour is one such case, whose Fabian Society ridiculed PR in a 1924 pamphlet (H. Finer 1924). But American unions had little influence in either party until well into the century (Schlozman 2015).

Labor's relative lack of influence may explain why, in many cities, there are records of unions backing PR campaigns. These include four of the five Ohio cities: Ashtabula (1915), Cleveland (1921), Cincinnati (1924), and Hamilton (1926) (Busch 1995: 91; Barber 1995b: 122; Kolesar 1995: 168; Weaver and Blount 1995: 214). Only in Toledo did unions oppose PR, and that was on a basis of opposition to at-large elections of any type (Anderson 1995: 244). Organized labor also figured prominently into the 1936 New York City adoption, here under the guise of the American Labor Party (McCaffrey 1939; Prosterman 2013), which also supported Franklin Roosevelt in that year's presidential election. Non-Federation unions also supported the new charter in Worcester.[33]

Some anecdotes buttress the point about labor. In Waterbury, for example, Monti (2011: 172–73) finds that labor leaders threatened to back the reform charter, in order to extract concessions from the Democratic Party.[34] In Cincinnati, Millard (1924: 604) notes "charges being made that fraud at the Republican primaries resulted in the counting out of a group of labor candidates for the legislature." Finally, one of the final acts of Worcester's pre-PR Board of Aldermen was to go on record opposing the Taft-Hartley Act.[35] Congress passed this anti-labor law in 1947, over President Harry Truman's veto, but it took the Worcester Democrats two more years to act. Notably, this was on the eve of the first "reformed" election. It is possible that, having lost the reform fight, Democrats now sought to court labor overtly.

---

[33] "Proportional Representation," *National Municipal Review*, October 1954, p. 422.
[34] Waterbury also had the largest manufacturing sector, in terms of persons employed, and the lowest number of manufacturing establishments per capita (Table 4.2). This suggests a city in which one or a few unions might have found it easy to extract concessions from government.
[35] See minutes of the Board of Aldermen for May 12, 1949, on file at Worcester City Hall.

4.4.2 STV and "identity politics"

Others have emphasized the role of group recognition in local campaigns for STV charters. In the Canadian cases, for example, Jack Lucas (2019) argues that diversity concerns gave "ideational glue" to reform coalitions. And R. A. Burnham (1990) argues that STV in Cincinnati was part of a larger push for more inclusive urban planning, based on a view of cities as "fundamentally made of groups." Beyond these general observations, we can point to three sorts of groups whose political activation gave grist to reform: ethno-racial minorities, women, and academics.

Racial and ethnic diversity intersected with class in ways that split local parties. In Cincinnati, for example, poorer African Americans remained loyal Republicans in the 1924 reform fight, but the local Black newspaper and the Universal Negro Improvement Association did not. R. A. Burnham (1997) shows that Blacks who supported the measure also opposed what they saw as a patronizing relationship with the Republican "machine." Some Jewish Republicans were prominent reform supporters both here and in Cleveland (Barber 1995b: 148-49). At least some white-collar Jews played a similar role two decades later in Worcester (MA), breaking with a predominantly Irish-American and working-class Democratic Party (Banfield and Wilson 1963: 97; Binstock 1960: II-41).[36]

The women's movement also was a frequent "P.R." supporter. Barber (1995d) and coauthors give evidence of their role in four of five Ohio PR cities. According to Millard (1924: 601), writing on Cincinnati, "The bulk of the organization work is done by women, in fact every ward has a woman chairman and many have a woman captain in each precinct." More evidence comes from Boulder (CO), where a woman member of the original charter commission won in 1919, in the second STV election (Winter 1982: 5; Lien 1925: 255). Also, in New York City, the League of Women Voters actively campaigned for the reform charter (McCaffrey 1939: 847).

Finally, we have evidence that university types were reform supporters in some cities. The vignette on Worcester named Morris Cohen, a Clark University political scientist who supported the campaign. In Cambridge (MA), Harvard Law School Dean and prominent New Deal Democrat James

---

[36] My fieldwork turned up living memories of anti-semitism in the mid-century Democratic Party. One example involved a regular Democratic council member (George B. Wells) taunting a Jewish CEA member (Joe Casdin) who had changed his surname from "Cohen." Source: conversation with former Mayor John B. Anderson (elected 1986) on a car ride to the municipal archive.

M. Landis chaired the campaign for "P.R.-manager" in his city.[37] Finally, the gift of the 1934 University of Toledo graduating class was support for the campaign there, under political scientist O. Garfield Jones.[38]

All of this is to say that social movements matter. Strategic dynamics shaped reform outcomes, but reform would not have happened without grassroots pressure on established, local party systems. And that set up a tension. In the case of STV, anyone might win, it seemed, given 10 percent of votes citywide. But after the election, someone would need to govern.

4.5 Recap

As Chapter 2 argued, the reform coalition shapes the rules. This chapter has documented reform coalitions as well as possible, for as many STV cities as possible. All were of the realigning type, enabled by prior "home-rule" legislation. (Again, an insulating STV adoption is theoretically possible, and some will appear in Chapter 8.) Note that there were no strictly multiparty reform coalitions. All included incumbent-party defectors, and very few included minor parties (with New York and Cleveland as key exceptions, both in terms of composition and the resulting reform designs). This explains why STV was never reconsidered—nor non-partisan elections, nor the small assembly. It also explains the messaging, which, once perfected, attacked "party responsibility" (Millard 1924). In a two-party system, realigning coalitions must be of the anti-party variety.

Meanwhile, far more cities adopted Model Charters without STV, in both realigning and insulating fashion. Among realigners, the difference between adoption with or without STV was the degree of local interparty competition.

[37] "Proportional Representation," *National Municipal Review*, October 1941, p. 609.
[38] "Proportional Representation," *National Municipal Review*, July 1934, pp. 398–99.

5

Rediscovering Party Government

> The councilmen are elected by a so-called proportional representation
> ballot. Just what proportion and what the proportion is, with regard to any
> particular councilman, I have never been able to discover.
>
> Cleveland Mayor Newton D. Baker (D) to Harris (1930: 48)

Political parties organize politics. They set the agenda, develop their brands, recruit candidates, and get people to vote for (rank) those candidates. Each stage of this process can leave someone feeling left out: avoiding divisive issues, discouraging would-be candidates, and shaping voters' preferences in ways that seem artificial. Anti-party reforms were meant to scramble the process.

By the mid-1920s, though, reformers were discovering that their reforms did not "work." Double-digit shares of ballots were invalid or blank, and coalitions shifted rapidly within councils—sometimes from election to election, often between elections. The solution was to combine the groups that had imposed reform in the first place, call them a "good government" organization, screen a set of candidates, and coordinate their campaigns. Strategy caught up with the logic of reform: coalition realignment.

Strategies tend to disseminate through networks, and the movement was no exception. In 1932, the PR League folded completely into the National Municipal League. Formally, the groups would "remain separate legally, however, and either [would] be free to break the connection, with due notice, at any time." But the entire PR staff relocated to New York City, now under the direction of George H. Hallett, NML's Associate Secretary (Hoag and Hallett 1932). Hallett had been with the PR League since just after World War I, under Clarence G. Hoag, architect of the PR-manager charter (Zimmerman et al. 1986).

In its final publication as a separate entity, the PR League announced the following policy: "to advocate for other cities, as completely as seems feasible, the program which has revolutionized Cincinnati: (1) the city manager

More Parties or No Parties: The Politics of Electoral Reform in America. Jack Santucci, Oxford University Press.
© Oxford University Press 2022. DOI: 10.1093/oso/9780197630655.003.0005

plan, (2) proportional representation, and (3) the permanent organization of citizens for good government" (Hoag and Hallett 1932).

5.1 Chaos in Cleveland, Cincinnati solution

News from Cleveland filled the pages of that final *PR Review* (January 1932). In back-to-back paragraphs, it was noted that the city had abandoned not just STV, but city-manager government in its entirety. No other STV city would—not even New York, which retained its analogous Board of Estimate. Meanwhile, the article's author claimed that Cleveland had not been "a failure." Several local groups had rallied to the charter's defense: Republicans, "all but three newspapers," the League of Women Voters, the Chamber of Commerce, and a host of other good-government groups (p. 1).

Sixty-five years later, however, Barber (1995b) painted Cleveland very differently. There had been five repeal efforts in the span of six years, and "the parties switched sides" over the course thereof. The large city council had resisted organization, and efforts to screen candidates had been too little, too late. Rather than enter a slate of their own, multiple good-government groups just endorsed candidates from the set of people who had nominated themselves. "Only in the 1929 election," she writes, "was a party-like independent organization created to raise money, defend the charter, and elect reform-minded candidates" (133).

Meanwhile, in Cincinnati, Walter J. Millard (1924: 601) was trying something different: combining reform elements into a party from the start. "It is risky to make prophecies concerning the results of elections," he wrote, "but because the writer took part in the Cleveland campaign, comparisons are forced upon him."[1] The Charter Committee, later known as the Charter Party, would be a formal slating deal between Progressive Republicans and the regular Democratic Party. Later Republicans would call it the "Charter-Democrat Party."[2]

---

[1] Millard also took part in the Boulder campaign, in 1917, "to do such educational work on the Hare system as opportunity might allow" (Lien 1925: 256). Harris (1930: 42) notes that ballot invalidity had been acute here. It is likely that this problem informed Millard's later work.

[2] See, for example, a statement on municipal annexation issues in the *City Bulletin* of October 15, 1952. Mayor James G. Stewart (R) was using such language as early as 1936, referring to an "unholy alliance of disgruntled Republicans and Democrats." See "Good Job," *Cincinnati Enquirer*, Oct. 27, 1937, p. 12.

5.2 Lessons learned at the top

It is common for nonprofits to compile "lessons learned" at certain stages in their work. One report of these exists from just before the PR League's absorption.

In 1930, Joseph P. Harris wrote a lengthy article on STV elections in the cities so far. Much of it concerns trouble electing mayors and city managers, both meant to happen via majority vote in council. It is noteworthy that Hermens (1941) repeated these concerns in *Democracy or Anarchy?*, long the going text on proportional systems in general. Further, Harris posited a tendency of large city councils to "facilitate racial voting" and observed that "P.R." elections "do not attract first-class candidates" (49). He dedicates several pages to voter error and abstention, noting voters' use of X-marks, not rankings.[3] He lampoons the claim that "P.R. will stimulate voting" and even the term "proportional representation." Instead, he suggests "choice voting."[4] And he quotes a former Cleveland mayor: "Just what proportion and what the proportion is, with regard to any particular councilman, I have never been able to discover."

Harris's core recommendations were two. One was to organize slates— to "draft capable candidates and secure their election." Further, he writes, "Where P.R. has been a decided success, a Charter Committee (Cincinnati), Charter Commission (Hamilton), Civic Government Association (Calgary), or Progressive Government Association (Cleveland in the last election) has been formed to make it a success" (46). Second, he called for strict adherence to the Model Charter's small-assembly provision. Clearly with Cleveland on his mind, he writes, "The election of a large council under P.R. has serious defects. Large councils do not attract first-class candidates. When used under P.R., even with a district system, a large council facilitates racial voting" (49).

How did the slates operate? Straetz (1958: 185–86) gives some evidence from Cincinnati, where Millard had developed the strategy.[5] In short, they worked just like modern parties: screening candidates, turning out vot-

---

[3] See Mott (1926) for the figures he cites.

[4] "The voter has to express choices on the ballot," writes Harris (1930: 48), "and therefore it is choice voting."

[5] For more information on the internal working of slating committees, see records of the Citizens' Plan E Association (unsorted) at the Worcester Historical Museum, Massachusetts. These include minutes from candidate recruitment meetings, which, in turn, include names of persons considered and biographical detail on each.

ers, looking for issues that divide their opponents, and building a policy brand with voters:

The City Charter Committee on the other hand, proving that reformers can be as hardheaded as regular organization people, announced early in its career that it was not just a slate-making organization but that it was a body expecting to nominate candidates, campaign to elect them, and maintain a lively and continuing political outfit between elections.

Further:

Charter is run by a Board of Directors which in turn hires a perma-nent executive secretary and director of women's activities. It maintains a year-round suite of offices and a small secretarial staff which expands, largely with volunteers, during an election campaign. The organization maintains an accurate and up-to-date card file of members and supporters throughout the city. It carries a regular campaign for funds and usually achieves its goal through the hard work of Charter volunteers aided by the unanimous support of the newspapers in the community, which overtly support Charter even if not PR.

Finally:

Charter headquarters is a pamphleteering, speech-writing, publicity spreading organization constantly on the lookout for strategic ways to gain advantage over the Republican opponent. Continuous efforts are made to keep up the precinct and ward groups because, as early as their first election, Charterites learned that one vote in a precinct could mean the difference between victory and defeat.

Three years after Harris's report, the Municipal League published a book, *City Management: The Cincinnati Experience*. Its author was a local Progres-sive hero, Charles Phelps Taft II, son of President William Howard Taft (R) and brother to U.S. Senator Robert A. Taft (R-OH). The purpose of the book was to market the slate strategy (Taft 1971 [1933]), plus the city's reputation as America's "best governed" (Roher 1939).

Some slates even had logos. Figure 5.1 gives examples from Worcester and Cambridge. Both come from mailings sent out to voters. Worcester's

Fig. 5.1 Example logos from good-government slates, 1949 (Worcester) and 1951 (Cambridge).

logo incorporates a heart because, for many, Worcester is the "heart of Massachusetts."[6] The Cambridge Civic Association does not seem to have used a graphic icon. Rather, mailers from this period (mid-1940s to mid-1950s) used the "CCA" acronym, sometimes with an oval, and sometimes with letters separated by periods. (See the next chapter for additional materials emphasizing "good government.")

5.3 Incidence of good-government slates

Table 5.1 gives the slate status of STV cities, based on the historical record. For the earliest cities, I cross-checked Harris's report against a 1929 dissertation from the University of Chicago. No STV adopter prior to Cincinnati developed a pre-election good-government slate—except for Cleveland, in its final election. After Cincinnati, though, twelve of eighteen adopters had slates going into their first elections. Of the remaining six, outcomes were as follows. In two cities, authors explicitly report reformers' failure to organize slates (Saugus and Lowell, MA). In Norris and Oak Ridge (TN), there is no mention of slates.[7] Two more—Coos Bay (OR) and Hopkins (MN)—had

---

[6] See, e.g., Andy Rosen, "A rejuvenated Worcester won't be ignored, and home buyers are noticing," *Boston.com*, July 7, 2021. Online at https://realestate.boston.com/buying/2021/07/07/a-rejuvenated-worcester-wont-be-ignored-and-home-buyers-are-noticing.

[7] One of these (Norris) had an advisory council and was "owned and controlled entirely by the Tennessee Valley Authority" (Stephenson 1938: 173).

Table 5.1 STV cities with and without pre-election good-government slates.

City	State	Adopt	Repeal	Slate
Ashtabula	OH	1915	1929	None
Boulder	CO	1917	1947	None
Kalamazoo	MI	1918	1920	None
Sacramento	CA	1920	1922	Board of Freeholders
West Hartford	CT	1921	1923	None
Cleveland	OH	1921	1931	Progressive Government Association (final election only)
Cincinnati	OH	1924	1957	Charter Committee
Hamilton	OH	1926	1961	Charter Commission
Toledo	OH	1935	1949	City Manager League
Wheeling	WV	1935	1950	Wheeling Association
New York	NY	1936	1947	Citizens' Non-partisan League
Norris	TN	1936	1948	None
Yonkers	NY	1940	1948	City Manager League
Cambridge	MA	1940	—	Cambridge Civic Association
Lowell	MA	1943	1957	None
Long Beach	NY	1943	1947	Citizens' Non-partisan Committee
Coos Bay	OR	1944	1948	None
Saugus	MA	1947	1951	None
Worcester	MA	1947	1960	Citizens' Plan E Association
Medford	MA	1947	1952	Medford Plan E Association
Quincy	MA	1947	1952	Quincy Civic Association
Revere	MA	1947	1952	Committee for Plan E
Hopkins	MN	1947	1959	None
Oak Ridge	TN	1948	1958	None

1950 populations of 6,223 and 7,595, respectively. The general conclusion is that, after Cincinnati, populous cities twinned adoption with a good-government party.[8]

Yet there are signs that slates were shaky devices—in the sense of organizing politics, defending reform charters, and recruiting "better men" to run for local office. For better or worse, slates eventually recruited candidates whom Harris might not have cast as "first-class." These include Theodore Berry, long held up by modern reformers as a Civil Rights success story, and a menu of "white ethnics" in Worcester (Santucci 2018a). Surely, there

---

[8] Data for Ashtabula, Boulder, Kalamazoo, Sacramento, West Hartford, and Cleveland are from Holcomb (1929: 10–12) and Harris (1930). For Cincinnati and Hamilton, Harris (1930). Other sources: Toldeo (Anderson 1995), Wheeling (Hallett 1937), New York (official returns), Norris (Stephenson 1938), Yonkers (Hallett 1941), Cambridge (L. Weaver 1982), Lowell (Dobrusin 1955: 362; Hallett 1944: 48), Long Beach (Hallett 1945), Coos Bay (Hallett and Woodward 1947), Saugus (Hallett and Woodward 1948b), Worcester (Binstock 1960), Medford (Dobrusin 1955: 451), Quincy (p. 477), Revere (p. 427), Hopkins (Hallett and Woodward 1948a), and Oak Ridge (Hallett and Woodward 1950).

are examples from other cities (Barber 1995d; Frazier 2020). Note the usual explanation for STV repeal, frequently invoked by modern-day reformers: that the system "worked too well" (Amy 2002: 274). In Cincinnati, where the slate strategy was perfected, the very person who marketed the idea (Taft) went on preside as mayor amidst a vitriolic repeal campaign. And even Cleveland's slate, organized to contest the last PR election, could not forestall repeal in 1931.[9]

5.4 Recap

Chapter 2 restated the well-known theory that politics tends to generate party organization. It also restated several features of party politics: organizing government, recruiting candidates, mobilizing voters, and cultivating party brand. None of this should surprise a student of political science. This chapter simply points to the attendant dynamics in STV cities. Recall the old Socialists' warning: "astonishing...that our whole host of municipal reformers...have been swept off their feet with the so called non-partisan idea" (Thompson 1913: 421).

A few other points are worth note.

First, I argued earlier that realigning episodes could be "messy," in that it might not be clear who would govern after the fact. But a simple model predicts that the reform coalition will be tempted to turn into a governing one. This is precisely what happened in the STV cities.

Second, "good government" became its own brand, polarizing politics along a "reform" dimension. This feature of American politics may not be unique to cities. Future research might ask whether it is useful to treat reform/anti-reform as more-or-less independent of the liberal/conservative dimension—at least at certain points in history. Recent work on "process" and "anti-system" attitudes points in a similar direction.[10]

Third, from the perspective of electoral-systems scholarship, is the under-appreciated role of assembly size. Many view "proportional representation"

---

[9] The Worcester (MA) Historical Museum contains extensive records on the deliberations of the local slating committee, the Citizens' Plan E Association (CEA). As of this writing, those records are not catalogued.

[10] See, for example, Hibbing and Theiss-Morse (2002), Dyck and Baldassare (2009) Dyck et al 2018, and Uscinski et al. (2021). For a comparative perspective, see Mudde and Rovira Kaltwasser (2017) on "ideational populism."

as sufficient on its own to generate more parties and/or office-holder diversity. Here, the crucial factor seems to have been a large assembly, relative to those in other reformed cities. The Cleveland debacle led not just to "good government," but also advice to keep councils small. Harris (1930) saw the two as inseparable. Consider recent work on electoral systems, which predicts 2.08 parties for a nine-seat council with PR elections (Shugart and Taagepera 2017: 101–103). Reformers now focused on proportional representation may want to avoid compromising on assembly size, especially if the goal is to improve representation (Bowen 2021; Latner et al. 2021). Similarly, some may want to revisit views of Duverger's Law.

6

The Price of Coalition

Does good government mean large numbers of candidates or small numbers of candidates? A heavy vote or a light vote? Quiet platonic campaigns
or vigorous campaigns with much mudslinging? Specific issues or decisions
on general tendencies? Or what?

Ralph A. Straetz (1958: 5), *P.R. Politics in Cincinnati*

Movement slates never fully "gamed" the local STV systems. Ten percent of
votes is not a low threshold, especially in a city with thousands of people,
but a well-provisioned independent could break through. Such candidacies
posed threats to post-reform establishments. In the medium term, then,
these political systems were responsive. When a party (or slating group)
found itself in the minority, it changed slating strategy to win back its majority. The tradeoff was a dip in party cohesion, temporary if the organization
could remake itself (Santucci 2018a).

This chapter takes a second look at the slates. Their purpose was to screen
candidates, get them elected, and organize the resulting councils. The glue of
these parties, however, was pork. Data on spending are available from 1930
onward, right around the time that the National Municipal League settled
on twinning reform wins with slates. We will see that spending in STV cities
was systematically higher than in both (a) non-reformed and (b) non-STV-
reformed cities.

Why do we see the spending pattern we do? One possibility is that the STV
charter combined two institutional logics. Council-manager systems (later
"at-large elections") are widely thought to promote "citywide focus." And
district-based systems (typical of mayor-council government) are reputed to
privilege "neighborhood issues" (see, e.g., Johnson 2014). Yet campaigning
under STV systems is thought to promote what some call "localism" (Carty
1981; Farrell 1985). Therefore, citywide good-government parties may have
been coalitions of neighborhood groups, combining local representation
with the "citywide focus" attributed to at-large elections.

More Parties or No Parties: The Politics of Electoral Reform in America. Jack Santucci, Oxford University Press.
© Oxford University Press 2022. DOI: 10.1093/oso/9780197630655.003.0006

Note that these patterns are not necessarily special. Distributive politics exist in many PR systems, even those with closed party lists (Latner and McGann 2005; Fiva and Halse 2016; Catalinac and Montoya 2021). What does seem special is the within-country difference: between STV charters and those based on non-PR rules (hereafter "plurality").

After dealing with spending, the chapter turns to campaign strategy. Anecdotes, secondary sources, and original data all point to "bailiwick" (or neighborhood-based) campaigning.

6.1 Electoral systems and public spending

This chapter suggests that the slates were distributive logrolls, meant to hold down the seat share of a city's largest party. The argument is based on some electoral-systems theory, as well as one key observable implication: that per capita spending was higher in STV cities than in both non-reformed cities and those with plurality charters.

The core of the logic is as follows. When people can force their way into an agenda-setting body, they can extract concessions in return for supporting the majority. In a large-scale legislature, the relevant agents are party leaders. Recall from Chapter 2, however, that small assembles may be attractive to anti-party reformers precisely because they imply weak agenda-control mechanisms.[1] That moves the problem of agenda control to the electoral arena, where the electoral system may matter (cf. Burnett 2017; Bucchianeri 2020). If the electoral system is too candidate-centered, there can be as many "mouths to feed" as there are legislators in the majority. And if that is the case, the only solutions are to (a) permit coalitions with the opposition party or (b) find some way to bind and insulate the majority.

6.1.1 The number of agents

Government spending tends to be higher where there are more parties in cabinet. The logic is that multiparty coalitions have to satisfy voters

---

[1] See, for example, the standing rules of the Worcester City Council, which permitted any member to offer a motion (Rule 98). These were published as annex to the Binstock (1960) report, but they do not accompany most library versions thereof. The annex is separately available from the Banfield Collection at the University of Minnesota.

from each party, whereas coalition parties in a two-party system can refuse benefits to their own voters because, due to third-party weakness, those voters cannot credibly threaten to exit (Bawn and Rosenbluth 2006). If we take this logic to the city level, the analogue of "cabinet" is the legislative majority. This may hold especially in a council-manager system, where the city manager's job depends on pleasing five of nine members (or four of seven, or seven of eleven, and so on).

Note that the core issue is the number of "bargaining units" who comprise the majority. It is not PR versus plurality-majority. While some have argued that PR leads to more generous welfare states (Lijphart 1999; Cusack et al. 2007; Persson et al. 2007), others have shown no immediate effects from adoption (Aidt et al. 2006). If I am right about the insulating nature of most national-level PR adoptions, the null result for adoption is not surprising. If anything, "social democracy" happened *in spite* of PR—which also is not the same as overall public spending.

6.1.2 The electoral system affects the number of agents

Obviously, factors like district magnitude will affect the number of parties that end up in government. Again taking this logic to the city level, any person could run, then become a winner with 10 percent of votes citywide. Or, if they could secure transfers through preference-swapping deals with other candidates, they might win with even less than 10 percent (of first choices). In the extreme, this system could turn every winner into their own party.

One technical name for the system used in STV cities is single transferable vote with "open endorsement."[2] The formal properties of this system are as follows: (1) the candidate does not depend on party organization for ballot access; (2) parties do not control the use of their labels; and (3) a vote for some candidate only helps their co-partisans if partisanship guides voters' rankings, and if that candidate has surplus to transfer. The net effect of these properties is to make it rational for candidates to build personal followings, at the expense of their parties' brands, assuming such parties even exist

---

[2] Note that New York City had something between "open" and "closed" endorsement. Any candidate could appear on the ballot, but they needed permission from a county committee to appear with the party's name next to theirs. Even still, according to Powell, Jr. (1971: 69), county committees might defer to candidates with strong personal followings.

(Carey and Shugart 1995: 428). Seen from a party's perspective (again, if it exists), there is little control of individual candidates' messages, as party leaders do not regulate ballot access.[3]

6.1.3 Why have slates at all?

Given the properties of open-endorsement STV, why would candidates agree to go with a slating group? And why would group leadership want the headache of managing them, given their incentives to campaign as individuals? Part of the answer is that slating groups provided name recognition in low-information environments. Figures 6.1 and 6.2 give examples of this, and others can be found in historical newspapers.[4]

Another part of the answer was the movement's need to produce sets of winners that very many voters had given high rankings. Harris (1930), for example, was obviously concerned with the types of people elected, but also voters' acceptance of election outcomes. Perplexity at transfers has long been a source of reformer frustration, as reform opponents tend to mobilize this sentiment.[5] Slates mitigated this problem in complementary ways: making candidates popular in the eyes of the voter (Figs 6.1 and 6.2), then causing those candidates to win.[6] Figure 6.1 gives an example of how slates guided voters rankings: 1 for the first choice, then 2 through 9 for the rest of the slate.[7]

Finally, we can turn to the perspective of policy entrepreneurs who care about influencing the legislative majority. Laver (2000) has argued that non-dominant parties in STV elections have a shared incentive to keep votes away from the largest party. This means getting voters to rank, first, a party's candidates and, second, anyone viable who is not from the largest party. This is to avoid transfers—either surplus from winners, or from eliminated

---

[3] These points are drawn from Carey and Shugart (1995), with some rethinking of multiple votes in STV. It is only weakly true that the voter gets several votes in an STV system. Rather, they get one vote (but potentially many markings), which may or may not transfer.
[4] Sources: "Historic Media," http://www.chartercommittee.org, Accessed April 2017; *Worcester Sunday Telegram*, Nov. 1, 1959, p. 16A.
[5] Harris (1930: 48) writes: "The average voter does not understand the system, and resents this fact. In some cities he is told by political organizations that it is complicated, mysterious, un-American, socialistic, and undemocratic."
[6] On whether elites can make candidates popular, see Riker (1982: 764) and Cox (1997: 98). Riker is worth quoting here: "The direction one must go, I believe, is to turn attention away from the expected utility calculus of the individual voter and to the expected utility calculus of the politician and other more substantive participants in the system."
[7] See Schulze (2011) for analysis of "vote management" in a larger set of STV cities.

BE PROUD OF YOUR CITY —
BE PROUD OF YOUR VOTE !

Vote for these
Charter-Endorsed Candidates
ELECTION DATE: TUESDAY, NOV. 6, 1951

THEODORE M. BERRY
Tireless crusader for civil rights

ALBERT D. CASH
A truly great Mayor and leader

PHILIP M. COLLINS
Able lawyer and experienced legislator

Dorothy Nichols Dolbey
Outstanding churchwoman and leader

HAROLD K. GOLDSTEIN
World War II veteran and civic leader

HARRY D. PROCTOR
Calm, clear-headed leader of A.F.L.

A. E. ROBERTS
Former Scout Chief — a great Cincinnatian

JOHN H. STEWART
Young man with a big future

EDWARD N. WALDVOGEL
Popular, hard-working Vice Mayor

SAVE THIS PAGE

Put it in your purse or wallet as a reminder when you go to vote!

BE SURE YOUR VOTE COUNTS

HERE'S HOW:

A. Vote for ALL NINE of the Charter candidates.

B. Do NOT use an "X".

C. Mark "1" in front of the name of your FIRST choice.

D. Mark "2" in front of the name of your SECOND choice.

E. Mark 3, 4, 5, 6, 7, 8 and 9 in front of the other Charter candidates in the order of your preference.

CLIP THIS PAGE AND TAKE IT WITH YOU TO THE POLLS

— Issued by City Charter Campaign Committee
B. Gates Dawes, Jr., Chairman

Fig. 6.1 A joint Democratic-Charter Republican ticket from the Cincinnati PR elections of 1951 (Cash, Democratic leader; Proctor, Charter Republican leader).

Fig. 6.2 A joint Republican-CEA Democratic ticket from the Worcester PR elections of 1959 (Holmstrom, Republican leader; O'Brien, CEA Democratic leader).

losers—helping to elect an opposition majority. The strategy, in other words, is to gang up on the largest party. Straetz (1958: 63) gives an example from Cincinnati (emphasis mine):

> PR opponents deny that a minority is elected. Instead they insist that the minorities usually consist of representatives of groups or blocs; as Republican leader Donald Hall put it in 1933, Charter was a coalition of Democrats and Republicans "which *promoted log rolling, petty trading of patronage, and prevented the Republican Council members who represented the dominant group* in Cincinnati from having any voice in the conduct of the city." The implication here of course is that Charter, even when it wins a majority of five, is actually nothing but a coalition of representatives of minority groups.

The spending implications of a gang-up are clear. In order to hold together a motley coalition—be it of two or more parties, or personal-vote-seeking candidates—there will need to be agreement on pork.

6.2 Spending in three types of cities, 1930–60

This section seeks to answer two related questions. First, was spending under STV charters greater than in non-reformed cities? Second, was it greater than in reformed cities with plurality elections? The answer in both cases will be yes.

I use panel data on total government spending, 1930–55, with indicators for plurality and STV reform charters. The data come from Choi et al. (2013), who built the set to analyze correlates of council-manager adoption and abandonment.[8] These data come from the *Municipal Year Books*, *City Data Books*, and U.S. Census. Observations come in five-year intervals and are interpolated if necessary. I combined those records with data on STV incidence from Childs (1965) and L. Weaver (1986). In order to minimize the number of comparisons, I omit cities with the commission form of government, the movement for which collapsed around 1920 anyway (Riçe 1977).

Table 6.1 STV cities included in analysis.

City	State	Adoption	First election
Cambridge	MA	1940	1941
Cincinnati	OH	1924	1925
Cleveland	OH	1921	1923
Hamilton	OH	1926	1926
Lowell	MA	1942	1943
Medford	MA	1947	1949
Quincy	MA	1947	1949
Revere	MA	1947	1949
Toledo	OH	1934	1935
Wheeling	WV	1935	1935
Worcester	MA	1947	1949
Yonkers	NY	1938	1941

---

[8] Significant predictors of manager-form adoption were county-level Republican vote share, unemployment, and percent employed in manufacturing. The authors did not distinguish STV from non-STV cases.

Twelve of the twenty-four STV cases are included. Some drop out due to date coverage, as their systems were repealed before 1930: Ashtabula (OH), Kalamazoo (MI), Sacramento, and West Hartford (CT). Others do not enter the data because their populations were too small: Boulder (CO), Coos Bay (OR), Hopkins (MN), Long Beach (NY), Norris (TN), Oak Ridge (TN), Saugus (MA). I drop New York City because it did not have a manager system.[9] Critically, all but two cities had good-government slates. The exceptions are Cleveland, which did have a slate in the election included, and Lowell, where there is no record of a slate.[10]

The dependent variable is per capita spending on all government expenditures, expressed in 2008 dollars. To merge the Choi et al. (2013) data with my STV cases, I needed to ensure that an STV-elected government would have had time to craft a budget, then that this budget would be reflected in the spending data. I did this by adding one to first STV election year, then rounding up to the nearest multiple of five. Toledo (OH) illustrates the logic. That city adopts STV in 1934, elects a government under those rules in 1935, and first shows up with STV spending in its 1940 observation.

Estimates come from a series of two-way fixed-effects models estimated via least squares. These models include variables for city and year. One model estimates the effect of "STV" reform, a second estimates the effect of "plurality" reform, and a third estimates both effects at the same time.

Table 6.2 gives results. They suggest that STV-reformed cities tended to outspend both other types: those with non-STV manager charters, then those with no reform at all. Relative to a non-reformed city, the estimated effect of an STV charter is just about $120, 30 percent more than a non-reformer, and 40 percent more than a "plurality" reformer. Note that the data for this analysis was based overwhelmingly on cities with the very slates that Harris (1930: 40) had called for—to make voting easier, increase reform longevity, and improve candidate "caliber."[11]

[9] Again, New York had a bicameral assembly, borough-level multi-seat districts, district magnitudes that fluctuated with turnout, varied supermajority requirements in the lower chamber, a separate executive, and partisan ballots with cross-endorsement potential (alongside nomination by petition).
[10] However, there is evidence that "everyone but the Irish" was Lowell's de facto slate (Frazier 2020).
[11] Elsewhere, I have analyzed data on earlier STV cases. Regression-discontinuity analyses with referendum vote shares point to a null effect on per capita spending. This may be due to pre- and post-1930 effects, i.e., higher spending after the decision to organize slates, versus lower spending before. More work is needed to build out this data set, possibly from records in the cities themselves.

Table 6.2 Two-way fixed-effects results for effect of STV and non-STV reform charters on per capita spending (2008 dollars).

	Model 1	Model 2	Model 3
Intercept	377.36***	373.22***	375.78***
	(58.79)	(58.74)	(58.55)
STV charter	121.59**		118.51**
	(43.53)		(43.36)
Plurality charter		−93.99**	−91.97**
		(31.09)	(30.99)
R^2	0.86	0.86	0.86
Adj. R^2	0.82	0.82	0.82
Num. obs.	1138	1138	1138

$^{***}p < 0.001, {}^{**}p < 0.01, {}^{*}p < 0.05$

6.3 At-large election, local representation

The STV charter combined two logics: of citywide and neighborhood representation. This may explain the spending patterns noted above, and it is consistent with campaign incentives in STV.

Municipal forms of government differ: in terms of spending priorities and how they relate to voters. There are different ways to talk about this: "comprehensive" versus "symbolic" policy output (Carr 2015: 677–78), "expansive growth policies" under "reform monopolies" (Trounstine 2008: 141), "citywide focus" versus "neighborhood concerns" (D. Johnson 2014), and "programmatic" versus "particularistic benefits." With respect to voters, council-manager governments reflect more "budgetary solvency" due to their relative political insulation (Jimenez 2020). Similarly, under council-manager government, voter turnout has tended to be lower due to the combination of non-partisan elections, geographically large districts, and possibly more frequent use of off-cycle elections (Hajnal 2009; Carr 2015).

Types of "at-large" elections also differ. If a voter has as many votes as there are seats to fill (i.e., under standard MNTV), the party can instruct voters to vote the whole slate. That logic also holds for two-round elections in multi-seat districts.[12]

---

[12] Compare Cox (1997: 144) on runoffs and AV.

But parties in STV elections face two problems, as the vote is *single* and *transferable*. First, the party must maximize its collective vote share by ensuring that transfers stay within the party.[13] Second, the party must ensure sufficient first-choice votes for each candidate, in order to prevent early-round elimination. Optimizing these problems is known as "vote management"—guessing how many seats the party is likely to win, nominating that many candidates, and dividing the district among them for campaign purposes (known as creating "bailiwicks").[14] Hence a common feature of STV elections: geographically targeted campaigns.[15]

The record on STV in U.S. cities reflects a bit of both dynamics: tension between citywide and neighborhood policy, as well as bailiwick campaigning. For example, Worcester was famous in the planning literature for reliance on "spot" zoning, long after other cities had adopted comprehensive zoning ordinances (Natoli 1971). In Cambridge (MA), it was common to equate STV with "neighborhood representation" (The Editors 1961). Someone from Cincinnati repeated the same phrase when I asked about his father's time in council there: "proportional representation is neighborhood representation."[16] This city also achieved public-sector desegregation before comparable Midwest cities (cf. Sugrue 2014: xliv, 13), possibly due to the work of Theodore "Ted" Berry, 1949–57 (Gray 1959: II–II). As chair of council's Housing Committee, Berry also worked to delay slum clearance until relocation housing could be built (V-5). Later, he and others in the Charter Party would implement an unpopular income tax, designed, in part, to finance the city university without increasing taxes on homeowners. Finally, on New York City (without manager government),

---

[13] Seat-maximization incentives may be stronger in multiparty systems, where the goal is to enter government. In two-party systems, such as some studied here, the goal may be to win just a seat majority.

[14] The optimization problem is less pronounced in a multiparty system, as party identification gives a rough signal of how many seats each party might expect. Further, party members may occupy or have connections to other local offices, making "bailiwicking" relatively easy. On Ireland, see Bowler and Farrell (1991). On Scottish local elections, see Clark (2012). Maltese parties face fewer optimization problems, given first-choice votes' role in party-level in seat allocation. In U.S. cities, the STV parties could not refer to opinion data, nor even voter-registration records (as the STV party systems defied the major-party divide). This may explain why the norm was to run a full slate, plus an apparently widespread belief "that vote management does not work in the USA" (Schulze 2011: 22).

[15] Also note that, as guessing expected seat share becomes difficult, co-partisans face increased incentives to run against each other (e.g., invade each other's bailiwicks).

[16] Source: conversation with Willis D. "Bill" Gradison about his father's time in City Council, mid-1930s to early 1940s. I had this conversation in the early stages of data collection, probably in Spring 2016. I did not take notes, but the statement stuck with me.

Shaw (1954: 213) writes: "Councilmen just didn't seem able to resist their constituents' requests on place names—more than half the local laws of 1938 related to the naming of streets, parks, or squares. Financial powers were still regarded as a convenient weapon for belaboring a Fusion administration, rather than an opportunity for framing municipal policies."

Evidence of bailiwicks exists for at least a few cities, even though the norm was to present a full slate. This is likely because operatives could not project how many seats they might win—voter registration did not track these party systems—but were banking on transfers from trailing candidates. In Cincinnati, where slates were perfected, Bentley (1926: 466–67) writes: "The question was whether under the system of proportional representation, there was more likelihood of electing five, by nominating nine, or by nominating a lesser number." Yet the Republican opposition, in 1925, "divided Cincinnati into 6 bailiwicks and nominated 6 candidates" (Schulze 2011: 21). Both parties quickly converged on nominating nine, but Gosnell (1939) shows that most results would not have differed under open-list PR, i.e., that trailing candidates' role was to supply transfers. Later work by Heisel (1982: 10) showed that all well-populated neighborhoods were represented. Further, newspapers regularly reported candidates' first-choice vote totals by ward (and sometimes precinct), suggesting an audience for neighborhood-level data.

Other signs of neighborhood campaigning exist. In Cleveland, Harris (1930: 49) laments "many councilmen still regarding themselves as representatives of a particular ward." In Worcester, which *kept detailed records* of candidates' ward-level totals, Fain (1991) finds evidence of two "Favulli wards" (an Italian-American candidate on the good-government slate, representing two wards that had opposed the charter). A review of the records, 1953–59, turns up three or four plurality candidates across the city's ten wards—all of them final-round winners.[17] Finally, in New York City, Democratic leaders "evolved their own technique for obtaining maximum representation. Each borough was divided into the same number of zones as the number of councilmen it seemed likely to select. Within each zone the district leaders agreed upon a candidate" (Shaw 1954, quoted in Schulze 2011: 22).

---

[17] These data are available on request. The result emerges after removing the slate's top vote-getter in each ward, almost always the ticket-leading candidate. This person must be removed because, in STV cities, the ticket leader typically became mayor. In other words, they were a slate's "citywide focus" candidate. For more on this, see Santucci (2018a).

6.4 Seeds of destruction?

Of twenty-three cities to combine STV with the council-manager charter, twenty-two retained the latter when abandoning the former (L. Weaver 1986). The sole exception is Cleveland, where Harris (1930) saw weaknesses in STV as *threats to the manager system*.[18] Even New York City, without a manager system, left many of its reforms intact. From the start, the

Fig. 6.3 Advertisement to repeal a PR-manager charter in Worcester (MA). Source: *Worcester Telegram*, p. 10c, November 11, 1959.

---

[18] He writes (page 3): "Is PR a vital reform for municipal government? Is it essential for the successful operation of the city manager plan?"

movements for STV and "non-partisan" local government were in tense alliance. Governing gradually pulled them apart.

Consider Worcester. In 1959, during an effort to repeal the whole charter, politicians ran the following newspaper advertisement (Fig. 6.3). It depicts the tax rate as a passenger balloon in unrestrained ascent. Clearly, this was meant to appeal to homeowners, and possibly also industrialists, both of whom had backed PR in 1947 (Eisenthal 1983).

Strangely, though, the repeal effort was led by regular Democrats, who had lost control of government in the first STV election. Their goal was to return to a partisan mayor-council system—a streamlined version of the pre-reform institutions, known in state law as Plan B. The Citizens' Plan E Association (CEA) opposed this change, allegedly because it would have thrown out the council-manager system.[19] STV in Worcester would last one more year.

6.5 Recap

Electoral systems shape public policy by shaping the number of bargaining units. This chapter has analyzed aggregate spending under the twentieth century's leading "reform" charters: council-manager government with and without STV. Based on data consulted here, government spending was generally higher with STV than "plurality."[20] This is despite the fact that the period covered was that of "good government" slates (i.e., post-1930). Then the chapter turned to accounts of campaign strategy, which point to a party-of-neighborhoods logic. This is consistent with accounts of STV elsewhere, especially Irish "localism" and "bailiwick" strategy.

Distributive politics are not unique to STV, which I noted at the start of this chapter. Several recent studies have found "geographic campaigning" in other PR systems, even closed-list. We might even find it in "plurality-at-large," although the Americanist literature tends to point to pro-business bias. Why is this interesting? Popular commentary tends to hold that PR

---

[19] Southwick (2017) writes: "PR was Plan E's main weakness." Further, during my fieldwork in June 2016, it became clear that Democrats had warmed to the manager system. A former city clerk told me that, when he took office under a post-PR mayor, that mayor advised him to defend council-manager government. This was not an interview, and I did not take notes, but the statement stuck with me.

[20] Again, I used this as a blanket term for any non-PR charter. Most such charters would have been multi-seat plurality. Some may have multi-seat runoff instead. Limited-nomination rules would not have been possible under non-partisan elections.

would eliminate "constituency link."[21] It may be time to retire the idea—or at least qualify it. When we look at the issue from a *coalition* perspective, why would a group that seeks control of government *not cater* to localized interests? Neighborhoods are the raw materials of politics.

What may be unique to the U.S. cases is the use of STV to defy an overarching party system. One practical consequence was an inability to perform "vote management." In the very place where reform slates emerged, their managers decided not to limit nominations. This is a rational response to not knowing how many seats one is likely to win. Voter registration might have been a guide, but slate politics did not track the wider party system. Reformers instead threw a Hail Mary by running as many candidates as there were seats to fill. And their "machine" opponents responded in kind, seeking transfers from hopeless co-partisans.

---

[21] See, for example, the British Electoral Reform Society on "Constituency Link." Online at https://www.electoral-reform.org.uk/voting-systems/what-are-voting-systems/constituency-link. Accessed October 17, 2021.

7
Legislative Limbo, Polarizing Repeal

> Even though five of the nine city councillors are CEA endorsees, the organization does not have control of the council. The organization's tendency to back candidates who are not strong CEA supporters weakens its influence in city government.
>
> Robert H. Binstock (1960: II-48)

Holding reform coalitions together was inherently difficult. Anyone could run, and, in most cities, ten percent of votes would deliver a seat. This forced coalitions to be responsive—to slate figures who might have won as independents. This is why some scholars in the late 1990s saw STV as having promoted officeholder diversity. On closer inspection, though, this was by accident; new forces collided with old reform alignments. Like Progressives before them, the labor and Civil Rights movements reshaped parties at all levels of American politics.[1] So did the "amateur Democrats," a new crop of liberals in the postwar period (Wilson 1962). Anti-party reform made parties permeable.

Transferable votes were another dimension. These made legislators responsive to voters on the other side of the aisle.[2] Already with low thresholds, keeping control of government was a balancing act.[3] Vote transfers made it even more difficult. This is why, in the repeal literature, we hear about STV "lottery effects" and renewed frustration with vote counts.[4]

---

[1] While often cited as a PR "success story," R. A. Burnham (1997: 148) is explicit about this. He writes: "Within the next few years, however, Cincinnati, like other northern cities, experienced a wave of civil rights activism, which changed the racial politics of the city in ways that gave the Charter Committee an opportunity to win Black votes."

[2] Whether transfers have this property is an open question. See Sorens (2016) for a case that they do not, then Reilly and Stewart (2021) for a case that they do. Both focus on single-seat AV. This is even more impressive because Australia requires voters to rank all candidates, arguably (to the transfer skeptic) making third-party voting purely expressive.

[3] Note, however, that such thresholds are not low in *comparative* perspective. Further, once we account for attendant reductions to assembly size, these "reformed" councils may have been even less representative than the preceding legislatures.

[4] This was despite the fact that candidate entry fell sharply, reducing the number of counting rounds needed.

More Parties or No Parties: The Politics of Electoral Reform in America. Jack Santucci, Oxford University Press.
© Oxford University Press 2022. DOI: 10.1093/oso/9780197630655.003.0007

Opinion leaders must have gotten angry about transfers. That meant anger at "P.R." as well, since reformers had made the two synonymous in America. These two dimensions, low thresholds and transfers, could lead to stalemate in city council. The third factor needed was more realignment. Consider the following scenario. Some new force emerges and portends to win seats. Both parties bid to incorporate it. One side wins the majority, partly due to an influx of transfers from its opposition. The losing side can claim that those votes were its property—that STV reversed the result of the election. Further, the winning side is divided. Some in its delegation owe their seats to voters in the opposite party. Council is in a state of *legislative limbo*, and opposing party leaders seek some way out: a *polarizing reform* deal.

This chapter shows for three key cases a state of *legislative limbo* at the time of repeal. It also compiles suggestive evidence of similar states in other cities. Limbo refers to a situation in which neither coalition has full control of government. It turns up as legislative disunity, voter dealignment, and overall party-system change. The *polarizing reform* response turns up in case history as "collusion" by opposing-party leadership.

I will not claim "limbo" in all twenty-four cities. It is possible, in some of them, that repeal followed different logic: another round of "throwing the bums out" (*coalition-realignment*), for example, or an incumbent party trying to stay in power (such as in one failed repeal attempt, documented below). However, for the cases studied here, failure of either side to *control government* helps explain the odd pattern of opponent collusion. It also helps explain repeal in three of the cities to have used STV the longest. Finally, it subsumes other purported causes, drawn from inductive studies of other cases: lack of party discipline, deadlocked mayoral elections, and perceptions of a "lottery effect" from the vote-transfer process (Hermens 1941: 417; Straetz 1958: 13, 31, 37; Banfield and Wilson 1963: 97; L. Weaver 1986: 242–45). Looking back at the first wave of repeals, Harris (1930) already had noted several of these issues. Limbo also integrates the observation that many in politics at the time of repeal were different from the players at the time of reform adoption (Barber 1995a).

The cases are Cincinnati, New York City, and Worcester (MA). The first two are well-documented and generate conventional wisdom: that the election of Blacks and Communists galvanized repeal coalitions. This is only partly true, as such figures had held office for several terms prior to repeal. The fundamental problem was control of government, and Worcester shows us this logic in a different context: overwhelmingly white and largely without labor figures.[5] These cases also offer variation on institutional context: Cincinnati and Worcester had the model PR charter, whereas New York City had a bicameral legislature and separately elected executive. Limbo there mattered when the reform coalition lost control of non-council offices (the mayoralty and Board of Estimate). A final section comments on other cases, including Cambridge (MA), where STV survives. Why? Data suggest that its reform slate learned to limit nominations. This is in contrast with the tendency elsewhere to field one candidate per seat, following the old advice from Harris (1930: 46).

In addition to explaining repeal in each case, this chapter also analyzes failed repeal efforts. Many of the triggers were the same: inflows of votes from the opposition, outflows of votes to the opposition, and diminished control of government. Efforts like these failed for one or both of two reasons. First, repeal initiators failed to attract support from members of the reform coalition. Second, if they did succeed, reform coalitions replenished themselves with voters and candidates who had been independent. These data appear in the appendix. Therefore, failed repeal initiatives often (but not always) ended with local-level realignment. If there were no independents to incorporate, however, reformers could not replenish pro-STV majorities.

Overall, PR in general is long-term "stable" when politics contains some "third force."[6] Hence a multiparty system is better for having PR in the long-term—with the qualifier that it can discipline the legislature. Healthy multiparty politics mobilize (and keep mobilized) that third force.[7] Multiparty politics turn realignment into boilerplate coalition change (Cox 1997: 253).

---

[5] See Binstock (1960: I-2, I-4): "According to the 1950 Census, there were only 1,719 non-whites, constituting 0.8% of the population; there has been no significant change since then... Negroes in Worcester are not politically active; they have no political leadership and no influence as a group." On labor, he writes (V-15), "The political activities of organized labor in Worcester are not very significant. Participation in municipal election campaigns is essentially confined to sponsorship of an occasional non-partisan rally with debates between candidates for the council. No labor union official has ever been elected to the council. In 1950 two labor men were badly defeated although they were endorsed by the CEA."

[6] Where is the "third force" in Maltese politics? I confess to not knowing. However, Maltese STV awards a seat majority to the party with a plurality of first-choice votes, as noted in Chapter 1. Malta also has used STV for a century, originally in the context of a multiparty system. All of this may matter for making the system seem less "foreign" and/or "confusing."

[7] For an abstract statement of the affinity between PR and more than two parties, see Ergun (2010).

7.1 Illustrating legislative limbo

The defining feature of legislative limbo is failure of either side of the aisle to control government. It occurs during periods of coalition change, when voters' allegiances are in flux. This section lays out how I illustrate each: lack of control of government, shifting coalitions, and their roots in the electorate.

7.1.1 Coalition change: spatial mapping

For each city, I have prepared a two-dimensional "spatial map" of its PR-period roll-call record. These plots are based on the same kind of algorithm used to study Congress and many foreign legislatures. Every legislator gets a point in coordinate space, based on statistical analysis of the entire roll-call record.[8] If two legislators appear close to each other, that is because they vote together often.[9] Further, if coalitions are stable over time, all legislators will appear in either of two places: the reform-coalition point, or the opposition point. Poole and Rosenthal (1988) used a similarly visual approach to show Congressional realignment on either side of the Great Depression.

In the following plots, each legislator is represented by their party affiliation.[10] To keep the plots readable, I include only the names of key figures implicated in successful repeal attempts. This typically means opposing party (or coalition) leaders, then others who stand out in case history. Roman numerals next to such names give the instance in which that person appears in the data (e.g., "Smith II" has either switched parties or been re-elected after some absence). Plots with all names are available on request.

---

[8] I use the optimal classification (OC) algorithm (Poole 2000, 2005), a non-parametric alternative to NOMINATE and related procedures. In doing so, I follow Rosenthal and Voeten (2004) in "fitting a party-switcher model," i.e., recovering separate ideal points for a legislator who changes parties. I also recover separate points for a legislator with discontinuous service. This is intentional. For example, if John Doe returns to office after a break of two years, does so as member of the same party, and everyone continues to vote as they had, his coordinates should not change.

[9] Frequently, these methods are used to recover liberal-conservative ideology. However, a common critique of this application is that partisanship structures legislative voting, so that "sincere" ideology cannot really be measured. For the present analysis, this debate is unimportant.

[10] Party affiliations come from official election returns (Cincinnati and New York City) and biennial slate announcements in the *Worcester Telegram*. For the two cities with slating groups, I also include major-party affiliations (Republican, Democrat, or unaffiliated). For Cincinnati, this information comes from Straetz (1958) and R. A. Burnham (1990), plus candidate biographies in the *Cincinnati Enquirer*. For Worcester, it comes from voter registration cards, cross-checked against a notebook of candidate filings (with residential addresses), both at the Worcester Election Commission.

To give the plots a temporal dimension, I have boldfaced legislators who entered council after some critical juncture in reform-coalition evolution. By "critical juncture," I mean some noteworthy change in nominating practices, campaign coordination, or caucus organization. Such junctures may implicate one, two, or all of those features. The point is that, for each city, contemporary observers saw some year as important. For example, in Worcester, the local archive (still unsorted) contained numerous clippings from 1955. This collection appears to have come from someone in the leadership of that city's reform slate (the Citizens' Plan E Association). In the other two cities, case history is sufficient.

7.1.2 Voter dealignment: transfer leakage

In a well-defined party system, STV allocates seats like party-list PR. Voters restrict rankings to their preferred parties, and transfers only flow among co-partisan candidates. If multiple parties are in coalition, transfers will flow within that coalition (Laver 2000). "Transfer leakage" is the going measure of failure to achieve this (Gallagher 1978). I compute it as the share of votes cast for either side's candidates that end up counting for winners on the opposing side.[11]

7.1.3 Control of government: roll rates

A polarizing reform episode requires neither side being clearly in control of government. I illustrate this state of affairs by computing a "roll rate" for each city. Broadly, this is the percentage of roll calls on which some group of interest does not get its way. If the group does not get its way, this is because

---

[11] This is calculated from aggregate STV returns that proceed by surplus transfer and sequential elimination. These returns are almost always presented in candidate-by-round "transfer matrices." Sources include the Hamilton County Board of Elections, University of Cincinnati Libraries, Worcester Election Commission (with credit to Howie Fain and Robert Bowditch, Sr.), and the *Annual Report of the Board of Elections in the City of New York*.

In an ideal world, we would have access to voters' entire rankings. This would let us see, for example, the proportion of voters for Candidate X who also ranked Candidate Y highly. In turn, that proportion would convey information about efforts to form cross-party coalitions. But those data are not available for historic elections. All we can see are the redistributions from (a) winners with surplus and (b) eliminated losers.

some part of it has voted with the other side.[12] It tells us about the extent to which leadership is able to organize legislative voting (Cox and McCubbins 2005).

A "majority roll" is said to occur when *a majority of majority-party legislators* do not get their way on a vote. This is because a minority in their party (or coalition) have not voted in the same way. The majority roll rate is the percentage of votes, over a given term, that end in such an outcome. I calculate this figure for Worcester and Cincinnati, as both bodies operated under simple majority rule.[13]

For New York City, I calculate "minority frustration" rates. This is because the charter gave veto power to the council minority, always "the coalition" of anti-Tammany parties.[14] The charter distinguished two main types of legislation: local laws and budget measures. Both required approval from the Board of Estimate and Mayor, and, with respect to the budget, council only could delete items. Council could override the veto of either other body by a two-thirds vote, in the case of local laws, or a three-fourths vote, in the case of budget deletions (Tanzer 1937). Therefore, given a Mayor and/or Board of Estimate hostile to the council minority, that minority needed one-third or one-quarter of votes, respectively, to extract concessions from the other bodies. The *minority position* for either class of vote is defined as the position taken by a majority of coalition legislators, and the "frustration rate" is the proportion of times in a given term that such positions did not prevail. I also give data on partisan control of the mayoralty and Board of Estimate, both controlled by "the coalition" until January 1946.

7.2 Cincinnati, 1925–57

In 1957, after sixteen elections, voters replaced STV with non-partisan, plurality elections at-large. Proponents branded this system as "9X voting."

---

[12] Or abstained, depending on the rules of the chamber. This was common practice in Worcester, for example, where members did so by leaving the room. I thank former Mayor John B. Anderson for sharing this point on a car ride. For the purpose of scaling results in the final section, however, I have treated abstentions and "legitimate" absences equivalently, as there is no way to distinguish between them.

[13] On Cincinnati, see Werner (1928). On Worcester, see a "Plan E Government Summary," originally an appendix to the Binstock (1960) report. My copy of this appendix came from the Edward C. Banfield Collection at the University of Illinois. See https://www.library.illinois.edu/cpla/special/banfield/.

[14] See Shaw (1954: 211, 223, 225) for examples of this usage.

The repeal coalition included regular Republicans, ten of sixteen Democratic precinct captains, and the CIO-affiliated United Steel Workers.[15] It is widely thought that the measure targeted Theodore "Ted" Berry, president of the local NAACP. Evidence consulted here suggests wider concerns and that Berry was controversial for having cooperated with fiscal conservatives in the Charter Party. This new crop of legislators depended for election on transfers from regular Republicans.

It helps to understand the repeal fight in a larger context of party-building. The migration to Charter of Black and labor candidates is detailed at length by Straetz (1958: 109–54). Prior to 1948 and 1953, respectively, these groups essentially floated between the parties, propping up Republican majorities from 1939–47. By the early 1950s, the local party system came to mirror the national one, except that Democrats were subsumed in Charter. Democrats had not won a citywide majority since 1912, under the "reform" administration of Henry T. Hunt. To remedy this, in 1954, a group of young Democrats began organizing Black neighborhoods (Miller and Tucker 1990: 94). Some of these pointed to Black candidates winning state-legislative races in plurality districts. It is noteworthy that, in 1954, pro-repeal Democrats proposed a "6X system." They claimed it would deliver stable majorities without gutting minority representation (Straetz 1958: 10–14, 26–27).

Four big issues defined politics in the repeal years. One of them was who should lead the Charter Party. Even though Democrats were a majority of the delegation, the party sought to placate "independent" Republicans by making one of their number mayor. Glimmers of this fight appeared in early 1954, on the death of Edward N. Waldvogel, a Democratic mayor from the New Deal generation (R. A. Burnham 2013: 65–66). Notably, in the subsequent council, this office went to Charles P. Taft, II, a national reform spokesman since 1933.

Three more issues pit Charter moderates against the left-labor wing: desegregation, taxation, and collective bargaining. In 1948, Charter buried a CIO proposal to integrate forthcoming housing projects.[16] The race issue

---

[15] On Democrats, see Straetz (1958: 14). On the CIO, see numerous sources, e.g., Maloney, Michael. 1957. "Light Ballot Predicted in Fifth Challenge Here to System of Election," *Cincinnati Enquirer*, p. 5, September 30.

[16] Rollin Everett was Charter's inaugural CIO candidate. Late in 1948, he sponsored a resolution of intent to mandate nondiscrimination in "temporary" public housing. The motion spent more than a month in two different committees. We do not yet know whether the final report included that language. See *The City Bulletin* for November 3, November 10, and December 8, all 1948. As of this writing, I still await fulfillment of a public records request (January 5, 2016) for the final report on the bill.

Table 7.1 Five referendums to repeal STV in Cincinnati.

Referendum	Proposal	Registration	Total vote	Turnout	For STV	Margin for STV
May 12, 1936	9X	243,241	72,469	29.8%	36,650	759 (1.1%)
Jun. 7, 1939	9X	228,912	95,858	41.9%	48,300	820 (0.8%)
Nov. 4, 1947	9X	246,671	155,003	62.8%	81,365	7,592 (5.0%)
Nov. 2, 1954	6X	245,429	150,416	61.3%	75,544	607 (0.4%)
Sep. 30, 1957	9X	242,348	119,843	49.5%	54,097	−11,625 (−9.7%)

reappeared in the 1950s, first as a fight over Fair Employment Practices (FEP) legislation, then over police brutality. On FEP, the CIO called for non-compliance penalties. Charter and regular Republican moderates favored a bill without penalties, a compromise that Berry was willing to make.[17] It is not clear what happened with police brutality. Berry and Jesse Locker (a Black Republican regular) cooperated on this issue in 1950–51, and it appears to have split the regular Republican caucus in 1956–57.[18] On taxes, Berry brokered a compromise between regular Republicans (who wanted to cut spending) and Charter's left wing (who sought to increase property taxes). The compromise was an income tax, allegedly temporary, and opposed by the CIO as "viciously regressive" (Sigafoos 1955). Finally, the collective bargaining issue split Charter along party lines: Democrats in favor (including Berry), and the sole Republican opposed.[19]

Some readers will want to know about four prior repeal efforts (see Table 7.1).[20] Two of these coincided with dissolution of the original reform coalition, 1936–39, due to defections by Charter Republicans. Charter was able to defeat these measures with help from voters who had supported third parties.[21] Yet these left-wing groups tended to support Republican majorities

[17] On fair employment, see: "City FEP Ordinance Is Defeated after Stormy Council Debate," *Cincinnati Enquirer*, p. 1, July 8, 1955; Maloney, Michael. "Mrs. Gusweiler in Council Hot Seat after Vote Halting FEP Ordinance." *Cincinnati Enquirer*, p. 20, February 16, 1957.
[18] On policing, see Joe Green, "Councilwoman Is Personable, Feminine and Trying Hard to Meet the Challenge," *Cincinnati Enquirer*, p. 20, February 16, 1957.
[19] For public manifestation of this controversy, see *The City Bulletin: Official Publication of the City of Cincinnati*, December 23, 1953.
[20] The data are from Heisel (1982) and R. L. Engstrom (1990), and referendum dates come from official records. "Proposal" refers to the proposed alternative, with the number on "X" indicating the maximum votes a voter could cast in an at-large, plurality election to the nine-seat council.
[21] By 1953, the combined independent vote had declined from 7,127 (4.4 percent) in 1947, the year Berry first ran, as well as the year of the third initiative, to 189 (0.01 percent) in 1953. From 1935–39, when PR was subject to the first two initiatives, votes for independents ranged from 23,928 (16.4 percent) to 26,551 (19.3 percent). These numbers rebounded to 6.1 percent in 1955, due to Albert C. Jordan's run as an independent. Jordan was a CIO endorsee who defected from Charter

until 1947. In that year, the Republican Party replaced its own mayor, filled a Charter vacancy with one of its own, and used a rare six-seat majority to order the third referendum. Having defeated that measure, Berry and the unions essentially rebuilt Charter on a platform of modern liberalism.

The fourth referendum, in 1954, initiated with Democrats and ended in a year-long recount.[22] That set the stage for 1957, in preparation by February 1956 at least.[23] Each of these efforts lines up reasonably well with the data given below. There were two critical differences between 1957 and the preceding initiative: no more independents in the candidate pipeline, plus the CIO defection from Charter.

7.2.1 Party-system evolution

Figure 7.1 depicts Cincinnati's PR party system (96.2 percent of votes correctly classified). Font styles mark two critical junctures in the Charter Party's evolution: a 1936 decision to limit the set of re-nominated incumbents (italics), then a 1951 decision freeing candidates from coordinating their campaigns (boldface). Roughly speaking, the x axis captures economic conservatism, and the y axis captures racial conservatism, but these characterizations are not perfect.[24]

These data suggest three distinct party alignments, each of which corresponds to one of the changes in Charter campaign rules, plus a spate of repeal activity. The original reform-machine alignment runs from north to south. The slightly leftward position of James D. Wilson, Democrat and labor leader, portends the New Deal alignment to come. That alignment

in the 1954–55 term. Minus Jordan's total, the independent vote in 1955 was 1,055 (0.01 percent). See Reed et al. (1957: 39), as well as the official election returns. Precinct-level analyses are in the appendix.

[22] Council certified the result on February 24, 1955.

[23] The first reading of a repeal ordinance was on February 29, 1956. It failed, and the referendum proceeded by initiative.

[24] For example, three Black legislators appear toward the bottom of the space: Theodore Berry (as a Charter Democrat), R. P. McClain (regular Republican elected in 1931), and Jesse D. Locker (regular Republican who served in the 1940s). Toward the top are Charter's original Progressives, who courted Black opinion leaders in 1924 but did not nominate a Black candidate until 1937. At the left of the space are the New Deal Democrats, which include Rollin Everett and Albert C. Jordan, both CIO endorsees. Opposite them are Republicans of the late 1940s and early 1950s, one of whom (William C. Kelly) went on to run the local Goldwater campaign. Another (Gordon Scherer) later served on the House Un-American Activities Committee, 1953–62.

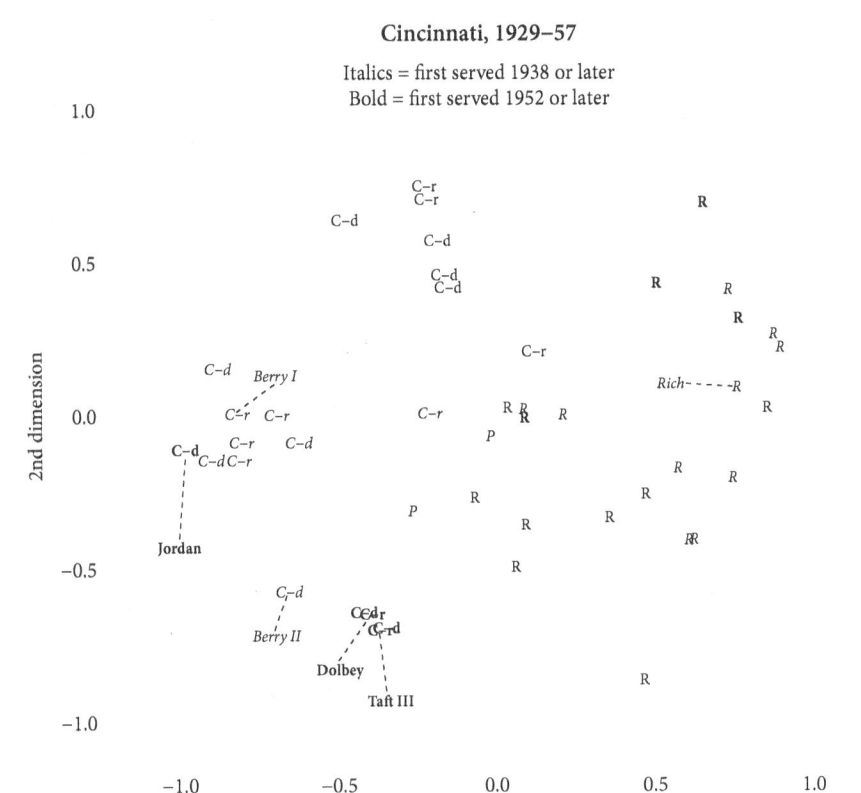

Fig. 7.1 Spatial map of voting in Cincinnati's STV council. C-d = Charter-Democrat, C-r = Charter-Republican, P = Progressive Democrat, R = Republican.

runs from east to west, with the right of this spectrum fairly scattered.[25] The transition between these states comes with several notable features: two repeal initiatives in the late 1930s, Republican departures from the Charter Party (e.g., Julian Pollak), two Progressive Democrats in tense alliance with Republicans, and Charter's change of nominating strategy in 1936. This was meant to rescue the party by facilitating absorption of third-party challengers. Figures elected after this decision are plotted in italics.[26]

---

[25] The right is scattered because, during the years of Republican majorities, both parties tended to cooperate on urban renewal issues.
[26] See Straetz (1958: 58): "To avoid the danger of discouraging new blood in the form of candidates, in 1936 the Charter Committee announced that it would adopt a policy of renominating

The transition that ends STV, however, is from the second to the third alignment. Despite again winning council majorities, Charter is visibly split between New Deal and white-collar wings. The white-collar bloc appears toward the bottom left. It includes John J. "Jack" Gilligan, who later brought the income tax to Ohio; Dorothy N. Dolbey, a Charter Republican who pressed to become mayor in 1954; and Charles P. Taft, II, veteran spokesman for the national PR movement. The New Deal bloc includes Albert Jordan, Rollin Everett's CIO successor, and Edward Waldvogel. These divisions led to the second change in Charter electioneering: allowing slate candidates to run separate campaigns (R. A. Burnham 2013: 64).

7.2.2 Control of government

If one were to predict repeal referendums from change in the majority roll rate alone, one would get three of five right (Fig. 7.2): Spring 1936, Spring 1939, and Spring 1954. September 1957 continued the fight of November

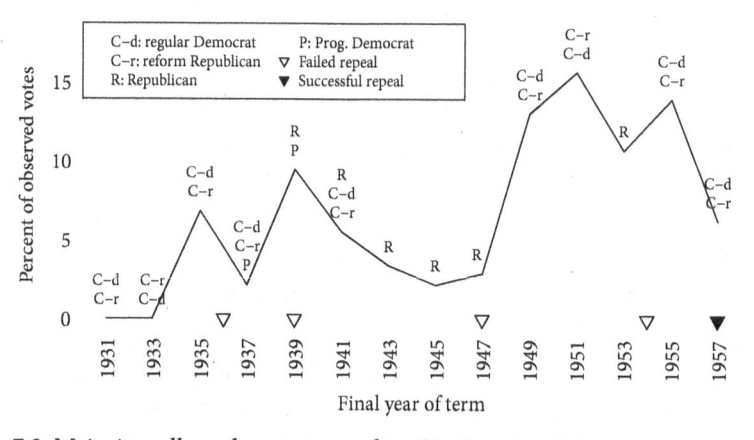

Majority rolls and party control in Cincinnati City Council

Fig. 7.2 Majority rolls and party control in Cincinnati, 1929–57.

only three or at the most four of the incumbents." On labor as a pivotal voting block, consult official election returns. In 1931, Charter successfully beat back a one-shot Labor Party: 67 percent of its transfers went to the Republican Party; 26 percent went to Charter Democrats. In 1937, the one-shot Roosevelt Democrats also entered a slate: 41 percent of its transfers went to Republicans, followed by 33 percent to Charter Democrats, then 20 percent to Progressive Democrats.

1954. November 1947 seems to have followed a *coalition-insulting* logic (see discussion under "voter dealignment" section below). The critical question is why it took until the mid-1950s to produce the last two initiatives. There are two overarching reasons.

First, the Democratic Party itself was unsettled. While CIO locals supported both PR and Democrats, the AFL supported PR and Republicans. Democratic organizers lamented these positions as late as 1954 (Straetz 1958: 27, 137). Black political leadership was in a similar situation. Primary representation had been through Jesse D. Locker, a loyal Republican until 1953, when he accepted an appointment as Ambassador to Liberia. Theodore Berry, also a Republican, did not join Charter until 1949, then the Democratic Party until the middle of his first term (1950–51). These conditions changed rapidly in the early 1950s, as the contemporary Democratic coalition took shape.

Second, the 1952–53 term galvanized Republican support for repeal. Despite having won a majority of seats, its own delegation was divided between two camps. One of these was moderate on racial issues and had history of cooperation with labor. This wing largely depended for election on transfers from Charter (see data below), following the 1951 decision to permit independent campaigning. The other wing was virulently anti-communist, to the point of having enlisted the Federal Bureau of Investigation in a purge of the local planning department (Collett 2002). These wings can be seen along the vertical dimension, toward the far right of Figure 7.1.

In June of 1954, however, a group calling itself the Charter Improvement League (CIL) announced bipartisan support for the "6X" system.[27] This announcement coincided with the start of the Democratic Party's internal re-organization.

CIL's announcement also coincided with another difficult term for Charter in city council. Charter Republicans had been reduced to one member: Vice-Mayor Dorothy Dolbey. Her role in frustrating Democratic Party leadership is well documented by Straetz (1958) and R. A. Burnham (2013). One new piece of information, however, is her role in blocking collective bargaining legislation. Almost immediately at the start of the 1954–55 term, Dolbey rolled her Democratic colleagues on two labor-related measures. The first concerned what to do about a strike at the nation's second-largest cemetery. Jordan called for council to investigate the issue, and Dolbey

---

[27] "New Proposal Made to Abolish PR; League Formed to Seek Amendment," *Cincinnati Enquirer*, p. 5, June 10, 1954.

joined Republicans in defeating the proposal. Second, on the same day, Jordan called for a formal report on the "feasibility" of a "local Wagner Act." With the Republicans, Dolbey voted to table it. On each of these items, all three Charter Democrats voted the Jordan position, including Theodore Berry.

Democrats in 1955 variously expected Taft to replace Dolbey or, better from their perspective, to win a Democratic-only majority.[28] Instead, Dolbey was re-elected, and Taft returned to council after a decade-long break. Charter also elected Taft mayor, in a bid to hold the party together.

7.2.3 Voter dealignment

The final part of the repeal puzzle involves candidates forming coalitions that defy the dominant alignment. Every repeal measure implicated this in some way, as shown in Figure 7.3.

In 1955, Republican candidates sent their largest ever share of transfers to winners in the Charter coalition. Of this 49 percent, half went to the Charter Republicans, Taft and Dolbey, then half to the new class of Charter Democrats. The single biggest beneficiary was Charles P. Taft, old Progressive advocate of "good government" parties. Jordan, meanwhile, lost this election because Republican transfers elevated Dolbey and Gilligan in the final two rounds of a fifteen-round count.[29] Finally, Charter won a seat majority despite Republican candidates having won more first-choice votes. In other words, transfer flows arguably reversed the result of the election (galvanizing Republican support for repeal), elevated Charter's lingering Republican wing (galvanizing support from labor-sympathetic Democrats), and helped a pro-income-tax Democrat defeat a union representative (leading labor in 1957 to join the 1954 repeal coalition).[30]

---

[28] On Young Democrats' expectations about 1955, see Al Schottlekotte's "Talk of the Town," page 4 of the *Cincinnati Enquirer*, November 28, 1953. Also see A. M. Forkner "Same Council Line-Up Predicted for '56, with Taft Replacing Dorothy N. Dolbey," *Cincinnati Enquirer*, September 5, 1955.

[29] Transfer flows are calculated from official returns.

[30] Some readers may wonder why the left wing of the labor movement joined a repeal campaign with racist undertones. One possibility, raised by a modern-day PR supporter, is that anti-communists had come to dominate the CIO, and that anti-communism colored attitudes toward the Civil Rights issue. Another possibility is that the ascendance of white-collar Democrats activated "authoritarian" attitudes among union rank-and-file. For a modern-day perspective on the second dynamic, see Zingher (2020), drawing on Lipset (1959).

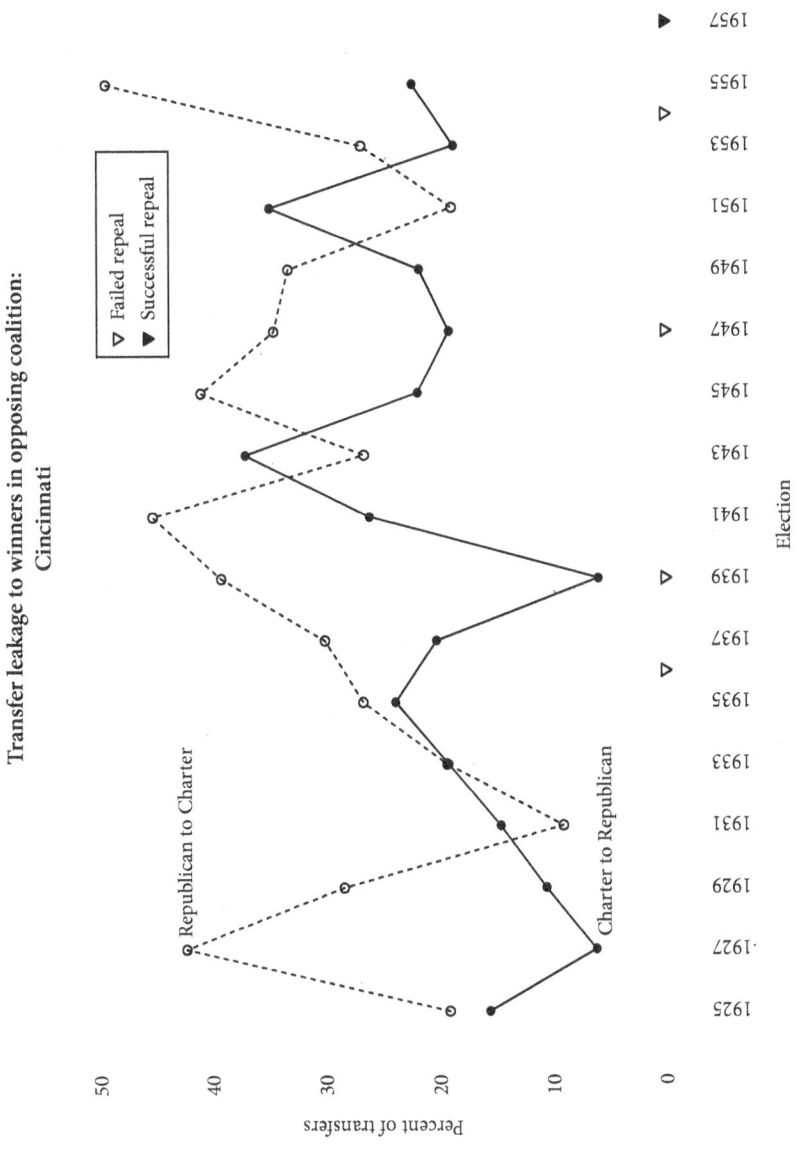

Fig. 7.3 Transfer leakage to opposing coalition winners, Cincinnati.

These data also shed light on the 1947 effort, which I have cast as *coalition-insulating*, i.e., one that initiates with the ruling coalition. There is no evidence in data, nor case history, that anyone but Republicans supported the measure.[31] For what follows, it is useful to recall the logic of several PR adoptions in Western Europe: incumbent parties facing threats from emergent coalitions in runoff systems (Cox et al. 2019; Emmenegger and Walter 2019).

For Republicans elected in 1945, the subsequent term was a window of opportunity to get rid of STV and its fickle vote transfers. In that year, more than 40 percent of their transfers benefitted Charter winners. (This rate was higher in 1941, but Republican control of council depended on Charter cooperation.) Yet a 5–4 majority gave Republicans the power to fill vacancies with conservative figures. The first came on January 2, 1947, when Republicans replaced a former Charter Republican mayor (Russell Wilson, recently deceased) with a party regular, Homer S. Toms. Then, in March, the party replaced its own long-serving mayor, James G. "Jimmy" Stewart, with Carl S. Rich, who went on to lead the party in the postwar PR years (Straetz 1958: 78–79). Four months later, with this six-seat majority, the party put repeal on the November ballot.[32] It failed, and, for the first time in a decade, power swung back to Charter.

Finally, these transfer flows help explain the first two repeal measures. Figure 7.2 showed that, during the 1934–35 term, divisions emerged in Charter's council delegation. In 1933 and 1935, Republican and Charter candidates alike sent 20–25 percent of their votes to winners in the opposing party. This coincided with a Republican effort to break Charter's majority by endorsing labor candidates. Instead of breaking that majority, however, the Republican strategy (a) returned Charter to control of council, (b) elevated its labor wing, and (c) favored Democrats (AFL's James Wilson) at the expense of Julian Pollak, a veteran Charter Republican who lost (127–8, 147). Meanwhile, the bulk of Charter's leakage to Republicans came from two candidates: ticket leader Russell Wilson (incumbent mayor and Republican), then Pollak on elimination.[33] In 1935, the Republicans tried their labor strategy again, this time endorsing two labor candidates. One of them lost in the twenty-seventh of twenty-eight counting rounds, transferring 2,698

---

[31] See Appendix A. For every Charter vote cast in the same election, I estimate that one voter also supported PR.

[32] Jesse D. Locker, then the only Black council member, also voted for this measure.

[33] In addition to Straetz, see the official returns. Further, transfers from Republican J. M. Dugan favored Wilson over Pollak by a factor of 2.4 (805 votes to 342 votes).

votes to regular Democrats (and the rest, 71 percent, to regular Republicans). All of this helps explain why many Charter Republicans, formerly the core of the pro-PR coalition, backed the May 1936 repeal initiative—and why Republicans might have wanted it. The effort of June 1939 reflects a similar fact pattern: symmetric vote flows across party lines (20–30 percent of total transfers in 1937), and disunity in the council majority.[34] In 1941, the mini-realignment was complete; Republicans would hold power for six more years.

7.3 New York City, 1937–47

In November 1947, after five elections, voters agreed to repeal STV. The replacement system called for plurality, using the same single-seat districts as state senate races. The repeal coalition included Tammany Democratic leaders, who opposed STV from the start, and Republican borough leaders, who did not sign on until October of that year.[35] Shefter (1986) and others have interpreted repeal as an effort to purge the left from city council. Yet Communists had been present since 1941; the American Labor Party (ALP) had split into factions, one of which was the new Liberal Party; and the ALP-endorsed City Council President also supported repeal.[36] Banfield and Wilson (1963: 97) offer the following alternative interpretation:

> PR breaks down party control over nominations and permits mavericks who owe nothing to party leaders to win office. For this reason, the Republicans in New York, although they gained seats by it, did not exert themselves to prevent the Democrats, who of course opposed it strongly, from succeeding in their campaign for its abolition.

Both views capture part of the story. The reform coalition in city council showed signs of failure from 1941 onward. Republicans withheld support for repeal, however, because ALP cross-endorsement allowed them to keep control of the Board of Estimate. In turn, that gave the Republican Party a check on whatever happened in city council. In 1945, however, the ALP

---

[34] However, the 1937 election was notable for a separate labor party, the Roosevelt Democrats. See the Appendix for their role in defeating the measure.

[35] See "Republican Leaders Join in Fight for Repeal of PR System in City," *New York Times*, pp. 1–2, October 17, 1947.

[36] "Impellitteri Asks Voters to Kill PR," *New York Times*, p. 2, October 30, 1947.

switched to supporting Democratic candidates for Board and mayoral elections. Having lost control of the upper chamber and mayoralty, Republicans now needed a cohesive council minority (due to supermajority rules) to bargain with the new administration. They had not controlled one since the start of the decade.

Substantively, issues of race and redevelopment seem to have broken the reform coalition. Early on, city planners decided to permit segregation in new public housing projects. This is partly why the ALP split into "left" and "right" wings (J. Schwartz 1993). Police brutality and job segregation were persistent issues, leading to the Harlem riots of 1943. Against this backdrop, and feuding with Mayor Fiorello La Guardia, Adam Clayton Powell in 1941 became the first Black member of city council (Capeci 1977). Another set of challenges concerned Robert Moses's plans for postwar urban renewal. In 1945, city council passed a resolution asking Mayor O'Dwyer to remove him. This vote drew support from both major parties, what remained of Fusion (the La Guardia faction of the Republican Party), and the left minor parties (ALP, Communist, Liberal). Finally, in 1946, the Republican Party splintered over government spending on school and park construction.

Stanley M. Isaacs deserves mention here, having gone all but unnoticed in STV historiography. According to his wife Edith's post-humous biography, "He remained a Republican throughout his career, but always a rather unorthodox Republican, fighting the reactionary wing of his party on every issue." In the 1912 presidential election, Isaacs had backed Theodore Roosevelt instead of William Howard Taft. As a young real estate developer, he earned ire from colleagues in a business association for pressing improvements to tenement housing: fire escapes, toilets, windows, and a ban on basement living. In 1937, as Manhattan Borough President, he appointed Si Gerson, whom he claimed was "not a real Communist," to a planning post in his office. This led La Guardia, under pressure from newspapers, to refuse Isaacs's renomination. Instead, in 1941, Isaacs ran for Council as a Fusion candidate. According to Edith, he did so with three goals: "saving money for the city," "spending it for the right purpose," and challenging the Board of Estimate on which he used to sit (Isaacs 1967: 27–54).

In 1945, Isaacs won re-election as a regular Republican. Banfield and Wilson (1963) did not offer evidence for the point they made above—that Republicans joined Democrats in STV's repeal because it deprived them of nomination control. Technically, party committees in New York City controlled use of their labels on ballots. However, other candidates had claimed an ability to force themselves on party committees (Powell, Jr. 1971:69). Based on the data that follows, it is likely that Isaacs was the Republican that Banfield and Wilson had in mind: a "Democratic Republican," in his wife's words.[37]

7.3.1 Party-system evolution

Shaw (1954: 223–24) described the council after 1942 as a "three-ring circus." He points to four big developments within the chamber: (1) the election of two Communists, the first in 1941, then another in 1943; (2) cleavage of the American Labor Party into its own left and right wings; (3) the entry of a new group of conservative Republicans; and (4) establishment by the left parties (both ALP wings, two Communists and, after 1945, the Liberal Party) of headquarters separate from the Republican and Fusion members. "The coalition," as it was known, was in trouble from the third election onward.

Signs of Shaw's "three rings" are visible in Figure 7.4 (97 percent of votes correctly classified). Legislators sitting in 1942 or later are boldfaced. Coordinates are jittered slightly to minimize overlap. The original fusion coalition appears at top, with several Fusion members, a few Republicans, and the early ALP. This group is visibly cohesive. If anyone "played both sides of the aisle," it was part of the early Republican caucus, elected 1937–39 (e.g., Abner Surpless, top-middle).[38] After the elections of 1941, however, the reform coalition scatters along the plot's second dimension. Adam Clayton Powell (ALP-Fusion) is in the dead center. Michael Quill and Eugene Connolly, both of the ALP left wing, appear toward the bottom, near Communists Benjamin Davis and Peter Cacchione. Isaacs also appears near them as a Republican (elected 1943–45). His earlier location, as a Fusion winner, is closer to the middle of the section dimension.

Shaw (1954: 217–18) also notes that, after 1945, the council became more productive in areas of rent control, housing, and automobile regulation. He attributed this to the Democrats, particularly the new mayor, William O'Dwyer (D), and Majority Leader Joseph Sharkey (D). This suggests that

---

[37] Also see Zeller and Bone (1948: 1128): "Although the Republicans enjoyed greater influence and representation in the new council, the leaders could not always prevent the nomination and election of so-called independent Republicans through P.R."

[38] Notable among ALP members is Baruch Charney Vladeck, the first Minority Leader, famous for having pushed rent control through the council.

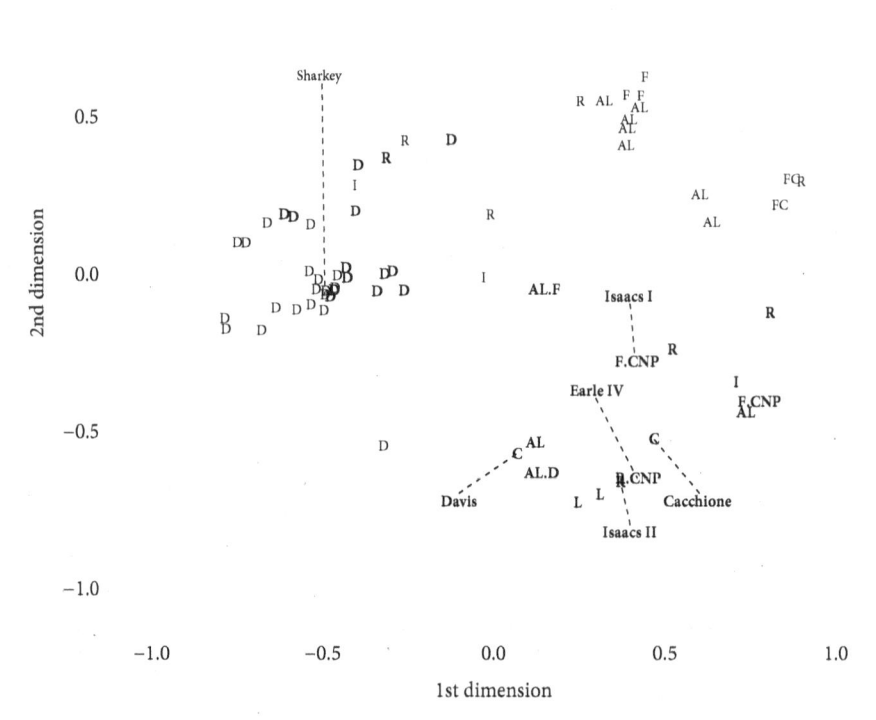

New York City, 1938–47

Bold = first served 1942 or later

Fig. 7.4 Spatial map of voting in New York City's STV council. AL = American Labor, C = Communist, CNP = Citizens' Non-Partisan, D = Democrat, F = Fusion, I = Independent, L = Liberal, R = Republican.

Shaw's "third ring," the Tammany Democrats, were cutting new deals with "coalition" elements.

Overall, the dissolution of the initial reform coalition in council lines up with increasing Republican support for repeal. The first attempt was in 1938, via a statewide referendum on an anti-PR constitutional amendment. A second was in 1940, when a citywide initiative lost. Neither of these attracted sufficient support from Republican leadership, at least within the city (Zeller and Bone 1948: 1127). After the elections of 1941, however, Republicans became increasingly anti-PR. In December of that year, in a bipartisan vote, City Council ordered another referendum. The Board of Estimate pocket-vetoed this.[39] Then, in 1943, Prosterman (2013: 183) notes that Robert Moses felt the need to urge Republicans against another initiative.

Why did it take until 1947 to galvanize Republican leadership? And why did Tammany always take the lead in organizing repeal campaigns? Part of the answer is in who controlled government. The other part comes from voting behavior.

7.3.2 Control of government

As noted above, the New York City reform charter had been built for minority rule. Legislation had to pass through the Board of Estimate, where each Borough President had equal voting power, regardless of their county's population. This put Staten Island, for example, on an equal footing with Brooklyn or Manhattan. The Mayor, Comptroller, and Council President (all directly elected) also controlled two votes each. Further, there were two kinds of legislation: local laws and budget measures. A typical local law might have have renamed a street (e.g., Avenue of the Americas), given city employees a holiday (e.g., Rosh Hashanah or Columbus Day), changed the building code, or regulated street vendors. On local laws, a two-thirds vote in council could override a Board of Estimate veto. The other class of legislation dealt with the budget. On these bills, by a vote of three-fourths, city council could delete items from the budget, over the will of the Board of Estimate. Therefore, a minority coalition could bargain from either of two positions: the Board or City Council's minority caucus. Further, if it controlled both, it might impose its will on the city.

Figure 7.5 gives the City Council "minority frustration" rate on the two major classes of legislation. Again, a roll-call vote is "minority-frustrating" if the majority position of anti-Tammany elements does not achieve a veto-proof threshold.

From 1942 onward, a faction of the City Council minority began sparring with the Board of Estimate, still controlled by Republicans until January 1946. This trend is stark for local laws, the lesser class of legislation, but we also see the start of conflict over budget issues. This helps explain why, in 1943, Moses needed to urge his party to forebear on repeal.

---

[39] See *Proceedings of the Council of the City of New York* for December 9, 1941, then Shaw (1954: 204) for the pocket veto.

Minority frustration in New York City Council

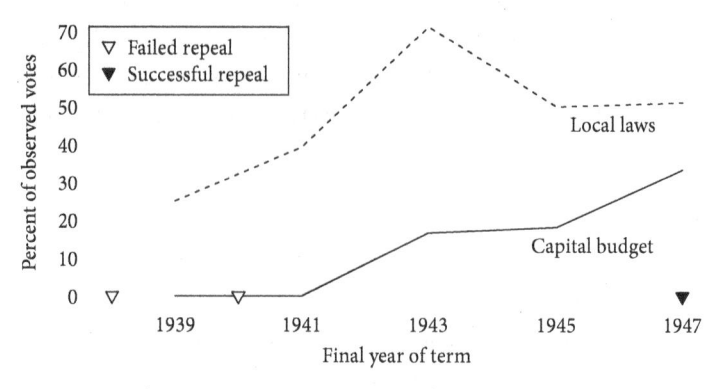

Fig. 7.5 Minority frustration rates in New York City Council, 1938–47.

In 1946–47, though, the minority's inability to cohere in council was fatal to Republican leverage. Table 7.2 gives the partisan balance of that body, as well as the number of votes controlled by each member. Cell entries reflect parties' cross-endorsement of the respective members, and borough names denote borough Presidents.[40] In November 1945, the ALP threw its support behind O'Dwyer and Tammany in every borough but Staten Island. This meant that Republicans' ability to bargain with the new Democratic administration would depend on a veto-proof coalition in council. On budget measures, this coalition had been eroding since the 1942–43 session. On local laws, it had been fractious from the start.

Some of these "rolls" are clearly responsible for the placement of the left bloc at bottom-right of Figure 7.4. For example, in July 1946, a package of budget amendments pit Isaacs (Republican-endorsed since 1943) and the left bloc (two Communists, two Liberals, one Laborite, and one Labor-Democrat) against three Republicans, including Minority Leader Genevieve B. Earle. Two more votes repeated the basic pattern, splitting the Republican delegation, and drawing some Democratic support.

In short, by 1946, the left bloc was backing Democrats in elections (except in Staten Island), Isaacs was defying Republican leadership, and, together, they were opposing both sides from a minority position in City Council.

---

[40] Data are from the *Annual Report of the Board of Elections in the City of New York*, 1937, 1939, 1941, 1943, and 1945. See Tanzer (1937) for voting strength on the Board.

Table 7.2 Partisan division of New York City Board of Estimate, 1938–47, as revealed by cross-endorsements. A = American Labor, AC = Anti-Communist, D = Democratic, F = Fusion, I = Independent, P = Progressive, R = Republican, TU = Trades Union, UC = United City.

Office	Votes	Election 1937	Election 1939	Election 1941	Election 1943	Election 1945
Mayor	2	R, A, F, P	R, A, F, P	R, A, F, UC	R, A, F, UC	D, A
Comptroller	2	R, A, F, P	R, A, F, P	R, A, F, UC	R, A, F, UC	D, A
Council Pres.	2	R, A, F, P	R, A, F, P	R, A, F, UC	R, A, F, UC	D, A
Manhattan	1	R, A, F, P	R, A, F, P	R, A, F, UC	R, A, F, UC	D, A
Bronx	1	D, TU, AC	D, TU, AC	D	D	D
Brooklyn	1	R, F, A, P	R, F, A, P	D	D	D, A
Queens	1	R, F, I	R, F, I	D	D	D, A
Staten Island	1	R, F	R, F	R, A, F	R, A, F	R, A, F

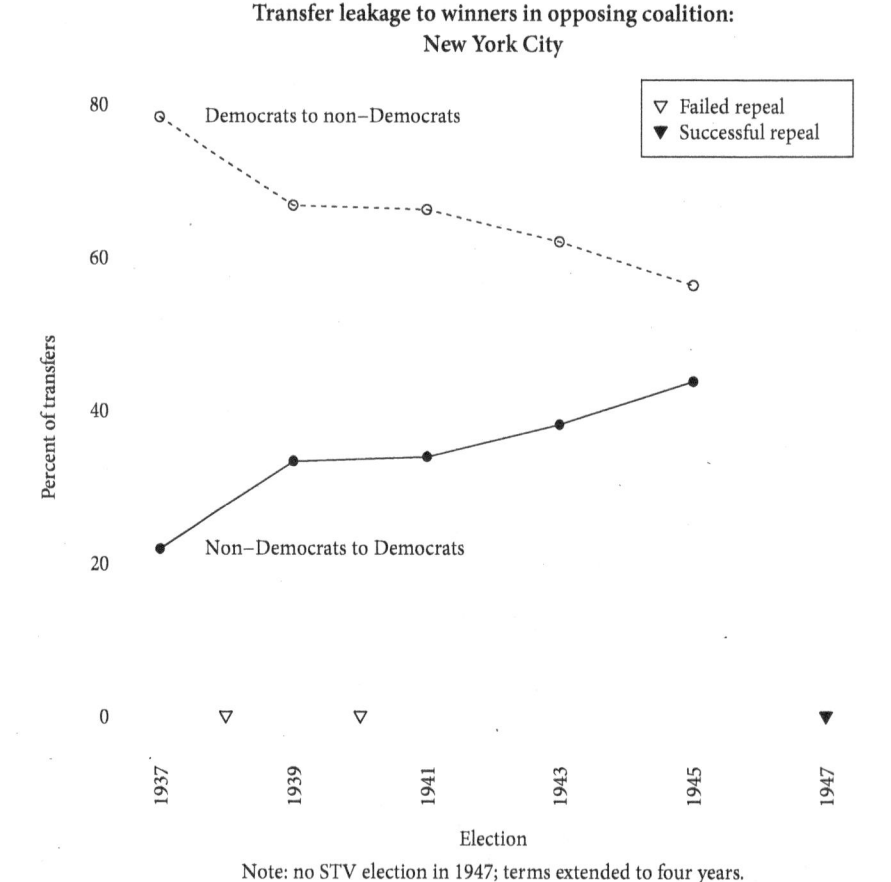

Fig. 7.6 Transfer leakage to opposing-coalition winners, New York City.

7.3.3 Voter dealignment

The Board of Estimate data suggest a sharp transition by the ALP from coalition with Republicans to coalition with Democrats. Rates of transfer leakage, however, suggest a more gradual process, which began at the very first STV election (Fig. 7.6).

Overall, the transfers point to persistently high levels of inter-coalition bargaining. At the first election in 1937, for example, nearly 80 percent of Democrats' observable transfers helped to elect "coalition" winners. This explains why Tammany attacked STV immediately in 1938, then again in 1940 and 1941. The rate of leakage from Tammany to anti-Tammany never fell below 56 percent, in fact.

Meanwhile, non-Democrats sent a fifth of their votes to Democratic candidates in 1937. That may help explain why "upstate Republicans" lent their support to the statewide initiative in 1938 (Zeller and Bone 1948: 1127). This rate increased to 43.7 percent in 1945, the final PR election.

Two Manhattan winners will reinforce the point: Stanley Isaacs (R) and Eugene P. Connolly (Democrat-American Labor), both of whom broke ranks with the reform coalition in the budget conflict of 1946. Of transfers that elevated Isaacs, 46 percent were from Republicans, 17 percent from a Citizens Non-Partisan group, followed by 13 percent from Democrats, then a scattering. Meanwhile, Connolly drew 25 percent of his transfers from Democrats, 24 percent from the Liberal Party, 15 percent from Citizens Non-Partisan, 13 percent more from Republicans, then a scattering. Despite formally being on opposite sides of the aisle, both Isaacs and Connolly drew substantial votes from both.

7.4 Worcester, 1949–60

In November 1960, with special permission from the state legislature, voters replaced STV with an at-large, non-partisan runoff system. The eighteen top vote-getters in a September preliminary would advance to a November general. Otherwise, as in most other STV cities, the nine-seat council-manager system remained unchanged. Permission from the legislature was necessary because the city had voted on repeal one year earlier, and state law forbade more than one referendum in a five-year period. The November 1959 repeal vote had been on a partisan mayor-council system (Plan B in Massachusetts state law). Data suggest that the Citizens' Plan E Association (CEA) rallied its voters to defeat Plan B.[41] Immediately after the election, however, several CEA legislators joined regular Democrats in petitioning the state legislature for the 1960 referendum.[42] According to Binstock (1960: A-2), "Some CEA directors . . . felt that the elimination of PR would, in the long run, improve the city manager form's chance of survival."

In practice, repeal came from two corners. One was the regular Democratic Party, opposed to reform from the start. A second was Republican

---

[41] Precinct-level results are available on request.

[42] Four months later, in March 1960, they attempted to walk back this position. Yet a CEA op-ed published at the same time claimed that it was "too late" to stop the referendum.

Party leadership, operating through the city's only daily newspaper, *The Worcester Telegram*.[43] Not all Republicans supported repeal. For example, veteran councilman Andrew Holmstrom opposed it. Yet a freshman Republican, Warren C. "Bud" Lane, abstained on the November 1959 vote to petition the state legislature. This replicated the *Telegram* position: getting out of the Democratic Party's way, now that the replacement rules would retain the manager charter (versus in November 1959). Binstock (1960: A-5) contends that the paper's editors shared the position of "some CEA directors" above: that STV endangered the manager plan.[44]

Urban redevelopment structured the major controversies during the STV years. This turned up first in 1953, with the city's adoption of an official map, paving the way for more systematic zoning and property tax assessment. Local lore holds that the devastating Worcester tornado (June 1953) was divine retribution. The late 1950s also saw conflict over construction of Interstate 290, as well as related land takings. Today, this highway runs through center city, formerly a working-class enclave.[45] What stands out most from written records, however, is zoning. Worcester was remarkable in the contemporary planning literature for not having updated its zoning regime since 1925, as well as for its frequency of case-by-case ("spot") zoning (Natoli 1971). At the time of repeal, a new zoning ordinance had been before council since 1955 (Binstock 1960: C-1). CEA leadership protested its own majorities' inaction with an op-ed in the *Telegram*, dated April 1960.[46] At some point in 1963, the post-STV council finally adopted "comprehensive" zoning (Natoli 1971).

Overall, the life of STV in Worcester tracked the life of CEA as device for keeping votes away from the regular Democratic Party.[47] In the mid-1950s, with help from Young Democrats, elements of the displaced "machine" began colonizing the party. Republicans threatened to run their own slate, ultimately deciding against this. Instead, in 1957, they tried to reverse the takeover by slating a new group of freshmen. This tug-of-war culminated in a difficult session for the CEA majority, 1958–59, and compromise rules to

---

[43] On the paper's Republican leanings, see Eisenthal (1983). The only other paper during this period was *The Worcester Yank*, published by George Wells. Wells was a regular Democrat and chief architect of both repeal measures.

[44] Also see Southwick (2017).

[45] On I-290 and the 1953 Worcester tornado, I thank Susan Ledoux.

[46] This appeared as an appendix to the original Binstock (1960) report. My copy of the op-ed came from the Edward C. Banfield Collection at the University of Illinois. See https://www.library.illinois.edu/cpla/special/banfield/.

[47] See Laver (2000) on this strategic imperative in STV systems.

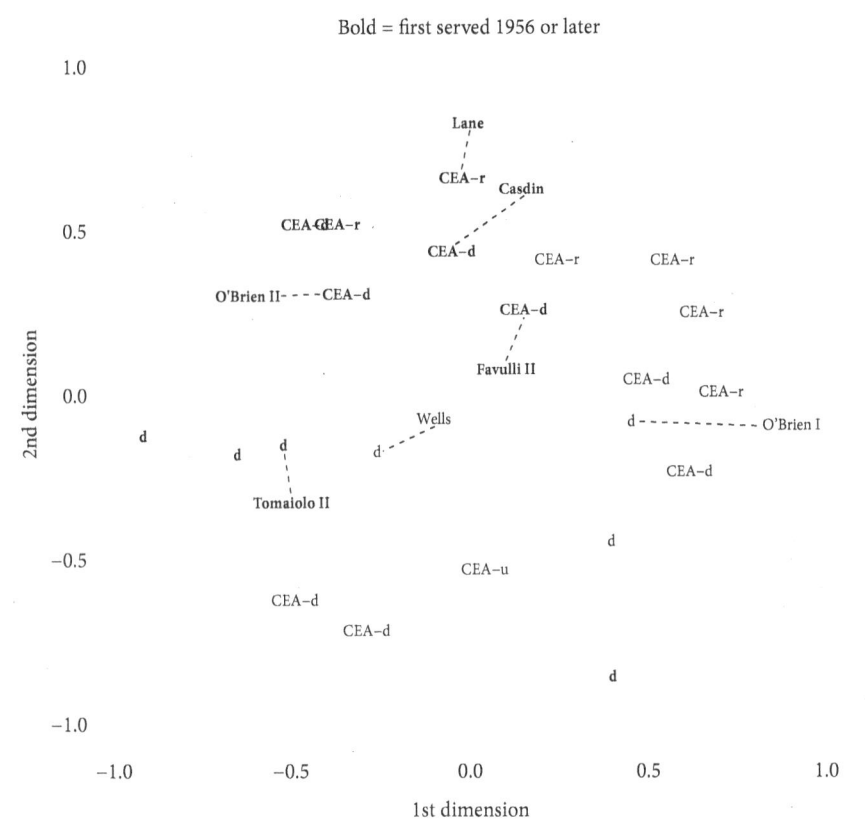

Worcester, 1950–60

Bold = first served 1956 or later

Fig. 7.7 Spatial map of voting in Worcester's STV council. CEA-d = Citizens' Plan E Association-Democrat, CEA-r = Citizens' Plan E Association-Republican, CEA-u = Citizens' Plan E Association-unaffiliated, d = registered Democrat (no official record of the Democratic slate).

(a) get rid of vote transfers, (b) preserve the manager system, (c) and resolve any lingering bargaining issues between the rounds of a runoff system.

7.4.1 Party-system evolution

Figure 7.7 maps the Worcester STV party system (94.6 percent of votes correctly classified). Legislators elected in 1955 or later appear in boldface. The CEA archives contain numerous clippings from this year, many of which point to infighting.[48] For example, the Republican Party threatened in May 1955 to run its own slate that November.[49] CEA board minutes around the same time record a failed motion to terminate a rule requiring endorsed candidates to support PR in public statements.[50] Further, L. Weaver (1986: 141) records a repeal effort in 1955, even though official records do not reflect one.

Part of the fighting in 1955 appears to have been related to changing personnel. In March of that year, newspapers reported an influx of Young Democrats into the CEA rank-and-file.[51] A former "machine" Democrat, James D. O'Brien, applauded this development.[52] Two years later, in 1957, the CEA endorsed two Democrats from the pre-PR party: O'Brien himself and Michael Favulli, the group's first Italian-American candidate since 1953.

The post-1955 policy space reflects two clear differences from that which came before. First is an overall leftward shift in the CEA delegation, closer to the positions of regular Democrats (e.g., George Wells, chief reform opponent). Second is that the vertical dimension captures substantial legislative conflict from 1956 onward. This dimension is defined by "Bud" Lane (at top), Republican collaborator in the 1960 repeal drive, and the regular Democratic bloc (left middle). CEA legislators after 1955 are essentially sandwiched between these figures. They include Joe Casdin (Democrat, elected 1957), Paul V. Mullaney (Democrat, elected 1959), and Carlton Payson (Republican, elected 1959).

7.4.2 Control of government

After 1953, and despite its majorities, CEA gradually lost control of city council. This decline came to a head in 1958–59, as shown in Figure 7.8, but signs were visible much earlier.

---

[48] As of June 2015, those clippings were still unsorted. They can be accessed at the Worcester Historical Museum by asking staff for "Plan E" and "CEA" materials. These items appear to have been collected by a local civic leader, then donated to the museum at some later date.

[49] Currier, Charles. "GOP to Run Council, School Board Ticket in Fall Plan E Election." *The Worcester Telegram*, May 15, 1955.

[50] Minutes of the CEA Board for May 16 and June 20, 1955, on file in the Plan E/CEA Collection, unsorted, at the Worcester Historical Museum.

[51] CEA doubled as a membership organization.

[52] Currier, Charles. "Many Democrats Here Supporters of PR." *The Worcester Telegram*, March 15, 1955.

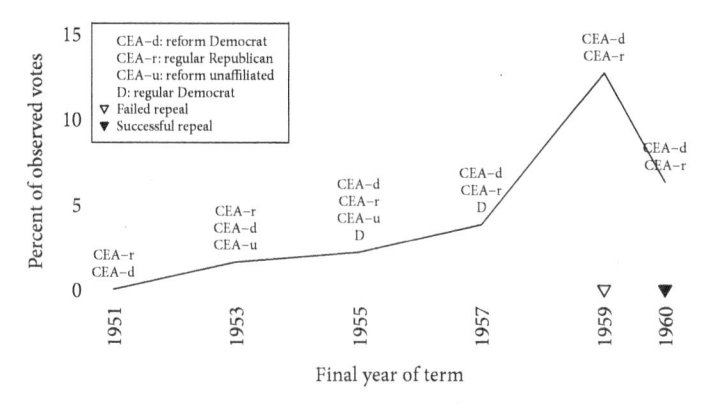

Fig. 7.8 Majority rolls and party control in Worcester, 1950–60.

The most obvious feature of the data is a spike in the roll rate just before repeal. CEA internal majorities did not get their way on seventy-eight votes in 1958–59. Of these, seventy-six occurred before the November referendum, and fifty-seven occurred in 1958 alone. The question then arises: why did CEA unanimously oppose the initiative of November 1959? Recall that George Wells, a regular Democrat, had proposed a partisan mayor-council system (i.e., Plan B in Massachusetts state law). Had he called for non-partisan plurality elections to the existing council (i.e., Plan D), Republicans and others might have gone along. They essentially did in 1960.[53]

The other thing to note, however, is diminishing CEA control of council from the second election onward. This appears first as slight uptick in rolls during the 1952–53 term. Then, in the 1954–55 term, we see a "grand coalition" government under Mayor O'Brien, then still a regular Democrat.[54] It was during this term that the Republican Party threatened to field its own slate.

The "grand coalition" persists into 1956–57, whereafter O'Brien is CEA-endorsed. Finally, in 1958–59, we see the critical session in council. At this point, the mayoralty passes to Casdin (born Cohen), a CEA Democrat elected in 1957. Choosing Casdin, however, took protracted negotiation: 318 roll calls and more than three months in early 1958.[55]

---

[53] See Schaffner et al. (2001, 2007) on the value to non-majority parties of non-partisan elections. On Republicans' loss of control in Massachusetts, see Lockard (1959) and Gamm (1989). On their loss of control in the city, see Eisenthal (1983: 67–68).

[54] Roll rates for 1954–55 and 1956–57 are nearly identical when Democratic members are excluded from these majorities, for the purpose of calculations. That plot is available on request.

[55] Official minutes.

Casdin appears to have led the faction caught between young Democrats, represented by O'Brien, and regular Republicans such as freshman "Bud" Lane. This is literally visible in Figure 7.7, toward the top of the plot's second dimension. Consider the following exchange, which Binstock (1960: VI-14) quotes from *The Telegram*:

O'Brien charged that Casdin said last fall that a plurality system of voting could give Worcester an Irish-Catholic-Democrat City Council similar to Boston's. "What's wrong with Irishmen?" O'Brien asked. "Don't forget Irishmen made you mayor, Mr. Casdin," he said.

The question is why the Republican Party, operating largely through the *Telegram*, permitted repeal to go forward. Banfield and Wilson (1963: 97) do not have an answer, having relied largely on Binstock's report, and having overlooked the paper's role in local politics. They contend: "PR produced a council in which two minority groups—Jews and Yankees—were represented. Its proponents (Republicans and Jewish Democrats) argued that going back to an ordinary plurality system would mean that Irish Catholics would elect all nine councilmen." Like their counterparts in New York, Worcester Republicans faced a difficult choice. PR elections gave them a lifeline in a city (and state) whose partisanship was changing.

But the STV system also worked against Republicans, as the transfer data below suggest. It also worked against regular Democrats, forcing figures like Joe Casdin to serve both groupings at once.[56] This explains why the replacement system was neither "ordinary" nor "plurality," contra Banfield and Wilson. It was non-partisan, based on runoffs, and designed to eliminate the logic of transfers.[57]

---

[56] Casdin voted for repeal in November 1959, then reversed this position in March 1960. Officially, the CEA explained the November 1959 vote as once in which "emotions ran hot." At the same time, however, the organization spokesperson said it was "too late" to reverse the process. See Binstock (1960: Document 6), a reproduced *Telegram* op-ed.

[57] The alternatives would have been some form of list PR, effectively *verboten* since 1913, or some rule like "limited" or cumulative voting. The latter options would have required substantial pre-election coordination. Given divisions in the Republican Party (i.e., Holmstrom and Lane were on opposite sides of repeal), the runoff system may have been attractive as a way to facilitate bargaining. Democrats faced similar coordination problems. In early 1960, in the final PR-elected council, Democrats agreed to rotate the mayoralty among three of their own deputies. Source: conversation with Judge Paul V. Mullaney, June 2015.

7.4.3 Voter dealignment

Almost from the start, the STV system worked against regular Democrats. Figure 7.9 plots transfer flows across the local-party divide. There is no available record of the official Democratic slate, and one may not have existed. However, candidate entry fell rapidly after the first election: from 152 in 1949 to 49 in 1951, 38 in 1953, then 28–31 in the remaining elections. Moreover, we can compute the *effective number of candidates*, which weights each candidate's contribution to the measure by their overall vote share.[58] This figure falls from 19.1 in 1949 to no more than 10–14, which, after the first PR election, strongly suggests both slates running as many serious candidates as each expected to win.[59] Despite the apparently rapid convergence on two-party competition, non-CEA Democrats repeatedly bled more than 80 percent of transfers to winners from the CEA slate.

STV also worked against the CEA from 1955 onward. Note once more that, in this year, the Republican Party threatened its own slate, that L. Weaver (1986) records a repeal effort (which never appeared on the ballot), that regular Democrat James D. O'Brien encouraged CEA's takeover by the Young Democrats, and that this election preceded his anointment as mayor. In 1951 and 1953, there were no CEA transfers to non-CEA winners. From 1955 onward, however, CEA vote leakage rises steadily, reaching nearly 60 percent in 1959.

At this point, it is useful to recall details from the post-election November meeting, in which City Council decided to petition the state legislature for a second initiative in 1960. This measure drew bipartisan support, as noted above, including from Mayor Joe Casdin (who went on to reverse position in March 1960). To quote the CEA's own leadership, in an op-ed four months later, "emotions ran hot."

I have noted in several places that inter-party transfers *can be seen* as having reversed the result of an election. According to Binstock (1960: VI-11): "Shortly after the 1959 election, two lame duck city councillors who blamed their defeat on PR urged their fellow councillors to support anti-PR action by the state legislature." One of these was Robert X. Tivnan, a regular Democrat. Contemporary analysis of the 1959 election data showed

---

[58] The *effective number of candidates* is equal to one over the sum of squared candidate vote proportions. More details are in the appendix.
[59] CEA did nominate nine candidates in each election.

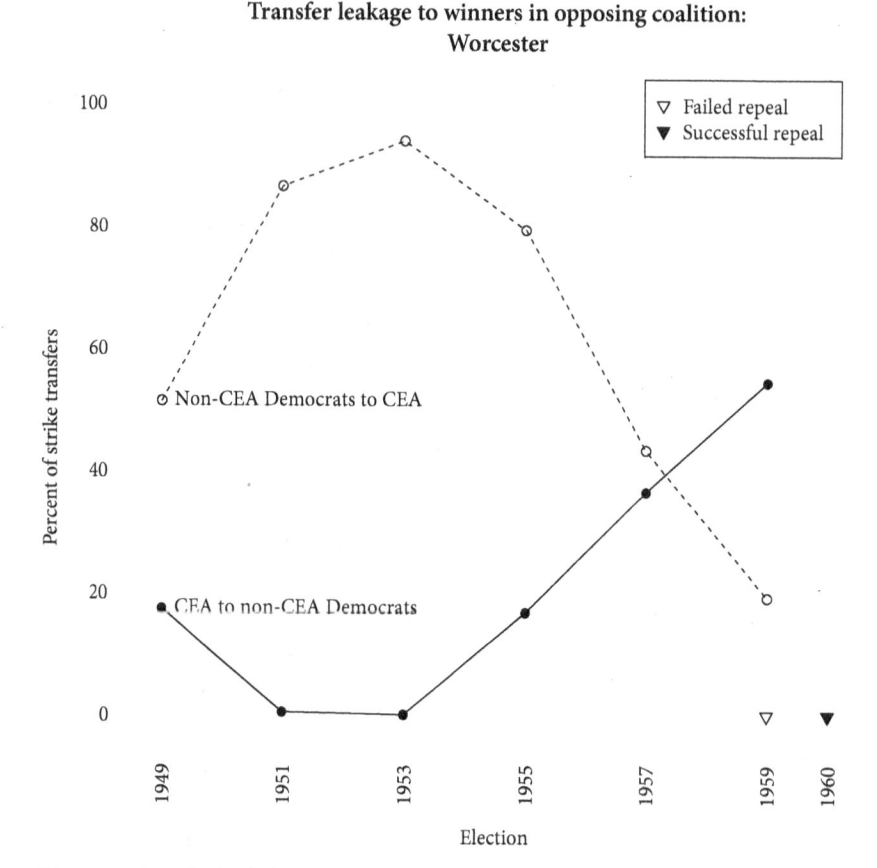

Fig. 7.9 Transfer leakage to opposing-coalition winners, Worcester.

that, under plurality-at-large, Tivnan would have come in seventh, handily winning re-election.[60] That this analysis even happened suggests important people cared about it.

The other "lame duck" member was Michael Favulli, first endorsed by the CEA in 1953, in an apparent bid to win support from Italian-American voters (II-48). At the 1959 election, however, this voting bloc split its support between Favulli and Peter Tomaiolo, a regular Democrat who had served in the pre-PR Board of Aldermen (Fain 1991: 1). Of 2,828 transfers from CEA candidates to Democratic winners (54.4 percent of CEA's transfer flow), 1,050 of these (37.1 percent) were from Favulli to Tomaiolo. The

---

[60] Binstock (1960: III-10) writes: "One out of every four ballots was tallied, allowing equal weight to the first nine choices [ranked on each ballot]."

CEA had failed in its core purpose, succinctly put by Laver's (2000) analysis of Irish coalition politics: "to keep lower preferences away from the largest party."

7.5 Stopping the leak in Cambridge, 1941–69

Cambridge is the only U.S. city not to have replaced its STV system. Robert Winters, a local PR historian, reports five repeal initiatives, plus the aggregate results of each (Table 7.3).[61] A full account of why these happened, as well as why they failed, would be based on the roll-call record, detailed information about candidates, and, ideally, precinct-level returns for elections and referendums alike. Given available data, however, we can analyze the nominating behavior and transfer flows of the Cambridge Civic Association (CCA). Note that this tells us nothing about where repeal initiated (e.g., in city council, as with Cincinnati in 1947, versus citizen petition), nor the extent of CCA participation.

Overall, the data show that CCA was relatively good at keeping votes within its slate (Fig. 7.10). In the period covered here (1941–69), leakage to opposition winners reached a maximum of 14.9 percent, in 1959. The average over these fifteen elections was 6.5 percent. In Cincinnati, by contrast, Charter bled more than a third of votes in 1951, the year that it freed its candidates to campaign as individuals. Worcester's CEA bled 20 percent or more of votes in four of six elections. Similarly, the New York City "coalition" sent at least as large a share of votes to Democrats in every STV election.

Nevertheless, there were spikes in the vote-leakage rate, and 1959 stands out. Two conditions here are strikingly similar to those in Cincinnati and

Table 7.3 Repeal referendums in Cambridge (MA).

Referendum	Keep PR	Replace PR	Margin for PR
1952	25,062	23,030	4.2%
1953	19,372	16,496	8%
1957	18,516	13,708	14.9%
1961	16,331	15,876	1.4%
1965	16,562	14,026	8.3%

[61] L. Weaver (1986: 141) lists four, omitting the 1965 effort.

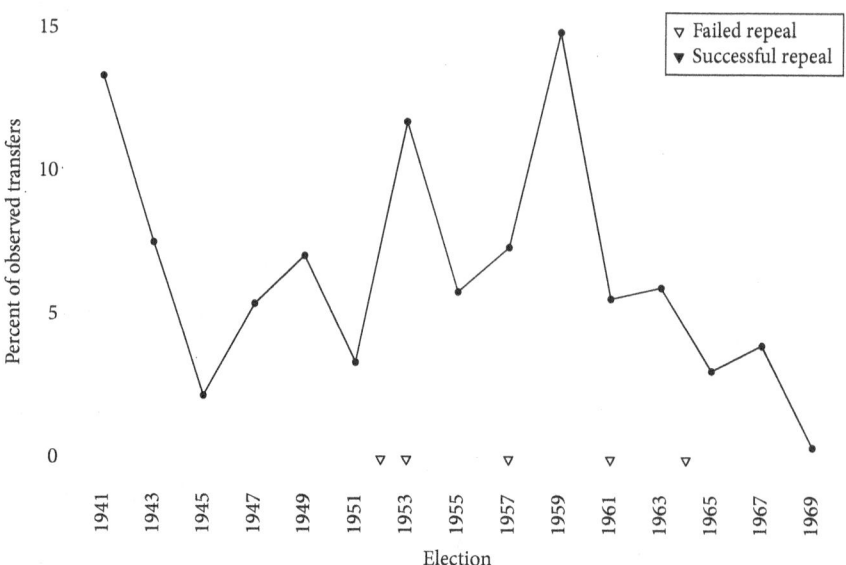

Fig. 7.10 Transfer leakage from reform slate to non-reform-slate winners, Cambridge.

Worcester at the time of repeal. First, the referendum result was the closest to date, coming within 1.4 percentage points of winning. Second, candidate entry at the preceding election had been the lowest under STV so far, suggesting relative shortage of independents to recruit to CCA's defense. Together, these points suggest two possibilities: (1) that CCA held fast, and that the 1961 initiative was the work of non-CCA actors; or (2) that CCA *was* able to refresh its numbers, possibly from among the twenty-two non-CCA candidates who ran in 1959.[62]

Whatever explains the failure of the initiative in 1961, CCA's immediate response was to reduce the size of its slate to only as many as it would need to dominate the council: five or six in every election from 1961–69 (Fig. 7.11). In turn, this brought immediate decline in the share of votes it bled: from 14.9 percent in 1959 to 5.6 percent in 1961, then eventually to 0.4 percent in 1969.

Why the relative success in Cambridge—both at holding down vote leakage, then at limiting reform-slate nominations? One possibility often

---

[62] There were thirty-one candidates total, and nine CCA endorsees, to the nine-seat council.

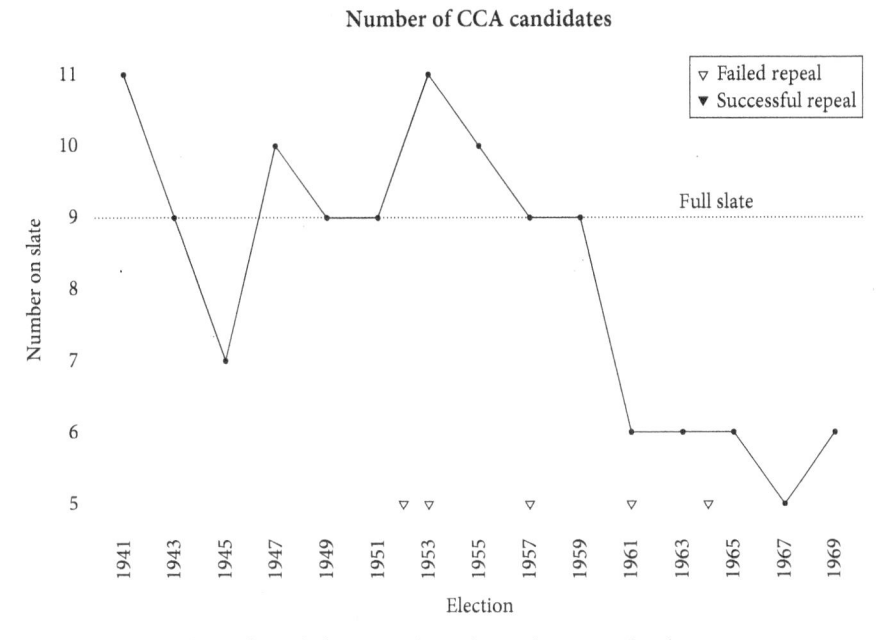

Fig. 7.11 Number of candidates on the reform slate, Cambridge.

raised is that "Cambridge is weird," highly educated, and/or proud of being the last STV holdout in the United States. Another possibility is that the CCA could learn from the many cities where STV had been repealed. Though the CCA no longer exists, recent Cambridge elections have seen similarly sized slates (Santucci 2019). Such slates are just large enough to capture legislative majorities, yet small enough not to include candidates who seek transfers from outside. Finally, such slates avoid the bargaining this entails: preference-swapping deals with non-co-partisans, leading to vote leakage and, possibly, more seats for the opposition.

7.6 Conclusion and notes on other cases

This chapter has argued that post-reform party-system change exposed flaws in the design of reform packages. Three of those packages (Cambridge, Cincinnati, and Worcester) were very similar: nomination by petition, non-partisan ballots, STV elections, and simple majority rule on small councils. In two of these cases (Cincinnati and Worcester), *legislative limbo* led opposing-party leaders to repeal STV wholesale. We do not know what happened in Cambridge city council, but transfer patterns suggest similar problems with *party control of voters' rankings*. The response was not to repeal STV, but instead to change nominating strategy (i.e., by no longer running a full slate).

Party-system change also exposed flaws in the design of New York City's charter, which did not follow the national reform template. STV permitted coalition formation among ALP-leaning Democrats, Democratic-leaning ALP members, and a group of Republicans (some in the remnant of La Guardia's Fusion Party)—all of these uncommitted to the post-1945 coalition deal between the Democratic and American Labor parties. It is telling that Vincent Impellitteri, the ALP-Democratic Council President, also signed onto the effort to repeal PR in 1947. All signs point again to *legislative limbo*, complicating the usual story about left-party "extrusion" at the hands of Republican and Democratic leaders (cf., Shefter 1986). Otherwise, as in Cincinnati and Worcester, key non-STV institutions survived repeal: the malapportioned Board of Estimate in New York's case.[63]

Future research will have to speak to political conditions *within* other STV cities. For now, however, some features of the macro environment shed light on developments in them.

7.6.1 Organized labor ascendant

First, organized labor increasingly turned against STV as it found a home in the Democratic Party.[64] The key event here was in 1955, with the national merger of AFL and CIO, but signs were visible in different places on both sides of it. Early evidence comes from Toldeo (OH), where, in 1949, local unions were pivotal to STV repeal. Unions would play a similar role in Hamilton (OH) in 1961 (L. Weaver 1986: 243). Additional evidence comes from Worcester, where the following appears in the council minutes for December 28, 1959: "A communication was received from the President of the Worcester Labor Council AFL-CIO that they have gone on record

---

[63] With respect to parties' role in elections, these include the rule that candidates secure party-committee permission to appear on that party's ballot line. However, with the resumption of partisan primaries, this rule was expanded to require party nonmembers to secure the same permission to contest the respective party's primary.

[64] Again, in comparative politics, Penadés (2008) finds that labor movements opposed PR when they could influence politics through a major party.

as supporting the appeal to the Mass. Legislature for a referendum for the repeal of P.R. voting."

We cannot rule out that labor opposition was informed by and/or reflective of the the Cincinnati story. To recap, in November 1953, Charter recaptured city council with substantial transfers from Republicans. This led to the election of one member, a Charter Republican, who voted with the opposing party on collective-bargaining measures. Later, when the local Steel Workers decided to back repeal, it was at a meeting convened by the national director of AFL-CIO's Industrial Union Department.[65] This conflict stretched back to 1954, when that same anti-labor figure had pressed to assume the mayoralty.[66] Just as "unpopular minorities" may have galvanized repeal coalitions nationwide, Cincinnati-type stories may have galvanized union opposition to PR.

Moreover, the best source on Massachusetts PR cases is the Dobrusin (1955) dissertation, cited elsewhere in this book. The study was reasonably objective. It gave statistics on voter turnout and the cost of election administration, as well as background information on local political contexts. One of its core findings, though, was that candidates with business backgrounds tended to win under "P.R.," and especially in Worcester. This was the finding that got headlines in local newspapers.[67]

One more set of facts points to labor's defection: loss of the movement's left wing. Despite losing the fight over non-partisan elections, Carl D. Thompson had continued to serve on the PR League Council. At the same time, he directed the Public Ownership League. Thompson appears to have been

[65] On the role of Al Whitehouse, head of the AFL-CIO Industrial Union Department, see page 3 of the Cincinnati Enquirer for September 18, 1957 ("Steel Worker Leaders Rap PR; Urge Its Defeat in Election; Charter Scored for Wage Tax").

[66] A CIO policy director, Ben Stoner, was present at the council meeting where this conflict reached its boiling point. The Cincinnati Enquirer dedicated front-page coverage to this controversy. See the issue for November 11, 1954 ("Rich Elected Mayor by Jordan Switch; Four Charterites Back Dolbey to End; Independent in Shift after Losing Struggle to Name a Democrat; Decision on 16th Vote; Arguments between Berry and CIO Leader Mark Council Session") At this meeting, the CIO-endorsed Charter representative, Al Jordan, was quoted as follows: "It is unwise for the Charter party to insist upon Mrs. Dolbey being mayor. I believe that because of this attitude, PR is gone forever and that the Charter party will eventually disappear."

[67] Whoever compiled the (unsorted) clippings at the Worcester Historical Museum (WHM) must have found this historically important. See: Currier, Charles E. 1955. "Study Shows PR Here Attracts Businessmen." The Worcester Telegram, August 19.

In its late years, CEA appears to have strained to win support from unions. The WHM archive also contains slate mailers for James D. O'Brien, as well as a bumper sticker. Going by the use of neon ink in this sticker, it looks to be from the late 1950s. It prominently displays a union bug and reads "Elect CEA Candidates" (all caps). The O'Brien mailer also contains a testimonial from someone in the local AFL-CIO.

friends with Walter Millard, the "Fabian socialist" behind three innovations: referendum strategy, voter education, and good-government slates. His work on voter education had begun in 1923, when Boulder (CO) made headlines for ballot invalidity (Millard 1923; Lien 1925: 256). He had been present in Cleveland, where trouble with STV led to the entire manager system's repeal. These experiences informed his work in Cincinnati, of which he was native, to organize the Charter Party (Millard 1924).

When Thompson died in 1949, Millard took his place at Public Ownership (Hallett and Woodward 1949). Curiously, though, he quit the PR League Council, possibly reacting to the New York City repeal. The *National Municipal Review* for January 1949 reports: "Walter J. Millard, field secretary of the league, called attention to an article in the *Scientific Monthly* for October 1948, entitled 'Three Methods of Voting,' by W. S. Taylor of Smith College." Taylor's paper (1948: 299) reads: "A recent example was the election of two Communists to the Council in New York City in 1945. Politicians and other opponents of P. R. made the most of that election to persuade the voters to repeal P. R.; and the voters did repeal it in 1947." If my account of repeal is right, Millard may have understood the politics (Republicans losing control of their own) and been dismayed by the optics (blaming Benjamin Davis).

7.6.2 Traces of legislative limbo elsewhere

Nevertheless, we find signs that limbo may have obtained in other cities. In Hamilton (OH), for example, a late-PR council majority declined to appoint a labor endorsee to a seat vacated by one of the same.[68] Presumably, labor had been part of the pre-election coalition.

Two more examples comes from Boulder (CO), which repealed STV in 1947. As an early adopter, Boulder did not randomize the order of candidates' names on ballots, and in normal elections, voters ranked candidates in they order they appeared. Winter (1982: 9) reports that, of thirty-three winners under PR from 1917–33, thirty had surnames beginning with the first nine letters of the alphabet (the council had nine seats). Boulder also saw a failed repeal referendum in 1933. According to Sowers (1934: 29–30), whom Winter cites, a controversy over electric and gas rates split the local political establishment in that same election. The next (and successful)

---

[68] See the *National Civic Review* for December 1960 (642).

repeal vote was in 1947. Winter (1982: 9–10) attributes this to the victory of A. Gayle Waldrop, "an iconoclastic, outspoken professor of journalism at the university [. . .] He was also among the mere handful of people with surnames beginning with letters in the last half of the alphabet who were elected." Winter continues: "As soon as Waldrop was sworn into office, he began upsetting the apple cart with motions to investigate private use of city-owned vehicles."

One more example comes from Lowell (MA), recently dissected amidst a 2019 effort to restore STV. This effort was part of a voting-rights lawsuit, seeking to overturn the city's at-large plurality system. Lowell voters had repealed STV in 1957, the first and only such initiative from 1944 onward.[69] This case had been notable for the absence of a "good government" slate. Rather, quasi-party competition pitted the Irish against everyone else, and the mayoralty passed among these groups accordingly (Yankee, French Canadian, Greek, and Polish). According to Frazier (2020: 6–7) the 1955 election was the first and only to produce a majority-Irish city council. Curiously, that council did not pick an Irish mayor, and a pre-reform mayor, William G. Geary, campaigned for repeal in familiar terms: "Proportional Representation has enabled Communists and fellow travelers to win elections in many places, including New York City" (Frazier 2020: 8).

7.6.3 Intellectual recognition of issues with STV

Gradually, thinkers "above the fray" came to see problems with STV. One example was David Austin, a Cincinnati journalist and occasional consultant to the local Republican Party. In 1945, he proposed a "majority-minority system," which came before voters as "6X" in 1954. The inspiration was an intra-party conflict over the city manager, with Wiley Craig (former Progressive Democrat) and Jesse Locker (Black Republican) pitted against the rest of their party (Straetz 1958: 16, 162, 290). Austin may have been trying to optimize (a) party discipline and (b) racial-minority representation, now a burning issue in postwar American politics.[70] A technical name for his system is the multiple non-transferable vote (MNTV) where the number of

---

[69] An earlier initiative, in 1955, was blocked by the courts.
[70] See, e.g., White (2019) on challenges of dealing with racial equality in the aftermath of World War II.

votes (*V*) is fewer than the number of seats (*M*) to fill. Today's reformers call this "limited voting." Given cohesive slate voting—finally acknowledged despite non-partisan elections—contemporaries could expect a majority with *V* seats and a minority with *M* − *V*. Variants of this, and "limited voting" more generally, can be found today in many cities (Bowler et al. 2003; R. L. Engstrom 2010).

Even the National Municipal League began to question STV, particularly without regulation of nominations. In 1951, two decades after his 1930 report, Joseph Harris led another NML study, titled *A Model Direct Primary Election System*. The report was ambiguous about STV, possibly reflecting mixed interests on the League's Committee on Direct Primary. One member, for example, was Richard S. Childs, eventual author of STV's nationwide eulogy (1965). Another was Hugh A. Bone, co-author with Belle Zeller of the classic text on repeal in New York City. Their 1948 paper was bold. It suggested, amidst rising McCarthyism, and in the *American Political Science Review*, that the repeal forces had used communism strategically. The second Harris report makes just two references to STV: that it does not require a primary, and that the report will not address it for this reason. Yet it *opens* with the story of Cincinnati, whose "experience [. . .] is typical. Unless qualified candidates can be induced to come forward, the voice of the people in elections may be only a weak and uncertain choice among mediocrities or self-seekers."

The second Harris report is rare for having cast "preferential voting" as *just one form* of PR.[71] No such distinction appeared in *City Politics*, possibly the definitive text on postwar urban institutional design. To quote Banfield and Wilson (1963: 97) once more: "PR breaks down party control over nominations and permits mavericks who owe nothing to party leaders to win office."

7.7 Recap

Reformers have long argued that STV "was repealed" because it led to the election of "unpopular minorities" and/or that it incurred ire from "party bosses." I have argued instead for a state of *legislative limbo*, brought

---

[71] It is possible that Childs, Bone, and/or Zeller pressed for this differentiation. Elsewhere, Harris (1934) had been critical of the entire PR project. He also sparred with old-line Progressives, such as Charles Merriam (Wickham-Jones 2018: 59, 64), both with respect to the primaries report and another, more famous, calling for "A More Responsible Two-Party System" (APSA Committee on Political Parties 1950). Note, however, that Harris supported non-partisan local elections and "blanket" primaries (Wickham-Jones 2018: 226).

about by fickle transfers and two-party politics. The key to reconciling these perspectives is realignment.

One realignment was national in scope and arguably killed STV as a cause. Americans were ready to have parties again in the mid-1950s. Race and labor liberalism fused, even if briefly, in the guise of the Democratic Party. This was very clearly on display in Cincinnati, as was what later observers would call "polarization." We see it also in New York City. The American Labor Party disintegrated, and what remained of it went into coalition with late-Tammany Democrats. In both cases, lingering "centrist" Republicans bucked the new party alignment. Given both cities' status as reform icons, the lessons were not lost on national "P.R." observers.

But other realignments were local in scope, involving the same basic dynamics: voter dealignment with attendant vote leakage and trouble keeping councils organized. We saw both in Worcester and the former in Cambridge. Stories from other cities, pre- and post-Harris, seem consistent with the overall pattern.

8

More Parties or No Parties?

> ...the same old remark that has done service in every other city manager campaign is heard on every side: "We don't understand all of this new scheme, but nothing could be worse than what we've got."
>
> Walter J. Millard (1924), Field Secretary, PR League

This chapter looks at prospects for reform going forward, drawing on the theory of "shifting coalitions," and based on its history in the United States. The national, state, and local levels get attention. I also speculate about AV's future, given its current popularity in reform circles.

For reformers, two-party politics is an overarching constraint. This limits adoption paths at the national level, directs reform energy into the states (to win "demonstration cases"), and makes it tempting to design reforms that attack party politics in principle. In short, two-party politics *pits reform against parties*. But reform is not a party. Post-reform change in a party system can expose problems with non-partisan rules, leading to frustration in opposing camps. A reform that permits candidates to defy their own parties does not sit well with competition between parties.

The chapter begins with a summary of the book's core points. This summary reminds us of how other countries have gotten reforms that seem to "support" multiparty politics, e.g., PR, majority runoff, the Alternative Vote. It also distills last century's reform trajectory: from visions of multiple parties in Congress to a set of brittle reforms at the local level. The chapter then turns to present-day reform politics, comparing the old and new movements. Common features include pressure for party and/or group proportionality, disagreement about majoritarian alternatives, and strategic inattention to nominations. Already, the nomination issue colors the *Fair Representation Act*, a sort of model charter for the twenty-first century. A final section looks at ways to mitigate that problem, all of which might force "independents" into their own parties.

More Parties or No Parties: The Politics of Electoral Reform in America. Jack Santucci, Oxford University Press.
© Oxford University Press 2022. DOI: 10.1093/oso/9780197630655.003.0008

8.1 Summary of core points

We can look at electoral reform, and STV's history in the United States, from at least three perspectives. One is the voter's perspective, e.g., "more choice," now on display in reform advocacy. A second emphasizes representation, understood as being present where decisions are made that affect one's community. Finally, we can look at reform through the eyes of those who control government (or hope to do so). This book adopted a control-of-government perspective.

8.1.1 Theory and comparative evidence

Chapter 2 derived three types of electoral reform: coalition-insulation, coalition-realignment, and polarization. It also laid out some bargaining dimensions in reform processes: district magnitude, assembly size, allocation formula, ballot type, and rules about nominations. Then it sketched implications for the substance of reform, i.e., whether it is hostile or hospitable to organized parties. Finally, it argued that the rules have downstream effects on governance.

Three types of reform
In coalition-insulation, the group that controls government installs a new electoral system to keep itself in power. When these episodes have resulted in "permissive" electoral systems (e.g., PR, AV, runoffs), some new party has threatened the dominance of one (or more) existing parties.[1] Examples were Belgium (1899), Norway (1919), Australia (1918), and New Zealand (1908). Later on, for Senate elections, an Australian Labor government replaced block-preferential voting with STV in 1948, facing imminent defeat by the Liberal-Country coalition. Following Kreuzer (2010), an ongoing research agenda is uncovering mechanisms that connect multiparty politics to PR adoption. A global survey by Colomer (2005) found that, in switches to PR from 1848–2002, the average effective number of parties (ENP) was 3.9 *on the eve of adoption*.[2] Similarly, new-party entry has contributed to fixing

---

[1] AV and runoffs really should not be seen as "permissive." Both typically rely on single-seat districts. Only with a dated reading of Duverger's Law—plurality rule in single-seat districts constrains the number of parties—can either of these systems seem "permissive."
[2] By contrast, in U.S. House elections, ENP typically runs at just under 2.0.

the size of the U.S. House of Representatives (1919, 1929) and adopting the secret ballot (many states, Populist Era). An exception to the new-party thesis was Congress's decision, in 1842, to reduce its own size and mandate single-seat districts. In this case, Whigs sought to contain a rising Democratic Party. Other exceptions, at the state and local level, have been manipulation of election timing and adoption of other reforms associated with Progressivism.

In coalition-realignment, one or more out-of-power groups joins forces with defectors from the ruling coalition. They strike a reform bargain reflective of their interests. Realigning coalitions may be internally fractious, such that "ideational glue" (Lucas 2019: 10) is needed to hold them together. Examples include some STV adoptions in Canadian cities, the imposition of PR in Switzerland (1918), and the adoption of mixed-member PR in New Zealand (1993).[3] Coalition realignment requires wresting control of the reform levers. In turn, this may require a "wedge" strategy, often deployed in advance, and possibly for other reasons. Examples include woman suffrage in U.S. states (pre-1919), power of initiative in U.S. states (1898–1918), Swiss power of initiative (1891), municipal control of municipal charters in the United States and Canada (various), and New Zealand's Royal Commission on the Electoral System (1985–86). "Wedging" of this type often involves minor parties working with reformist factions of existing parties.

In polarizing reform, opposing coalitions agree to change the electoral system because one or more players resists picking sides. Neither coalition can count on such players for consistent support across policies. Reform is therefore meant to get rid of such players, otherwise bring them to heel. Such episodes are likely where agenda control is weak *between elections*. Examples included France's turn from PR to majority runoff (1958) and the single-seat district mandate for U.S. House elections (1967).

One last note on realigning episodes. There is a tension in the theory sketched here. Insulating and polarizing episodes clearly *respond* to party-system change, but realigning episodes seem to *bring* such change about. More work is needed on the "trigger(s)" of that type. For now, two possibilities are apparent, each involving changes in the macro environment, e.g., a federal-level party system that nests state and local ones. For example, Karol (2009: 134–81) shows that national politicians sometimes "try out" new

---

[3] In Switzerland, the reform coalition split before it could go on to govern. There was not enough "ideational glue."

issue stances without much prodding from civil society.[4] One can imagine such experimentation at higher levels provoking local-level reform activism. Another possibility, which seems related, involves recent loss of power— due either to new voters entering the electorate, or to voters' prior party-switching.[5] The theoretical tension does not negate the general point about "shifting coalitions."

Implications for rule-choice and governance

The reform coalition leaves its imprint on the rules. The point will not surprise anyone. But in a two-party system, only two kinds of reform coalition are likely: single- and anti-party. Beyond that, pro-party reforms (e.g., larger assemblies, list PR) may seem anathema, even for people who say they want more parties. Evidence included opinion data from the American public (2018), research on the role of party cues in recent non-U.S. episodes, and a quick look at the Swiss (1918) "reform from below" (Lutz 2004). Switzerland again is an interesting contrast with the U.S., since it adopted list PR through popular initiative.

Finally, the electoral system affects costs of coalition maintenance. The core idea here is "bargaining unit." More parties obviously means more bargaining units, but so does a system that resists party organization.

STV and "vote leakage"

STV is special among PR systems for two reasons, both related to "vote leakage." First, it lets otherwise unpopular candidates seek votes from outside their parties. This can affect party cohesion in government. Second, it allows votes to leave a party (or to "exhaust"), rather than contribute to a party's overall total. This can affect nominal control of a legislature.

Other countries have developed ways to manage vote leakage (per Chapter 1). One solution, on display in Ireland and Scotland, is for parties to be sufficiently mass-based to dictate voter preferences. This keeps transfers within parties and, to some extent, among coalition partners. Australia

---

[4] See McCarty and Schickler (2018) for some reflection on these issues.

[5] Consider Eisenthal (1983: 3) on Worcester: "The third hypothesis, related to the second, is that whoever initiated and waged the Plan E campaign was motivated by fear of the growing political power of the largely Irish Democratic Party. It is possible that those behind charter change saw it as a way to stunt the growth of Irish and Democratic power; changing the arrangements of government would change power relations. Furthermore, Plan E would have non-partisan elections which would reduce the power of ward-based political organizations, many of which were dominated by Irish Democrats." But the Irish are only one part of that story. Compare with Gamm's (1989) account of Massachusetts realignment.

supplements this with ballot design (e.g., grouping co-partisans so that they can be ranked easily), an option to ratify some pre-existing rank-ordering, and the requirement of compulsory ranking (now in effect only for AV elections to the House of Representatives). With respect to transfers and nominal control (of a chamber or government), two solutions present themselves. In Northern Ireland, government formation is based on parties' overall seat shares, which ensures that the two largest parties control government together. In Malta, which now has a two-party system, a plurality of first-choice votes delivers a seat majority.[6]

One last point is worth restating. In every other STV country, adoption (or imposition) has been in a context with multiparty politics. Hence STV has developed other features, either formal add-ons to the rules (e.g., Australia) or informal strategies used by the parties (e.g., Ireland and Scotland). STV channels party competition in these places. In the United States, it was designed to crosscut the two-party system.

8.1.2 Key points from STV's history in America

The PR movement organizes in 1893, largely as a way to make more parties viable: Populists, Prohibitionists, and, eventually, Socialists. Others in this movement seek to mute Civil War cleavages, alleviate gridlock, and diminish corporate influence in politics (Spence 1893; Commons 1896). The movement spends two decades without traction.

Around 1900, a second movement emerges: for non-partisan local government. Its proposals include nomination-by-petition, party-free ballots, at-large elections, and small assemblies. Within that other movement, some are adding Bucklin voting (similar to AV) to the commission plan, which spreads to dozens of cities, 1909–17. The PR League shifts its focus to local government.[7]

Non-partisanship, ranked ballots, and small assemblies shape PR advocacy, via an alliance with municipal reformers. Dissenters say the emerging template will weaken political parties, both organizationally and as sources of cues to voters. They counter with a proposal for list-based PR,

---

[6] Again, this is since 1996. From 1987 until then, a majority of first-choice votes guaranteed a seat majority.
[7] Otherwise, AV and Bucklin are used for eleven states' party primaries (Weeks 1937).

whose defeat in Los Angeles, 1913, persuades reformers that this is a non-starter. Ashtabula adopts STV in 1915, and the "representative council plan" emerges victorious. The PR League and National Municipal League cement an alliance to promote this new Model City Charter.

From Ashtabula (1915) through Worcester (1947), PR League field staff build reform majorities from out-of-power parties and factions of ruling parties. Their campaigns emphasize anti-corruption, consistent with framing by the wider reform lobby. The STV charter spreads to twenty-three cities in ten states. One more, New York City, rejects much of that charter, yet retains the spirit of many of its features: substantial authority for a small upper chamber (the Board of Estimate), nomination by petition, and no graphic logos on ballots. All adoptions are *coalition-realigning* and cluster in three states: Ohio (five in the 1910s–20s), New York (three in the 1930s), and Massachusetts (seven in the 1940s). In other states (California, Connecticut, and Michigan), hostile courts and legislatures ban further consideration of "proportional representation." Finally, such charters lose when they do not attract support within ruling parties (e.g., Waterbury, CT, in 1939). Sources of ruling-party disunity include: organized labor, the women's movement, excluded ethnic and religious groups,[8] and party reformers in general (e.g., Progressive Republicans, as in Ohio, or "amateur" Democrats, as in Massachusetts).

Meanwhile, numerous cities adopt council-manager government without STV. Most of these are in lopsided jurisdictions, where there is little need to bargain with out-of-power parties. Others are in competitive territory, some imposed by incumbent parties themselves (e.g., "Boss" Pendergast in Kansas City), some by their oppositions (e.g., Republicans in Brockton, Massachusetts). PR League staff assist some of these efforts, giving rise to "plurality at-large" systems.[9]

By the late 1920s, three problems with STV are apparent: shifting coalitions on city councils, lack of "first-class candidates," and voters' rejection of the ranked ballot. A study by the National Municipal League attributes these

---

[8] However, Blacks tended to be skeptical. Consider Adam Clayton Powell, Jr.'s concerns about New York City's multi-seat districts (Powell, Jr. 1971: 68), or that, in Cincinnati, most Black voters supported repeal until Theodore Berry's run in 1947 (R. A. Burnham 1997).

[9] Consider Walter Millard, who quit the movement to work for the Public Ownership League. Hallett and Woodward (1949) write: "Mr. Millard has been field secretary of the P. R. League since 1918 and before the League's merger with the National Municipal League in 1932 spent most of his time travelling throughout the United States and Canada speaking in the interests of P. R. *and the council-manager plan* [emphasis mine]. He has probably participated in more city charter campaigns than any other living man."

to two factors: a large assembly, then only in Cleveland, and a lack of party organization. Harris (1930: 46) writes:

> Where P. R. has been a decided success, a Charter Committee (Cincinnati), Charter Commission (Hamilton), Civic Government Association (Calgary), or Progressive Government Association (Cleveland in the last election) has been formed to make it a success.

The PR movement undergoes reorganization. In 1932, the NML formally absorbs the PR League. It moves the PR office to New York City and replaces Clarence Hoag with George Hallett. Independent publication of the *Proportional Representation Review* ceases. A book by Cincinnati politician Charles Phelps Taft, II (1971 [1933]) popularizes advice from the Harris (1930) study. From Cincinnati onward, two thirds of new STV charters are twinned with good-government parties.

Party competition in STV cities combines citywide and neighborhood logics. The norm is to nominate a full slate of candidates, draw expected winners from important parts of town, and use trailing candidates to garner vote transfers. Aggregate spending is higher in cities with the STV charter than in: (a) unreformed cities, where district elections promote "neighborhood concerns," and (b) manager systems with plurality voting, said to promote "citywide focus." The campaign strategy is consistent with practice in other STV countries, where parties divide districts into "bailiwicks." However, American slating groups do not limit nominations, and their leaders run citywide campaigns.

As party competition shifts away from reform alignments, STV elections come under attack. Vote transfers cross the major-party divide (between reform coalition and opposition), and legislators defy party leaders in government. These developments precede *polarizing* repeal episodes, orchestrated by leaders from opposing coalitions. Data from three cases support this conclusion: spatial maps of realignment in government, rates of inter-coalition transfer leakage, and "roll rates" in legislatures. The cases are Cincinnati, New York City, and Worcester. Anecdotal evidence from other cities points to similar problems of party cohesion. Reform coalitions defeat repeal efforts when they can offset defections from their own ranks.

At the movement level, thinkers begin exploring non-STV approaches to combining party government with minority representation. A second report by Harris (1951) covers nomination rules, ostensibly at the state and national levels, but with several references to STV cities. Meanwhile, movement elites withdraw support for "P.R.," now associated with Civil Rights and communism.

By 1961, just two cities have STV. One is Hamilton (OH), which repeals it that year. The other is Cambridge (MA), where the Civic Association begins limiting nominations, bringing vote leakage down to single-digit rates.

8.2 Prospects for a proportional U.S. House

Once again, a large part of reform advocacy is focused on Congressional elections. Persistent two-party politics makes this an uphill battle, both theoretically and in light of comparative evidence. Any path *not involving* new-party entry is apt to face challenges found in STV cities.

8.2.1 Paths involving new-party entry

As the comparative examples show, it is rare for a national government to impose PR without more parties already on the scene. The main mechanism constraining this outcome is the ability of dominant parties to insulate themselves through districting instead (Walter and Emmenegger 2018). Research on the topic is ongoing,[10] but Calvo (2009) gives the theoretical point of departure: new-party entry disrupts the tendency of low-magnitude systems to deliver majoritarian outcomes. Otherwise, where PR has been adopted, the catalyst has been imminent formation of an alternative winning coalition. This has tended to happened under pre-existing runoff systems (e.g., Belgium, Germany, and Norway at the turn of the last century).[11]

Another path to PR has been party-system dealignment, combined with rank-and-file rebellion inside established parties. In turn, if those rank-and-file prefer cooperation with new parties, a path opens up to coalition realignment (e.g., New Zealand in the 1980s and 1990s). Notably, this is the only path that has seen list PR replace single-seat plurality (i.e., first-past-the-post). It is also the path that produced initiative-and-referendum

---

[10] See, e.g., Walter (2021) on establishment parties' cross-endorsement strategies in the face of "socialist threat."

[11] Also see Colomer (2005), whose cross-country analysis of PR adoption codes plurality and majority systems as equivalent. Blais et al. (2005) show that majority systems were the norm.

(Smith and Fridkin 2008), state-level woman suffrage (McConnaughy 2013), and possibly STV local options.[12]

8.2.2   Paths without new-party entry (in advance)

Four more options have been floated: minority rule, mutual disarmament, what might be called "centrist insulation," and then unilateral Democratic imposition. The third of these seems to be the most likely path, but it foreshadows old problems for coalition in government.

The minority-rule argument originated with S. E. Finer (1975) as the "adversary politics thesis." Finer thought that two features of mid-century British politics were fertile ground for PR adoption. First was frequent alternation between the dominant parties. Hence the old claim that, under first-past-the-post, policy can "swing like a pendulum." Second was that such policies were majority-opposed, in the sense that the opposition and some ruling-party rank-and-file both had to accept policy they did not want. Finer therefore saw demand for policy stability from multiparty coalition. For whatever reason, this demand never led to PR. Debnam (1994) suggests it is because the party system realigned in favor of the Conservatives.

A related path, which we have not seen before, is the parties' mutual agreement to break themselves up (Drutman 2020). This is essentially Finer's thesis applied to the U.S. presidential system. The logic is that neither party can gain control of national government, yet each is organized to keep trying. This produces a set of positive feedback loops, reinforcing "polarization" at the elite and mass levels. In turn, policy stalemate is thought to become mutually hurting. What presidentialism may add is a set of expectations that "normal" policy-making involves bipartisan coalitions that straddle constitutional offices (i.e., the Senate and President). The verdict is still out on this path. If sufficient politicians see *gridlock itself* as policy, the odds for PR may not be good (Rosenfeld 2020).

Nevertheless, some see potential in "centrist insulation." First, this involves Democrats recognizing that they are systematically disadvantaged under single-seat districts. This means that their voters are too

---

[12] The clearest example is Ohio, where Herbert S. Bigelow chaired the 1912 constitutional convention. As noted in Chapter 7, Bigelow then served in Cincinnati city council in the late 1930s and early 1940s.

geographically concentrated to translate modest vote majorities into seat majorities, and that "neutral" redistricting provides limited recourse. McGann et al. (2016) and Rodden (2019) compile strong evidence for this. Then some group of Republicans would need to break with their party, possibly shepherding the bill through the Senate. Presumably, with STV and weak nomination control, these Republicans would have an easier time surviving primary challenges in their districts.

Overall, the centrist-coalition path depends on several factors coming into alignment: Democratic recognition of districting problems, Democrats' willingness to tolerate new-party entry, their willingness to tolerate Republican seat gains (especially without House expansion), a sufficient number of "endangered" Republicans willing to turn to PR, and willingness of that group to cooperate with Democrats—at least on some issues, some of the time. It also presumes that "moderate" Republican-aligned interest groups cannot get what they want through an evolving Democratic Party (cf., Miller and Schofield 2008).

A final path might involve imposition by united Democratic government. Democrats then would be solving their districting problem at the costs of third-party entry (which is not guaranteed) and new risk to incumbents (which House expansion can offset). The reform would be insulating in the sense that it would contain a vote swing toward Republicans—and cut off Republicans' ability to gerrymander.

As of October 2021, the Democratic Party has not shown interest in PR. This is despite united government and decennial redistricting, which will produce a map drawn mostly by Republicans. When I say "party," I mean officeholders,[13] the Democratic National Committee, and interest groups long allied with the party.

What can explain the lack of interest? One answer is that there have not been enough plurality inversions (when the party with the most votes does not get the most seats). Or maybe the last such inversion, in November 2012, is too temporally distant from the current "trifecta" (cf. Shugart 2008: 15).[14] Another answer may be that PR just is not well understood—including by the party most likely to become the "party of reform."[15] But this

---

[13] Exceptions are Reps. Jamin Raskin (D-MD) and Don Beyer (D-VA), five more Democratic cosponsors, and possibly House Majority Whip Jim Clyburn (D-SC). Clyburn spoke favorably of cumulative voting in a late-2020 op-ed for the *Washington Post* (Clyburn 2020).

[14] The last "trifecta" was in 2009–10.

[15] See Shugart (2008: 17) on "act-contingent" factors in reform initiation.

leads us to ask where understanding originates. Maybe Americans need to experience more plurality inversions. Or maybe, following the discussion of party cues in Chapter 2, understanding improves amidst multiparty politics. Multiparty politics do not always lead to PR—witness the other Anglo settler democracies—but they do produce clarity about reform alternatives.[16]

Another answer may be that the party, taken collectively, is fine with the policy status quo. Focusing on parliamentary democracies, Pilet and Bol (2011) argue that parties are risk-averse about reform proposals, even if they might benefit (in a seat-maximizing sense). This aversion disappears if a party has not "often been in power" (571). But power, as we saw in Chapter 2, can be used to advance or block policy. Non-parliamentary systems tend to separate these functions, so that one can block from many "points" in the system. Recall Stanley Isaacs (R-Manhattan) from Chapter 8. Since members of the Democratic *coalition* have had blocking power quite recently (most notably in the Senate), their risk aversion should remain in place. In turn, it is enough to deprive the wider party of the votes needed to ram reform through.[17] This does not bode well for the "party of reform" path.

The *Fair Representation Act*, as we will see below, is built for a centrist-insulation adoption path. But how would such a coalition sustain itself? On what issues would the reform coalition cooperate? How might the "left" of the Democratic Party regard that cooperation? Like the old Model Charter of 1916, the FRA is silent on nomination control. It is designed to let in all factions qua *factions*.

8.3 Back to the future?

Although PR faces an uphill battle in Congress, we may see adoption efforts at the state and local levels. The national-level proposal reflects consensus among reform partners, who work primarily at the subnational level. Points of consensus include the ranked ballot and silence on parties' role in nomination politics. An unresolved issue concerns district magnitude, i.e., whether to promote AV or STV. This section looks at how reformers got here and

---

[16] Note that Fair Vote Canada, that country's main reform lobby, opposes the Alternative Vote. See: "Alternative Vote: From the Frying Pan into the Fire," *Fair Vote Canada*, February 15, 2020. Online at https://www.fairvote.ca/2020/02/15/alternative-vote-from-the-frying-pan-into-the-fire-lessons-from-australia. Accessed October 17, 2021. On minor-party skepticism of AV in the United States, see Sorens (2016) and Feinstein (2020).

[17] Witness the current state of voting-rights legislation.

the prospects for both "ranked-choice" systems. With two big exceptions— pressure for improved descriptive representation, then recognition of limits with independent redistricting—many intellectual forces behind the new consensus are similar to those of a century ago.

8.3.1 Reform template for the twenty-first century?

For those who have decided in favor of PR, the *Fair Representation Act* (FRA) serves as one point of departure, as well as signs of consensus on the role of parties. It calls for STV in districts of 3–5 seats and no increase in the size of the House. For states with just one or two seats, single-seat districts would be used instead, and STV would resolve to AV. With respect to nominations, the FRA is silent. For states with primaries, the first round would use STV to produce a full slate. For states with non-partisan two-round systems (e.g., California "top two"), the first round would use STV to generate twice as many final-round candidates as there are seats to fill.

The crucial thing to note, regardless of a state's primary type, is consensus on representation of party factions *as factions*. This manifests in two ways: generating a full slate (or twice that number in states with non-partisan runoffs), then using STV to arrive at these slates. As such, the focus is on *representation* and not so much *control of government*. That focus also is clear from how the proposal is sold. Consider David Brooks (2018): "A district in Southern California, for example, might elect a Bernie Sanders-type progressive, a centrist business Democrat and a conservative." To preview what is coming, might not the centrist be inclined to seek transfers from the conservative (and possibly vice versa)? What might this mean for congressional voting?

8.3.2 Forces shaping the template, compared

Broadly, four forces shaped the old PR movement and, by extension, the Model Charter of 1916. One was for institutions that might support multiparty democracy, i.e., some type of PR. The second was demand for non-partisanship, both in terms of removing party labels from ballots, but also in weakening parties' gatekeeping functions. Third was contention with majoritarianism, which also supplied pressure for non-partisan elections, as well as for small assemblies. These forces fused in the wake of 1912, which revealed deep division in the Republican Party (then the more liberal and hegemonic), as well as the role of "spoilers." Finally, and especially from 1924 onward, STV was sold in "anticorruption" terms.

The current movement has followed a similar trajectory. If we go back to its founding days in the early 1990s, we see calls for multiparty democracy, proportional representation based on party lists, and a national commission on electoral reform (Cossolotto 1993). For this new generation, New Zealand was Ticino—a place where the seemingly impossible had happened. But from there, the story turns to non-partisan elections. At the local level, old Progressives already had settled this question. Early STV adoption efforts were in Cincinnati (1988, 1991) and San Francisco (1996), both with non-partisan elections left over from the 1920s. And the San Francisco story was reminiscent of Los Angeles in 1913: defeated by a coalition of downtown business interests—Progressives and Republicans in 1913, Democrats and Republicans in 1996 (DeLeon et al. 1998). Not until 2006 would any city adopt STV: Minneapolis for local park boards. Several later measures also failed: Cincinnati again in 2008, then Lowell (where STV also had prior history) in 2009 and 2019.

Meanwhile, proportional representation *of any type* has contended with majoritarian ranked-ballot reforms. All of these have been on the heels of purportedly "spoiled" presidential elections: San Francisco (2002), followed by Berkeley (2004), Oakland, and Minneapolis (2006). Numerous other cities (and the entire state of Maine) turned to AV in or after 2016. Notably, many adoptions have been in cities with non-partisan runoffs, otherwise for party primaries.

The most recent developments have been at the state level, where a new group of reformers hopes to fuse "ranked choice voting" with a movement to abolish nominations altogether (Gehl and Porter 2020). This is similar to the fusion of Bucklin with commission government. The goal is to permit multiple candidates from the same party to appear before voters in an election's decisive round (122). These reforms go by different names: "top X" and "non-partisan" or "open" primaries, for example.[18] These rules are not the same as strictly non-partisan elections, but their intent is not much different: to diminish party control of nominations.

---

[18] Again, an election is not a primary unless its purpose is to nominate a candidate or slate. "Open" primaries, properly understood, do this without requiring voters to be registered with the party in whose primary they vote. "Blanket" primaries do the same on an office-by-office basis.

As of this writing (October 2021), the new state-level movement has shown little interest in PR of any type. Rather, it has promoted AV *within* party primaries or as a way to *eliminate nominations* altogether. The latter reform, known as "Final Five Voting," rests on a theory that primaries cause "extremism." In this theory, primary electorates pull candidates away from the "political center," and getting rid of primaries will produce "moderation." Another version of theory, more recently articulated, holds that bans on nominations can rescue incumbents from primary challengers. Whatever the rationale, this reform proposal fuses "top two" with the Alternative Vote, such that the top five candidates (or four, as in Alaska) in a first-round election proceed to an AV second round, regardless of party affiliation.

A key question is whether proponents of the new state-level fusion continue their commitment to AV. The *Fair Representation Act* already accommodates them: by preserving non-partisan two-round elections, but especially by pitting co-partisans against each other in the decisive round of an election. Even the bill's default provision does this: having parties run full slates and using STV to pick them. Finally, to the extent that AV supporters want to hold down new-party entry (e.g., by holding down district magnitude and/or House size),[19] the FRA proposal already does this. It calls for smaller districts than those recommended by fragmentation-wary political scientists (Carey and Hix 2011).

The last factor is "anticorruption" branding, which four groups now provide on some level. The most explicit is RepresentUs, whose model legislation, the *Anti-Corruption Act*, frames the ranked ballot as follows: "This makes it easier to elect independent-minded candidates who aren't beholden to establishment special interests."[20] On the right are three more groups: Unite America (formerly The Centrist Project), the National Association of Non-partisan Reformers (NANR), and the Institute for Political Innovation (IPI). So far, Unite America refers readers to a video by RepresentUs, titled "Ranked Choice Voting vs. The Establishment."[21] Meanwhile, NANR appears to be a catchall organization. Its list of reforms includes "ranked choice voting, other alternatives to plurality voting, open primaries, non-partisan primaries, and independent ('public') primaries." NANR brands these reforms as "all focused on putting voters first."[22] IPI focuses exclusively

[19] See Santucci and Diamond (2018) for a sense of this tension.
[20] https://represent.us/anticorruption-act/. Accessed December 2020.
[21] https://www.uniteamerica.org/strategy/ranked-choice-voting. Accessed December 2020.
[22] https://non-partisanreformers.org/policy-list. Accessed December 2020.

on "Final Five Voting," which would ban nominations in service of "healthy competition."[23]

8.3.3 The difference, for now, is voting rights

One difference between the old and new movements concerns voting rights, especially as related to people of color. For the old movement, we get little sense that racial representation mattered, except maybe for Catherine H. Spence (1893)—she argued that STV might have led to slavery's gradual abolition—and very early Civil Rights activists in Ohio (R. A. Burnham 1997: 136).

The Civil Rights project has a complicated relationship with electoral reform. In many ways, the "racial realignment" helped to end PR advocacy. The Cincinnati story suggests some reasons why: representation mainly through the Democratic Party, then a perception that STV (always called "P.R.") helped to break the alliance between race and labor liberalisms. Single-seat districts became the main way to secure descriptive representation. Glimmers of that settlement were on display in Cincinnati, when Democratic leaders of the last two repeal efforts pointed to people of color winning under plurality (Straetz 1958: 10–12, 27).

From the 1980s onward, however, skeptics of single-seat districts have been a constant movement presence. The argument is that social groups— ethnic, racial, or whatever—should be able to define themselves for purposes of interest articulation (see, e.g., Guinier 1992 and Charles 2003). This has been a theme in local efforts to restore STV. Cincinnati saw two such measures (1988, 1991), the first of which attracted support from Theodore Berry, Jesse Jackson, and the Rainbow PUSH coalition (R. L. Engstrom 1990). Two more measures (2009, 2019) sought to restore the system to Lowell (MA). More recently, STV has been enacted in Eastpointe (MI), Palm Desert (CA), and Albany (CA). Each of these adoptions has been a voting-rights cause in a city with non-partisan elections. So far, though, no city has made a switch from single-seat districts.

The presence of a voting-rights constituency does not guarantee that voting rights will remain a priority. I noted in the introduction that the old movement helped spread devices that reduced participation in the long

---

[23] https://www.political-innovation.org. Accessed September 2021.

run: citywide elections, small assemblies, low-information ballots, and so on. This was a go-along-to-get-along strategy, flowing from the alliance with "good-government" Progressivism. Pre-existing restrictions on voting facilitated many of these "wins" (Bridges and Kronick 1999). Now there is another attack on voting, proceeding state by state, and enabled by the federal judiciary. Key reformers have not taken a position on that issue.[24]

8.3.4 Prospects for AV in American politics

Political scientists do not yet know why majority-preferential systems disappeared from the map. We do know, however, most adoptions were between 1912–18, inclusive. The timing alone suggests two possible reasons why they stopped: elite consensus on STV instead, then diminished interest in solving "spoiler problems." Crucially, in 1916, the Republican Party worked to resolve issues that had split it four years earlier. With respect to STV consensus, Chapter 3 showed how Clarence Hoag (the second PR League Secretary) strained to educate reformers on "two objects of voting" (picking winners versus picking legislatures). We also know that he and others objected to majority systems' minority-representation properties, especially when applied to multi-seat districts (Thompson 1913: 420; Hoag 1914c: 54).[25]

As far as repeals go, majority-preferential systems seem to have become unpredictable—just as STV did in the cases analyzed here. But the issue with AV (and its Bucklin cousin) was not vote leakage. Rather, it was non-use of rankings (i.e., "ballot truncation"). On repeal in several states' party primaries, Weeks (1937: 37) cites "failure of party leaders and officials to educate the public in the use of the preferential feature, due partly to their opposition to it as a complicated device and one the results of which could not be easily anticipated." Silbernagel (2021a, 2021b) gives more evidence from Grand Junction (CO), the first city to fuse Bucklin with the commission form of government. Here, many candidates discouraged ranking, leading to victory by a Socialist (who did encourage it). Similarly, Cleveland was the only city to switch from Bucklin to STV. Maxey (1922) suggests this was due,

---

[24] See Gehl and Porter (2018): "We wholeheartedly celebrate the expanded awareness that H.R. 1 can bring to the national debate for fundamental, non-partisan election reform."
[25] Also see Gilpin (1844), reprinted in James (1896), for an early taste of Hoag's "two objects" and critique of majority systems.

in part, to dissolution of a preference-swapping deal between Progressive and "standpat" Republicans. Also, "it was discovered that the preferential-choice scheme could be turned to the advantage of the party by passing out the word to all regulars to vote only for a first choice" (85).

Ongoing work by Buisseret and Prato (2021) has formalized elites' incentive to encourage "truncation"—or at least not to discourage it. In a three-candidate divided-majority setting, the two majority-supported candidates are playing a game of cross-endorsement "chicken." The result is a typically unpredictable three-way race in which the lone minority-supported candidate has a good chance of winning.[26] Note how Australia makes AV predictable: compulsory ranking and multiparty coalition (including agreements between parties to not contest each other's districts).

The verdict is still out on AV's future in America. The vast majority of adoptions have been fairly recent, and there are glimmers of problems. According to data from FairVote, 96 percent of winners in modern AV elections have been leaders in first-choice votes. The other 4 percent, known as "come-from-behind" (CFB) victories, have preceded repeal activity when they implicate high office.[27] The only high-profile CFB outcome that has not preceded repeal is a 2010 mayoral election in San Leandro (CA) (Reilly and Santucci 2021).[28] Further, ongoing work by Cerrone and McClintock (2021) suggests that CFB outcomes make voters receptive to repeal messaging.

Two repeal cases have been subject to ballot-level analysis, and results are consistent with a predictability story. In Pierce County, Alvarez et al. (2018) found a two-dimensional structure in rankings from the CFB race. One dimension was partisanship, and they term the other "preference for independence." Because there was only one independent in the race, the orthogonal dimension suggests a candidate whose ballots did not flow reliably to either side. Similarly, in Burlington, AV critics have long argued that "the system failed" to elect a Condorcet winner. This suggests lack of coordination along the dimension that was salient to most voters (cf. Nagel 2006). Hence critics conclude that Burlington's repeal was due to "the surprise outcome of the election."[29]

---

[26] Note that Nagel (2007) gets similar results for Approval Voting.

[27] The Grand Junction Socialist, noted above, also won in CFB fashion.

[28] Data in the working paper are from: FairVote, "Data on Ranked Choice Voting," accessed October 21, 2020. https://www.fairvote.org/data_on_rcv#research_snapshot. These did not include recent results from New York City, which do not change the pattern. There were three CFB wins, all for low-level primaries, and the CFB rate was again 96 percent.

[29] See the *ElectoWiki* page for Burlington's 2009 election: https://electowiki.org/wiki/2009_Burlington_mayoral_election. Accessed October 13, 2021.

Nor are all reformers satisfied with AV, which, fundamentally, is still "winner-take-all." Skeptics include proponents of improved racial representation, those who aim for multiparty legislatures, and those whose main commitment is to undo Democrats' geographic disadvantage. As I write this, a new group called More Equitable Democracy is trying to steer the conversation away from single-seat districts and, by extension, majoritarian ranked-ballot systems. This group's stated mission is to increase minority representation in government.[30] On the proportionality front, Rodden (2019) includes Australia (with AV and independent redistricting) among cases where single-seat districts punish urban parties. He recommends PR instead. Finally, simulations of U.S. legislative elections show that very few maps based on single-seat districts can lessen the Democrats' geography problem (Chen and Rodden 2013; McGann et al. 2016).

One last source of dissatisfaction may be independents themselves. In the going theory of open-endorsement AV, the policy space is unidimensional, most voters are in its middle, and party nominations pull candidates to extremes (Gehl and Porter 2020: 46). Getting rid of primaries therefore should empower the "center."

There are reasons to question the centrist theory of reform. First, the policy space may be multidimensional (as presupposed by "shifting coalitions" theory, then shown with spatial maps in Chapter 7). Research on voters and elites alike shows that two or more dimensions are needed to model preferences, especially during realignments (Miller and Schofield 2003; Treier and Hillygus 2009; Poole and Rosenthal 1997). Second, there may not be much difference, policy-wise, between primary- and general-election voters (Ranney 1968; Sides et al. 2018).[31] Third, voters who appear (or place themselves) in the center have blends of policy views, not a single "centrist" position (Converse 1964; Kinder and Kalmoe 2017; Hare et al. 2018). Therefore, the process of choosing nominees—or coordinating on frontrunners in non-partisan races—is partly about choosing which dimension will be salient.[32]

---

[30] The organization's website reads as follows: "For communities of color, however, electoral systems have presented significant barriers to political empowerment. Either through the process of redistricting, whereby people of color are often strategically 'packed' into few or 'cracked' into several single-member districts, or the perpetuation of at-large elections by numbered positions when polarized voting patterns persist, the ability of communities of color to elect candidates of their choice is often thwarted." See https://www.equitabledemocracy.org/our-work/.

[31] The only exception of which I am aware, as of October 2021, concerns Republican attitudes toward immigration. I thank Nick Troiano for alerting me to this result.

[32] This is consistent with Cox (1997: 144), who expects two viable candidates in an AV election. It also is consistent with Reilly (2001), who casts dimension selection (i.e. coordination) under AV as "moderation."

As long as reformers control the salient dimension (e.g., by priming "corruption"), they will win most of the time. The question is how long they can control that dimension without party or "special interest" backing.[33] In turn, this may explain why last century's reformers rejected majority systems (Hoag 1914c: 50). STV may be better for small groups of uncommitted politicians—"independent of boss or party," per Porter (1914: 581)—than winner-take-all rules like AV. Maxey (1922: 84–85) gives evidence of this recognition in Cleveland, again the only city that switched from Bucklin to STV (emphasis mine):

> The party organizations soon discovered that although they could not nominate candidates directly, they could endorse candidates nominated by petition and *throw the whole force of the party organization behind such candidates.* Furthermore it was discovered that the preferential-choice scheme could be turned to the advantage of the party by passing out the word to all regulars to *vote only for a first choice.* Thus the alternative votes of the independent voters would tend to build up the aggregate vote of the party candidates, but the *regular party voters would contribute nothing to the aggregate vote of the independent candidates.*

If AV loses appeal, as Bucklin did in the last century, opponents of party politics may reconsider STV. The resulting conversation could recall the 1913–14 debate between PR League leaders and left-wing intellectuals (e.g., Walter Lippmann and Carl S. Thompson). As we saw in Chapter 3, the party skeptics won that fight, and nominating provisions in the *Fair Representation Act* suggest they might do so again.

8.3.5 Prospects for STV in subnational politics

I am reluctant to make predictions about where or when we might see STV. Three paths seem apparent, however. One is the path already underway: imposition in cases of minority-vote dilution. So far, these have been

---

[33] In Australia, by contrast, AV *works with* a multiparty system, which already existed when it was adopted. It also comes with features (e.g., compulsory voting and compulsory ranking) that push voters to ratify coalition deals among parties (Reilly 2021). These points cannot be repeated enough.

Eastpointe (MI),[34] Palm Desert (CA),[35] and Albany (CA).[36] Eastpointe involved an agreement between the U.S. Department of Justice and incumbents in city government. Palm Desert involved an agreement with plaintiffs under the *California Voting Rights Act* (CVRA). Albany did not involve a formal lawsuit, but the threat of one (under CVRA) otherwise might have led to single-seat districts, and several incumbents backed the referendum. All three adoptions might be classified as *insulating*, as incumbent governments set the terms for reform (by choosing STV over single-seat districts).[37] Notably, all three adoptions call for low district magnitudes: three and two (staggered) in Eastpointe, two and one in Palm Desert, and three and two in Albany.

A second path, which we have not seen, is new-party entry leading to *coalition insulation*. Related paths without new-party entry might involve the scenarios discussed above, with respect to the U.S. House.

A third path, involving *coalition realignment*, seems possible in places (cities or states) with non-negligible minority parties and internally divided ruling parties. What follows is a hypothetical reform trajectory, based on patterns noted in the rest of this book.

Consider Massachusetts, where Republicans are under-represented in proportion to their numbers, and where younger Democrats have crowded recent primaries. Assume that, for reasons of generational change, "affective polarization" has receded, as well as the salience of national issues. The Republican Party, still controlled by social moderates, seeks some way to improve its legislative position. Meanwhile, fiscally moderate Democrats become frustrated with decaying infrastructure, the state's pension obligations, and the fact that many know it as "Taxachusetts." At least some Republicans agree. Would-be contestants in party primaries are drawn to ideas about "more voter choice," "no more spoiler effect," and the prospect of winning on transfers. One of the national RCV groups swoops in with a message of "good government," plus a new model state constitution. It calls for a unicameral legislature and "proportional ranked choice voting" in districts of three to five seats.[38] Actors like Michael Douglas and Jennifer Lawrence

---

[34] https://www.detroitnews.com/story/news/local/macomb-county/2019/11/03/eastpointe-ranked-choice-voting-michigan-first/40538173/. Accessed September 2020.
[35] https://www.cityofpalmdesert.org/home/showdocument?id=28138. Accessed September 2020.
[36] https://www.voterchoicealbany.org/faq. Accessed September 2020.
[37] In Eastpointe, the previous at-large system was based on numbered posts.
[38] The Committee on State Government of the National Municipal League proposed something like this, minus the RCV reference, in the early 1920s. See National Municipal League (1921, 1924),

record YouTube videos to support the measure. It passes with 65 percent voting "yes": most Republicans and a large minority of Democrats.

Record numbers of candidates contest the first STV election. Reform-minded Democrats hold the balance of power in the state's first unicameral legislature. Several have been elected on transfers from Republicans, most in the rural western part of the state. Others, representing the Boston suburbs, won seats "from behind" on transfers from regular Democrats. Choosing a presiding officer takes several weeks. A Democrat is picked, but when pension reform comes up, several Democrats vote with the Republican caucus. Democratic leaders reach out to Republican counterparts, asking about interest in repealing STV. Republicans are reluctant, noting they have won on pension reform. Democratic leaders counter that, due to vote leakage, Republicans got 30 percent of seats on 40 percent of first-choice votes. As the agenda turns to policing reform, moderate Democrats kill the bill in committee. The *Boston Globe* reports on legislative inaction, with visualizations of key players' transfer flows.

8.4 Making reform work

This book has identified vote leakage as a weakness in past American STV systems. As party systems evolve away from whatever alignments produce reform, "centrist" politicians can survive in office by seeking transfers from the opposition. This can lead to *polarizing* repeal activity.

A related problem is when vote leakage changes nominal control of government. This occurs when transfers flow to the opposition instead of some candidate's co-partisans (taken to include coalition partners).

A third problem is "ranking truncation" or "ballot exhaustion," which also threatens control of an assembly. A ballot becomes exhausted when it does not enter a subsequent round of counting, either because the voter has ranked only weak candidates, or because that voter has used very few rankings. The problem may be negligible in single-winner settings, which have generated most studies of truncation so far (Neely and Cook 2008; Burnett and Kogan 2015; Kilgour et al. 2020; compare Coll 2021).

---

especially page 4 of the latter. Curiously, both versions were silent on nominations. Regarding "proportional ranked choice voting" (i.e., STV), see the newest messaging from modern-day reformers.

With STV, however, truncation can have voting-rights implications. Say we have some popular candidate, e.g., Ted Berry in Cincinnati, or Adam Clayton Powell, Jr., in New York City. It is plausible that some voters will rank only that person (cf. McDaniel 2018). Once such candidates have been elected, any votes in excess of the quota have no other place to go. Further ballots (or parts of ballots under fractional transfer) become exhausted. At this point, the STV fan may claim that those voters did elect a candidate of choice. But if this popular candidate is part of some *team that seeks control of government*, ballot exhaustion deprives that team of votes that might have increased its seat share. If certain kinds of voters are more likely to truncate rankings, ballot exhaustion penalizes whatever party represents those voters.[39]

8.4.1 Open-list systems

Open-list proportional representation (OLPR) obviates vote leakage and ranking truncation. In an open-list system, the voter marks one or more candidates. In turn, these votes (a) determine candidates' list positions and (b) contribute to the overall total of the party or coalition slate. There is no way in which a vote can leave one party's column, then contribute to the seat share of another party (unless those parties are in pre-election coalition). Ballot exhaustion becomes a non-issue, as does centralized vote tabulation. And open-list systems would let voters do what ranked-voting systems now promise: choose their most preferred candidate(s).[40]

---

[39] As noted in Chapter 3, reformers were aware of these problems with STV (Gove 1894; Harris 1930). They did not frame them in party-control terms, likely due to consensus on non-partisanship. Yet there were efforts to document both "bullet voting" (leading to ballot exhaustion) and voter confusion (typically using one or more X-marks instead of, or in combination with, numeric rankings). The key work is by Mott (1926). In the cases he looked at, rates of ballot invalidity ranged from 1.7 percent (Winnipeg, 1920) to 23.6 percent (Boulder, CO, 1919). On average, from 1915–25, American STV elections produced 6.3 percent invalid ballots. That figure in Canada was 4.7 percent. What about ballot exhaustion? In Cincinnati's first PR election, 1925, 7.7 percent of *valid* ballots did not continue to the final round—2.3 points shy of a seat-earning quota. The Cincinnati figures are notable because this is where the old movement learned to "get it right."

[40] The voter-experience point is worth emphasis. Evidence is accumulating that significant numbers of voters *may not like* ranking multiple candidates. For example, survey data analyzed by McCarthy and Santucci (2020) reveals lower support for "ranked-choice voting" when the rule is pitted against an alternative in which "the person with the most votes" wins. See Neely and Cook (2008) and Neely and McDaniel (2015) for precinct-level observational studies. Finally, two recent studies with national samples find that voters prefer just-choose-one systems (Blais et al. 2021).

On these points, it is worth reviewing Gosnell (1939), whose paper attracted (and still attracts) little attention. He made four big points. First, non-partisanship was on paper only in most STV cities. Second, open lists are easier on voters; they just pick their preferred candidate. Third, they are easier on election administrators, as there are no transfers requiring central-ized tabulation.[41] Finally—and critically—based on the elections he studied (New York City, 1937, and Cincinnati 1925–37), open-list allocation based on first-choice votes would have produced the same winner in 89 percent of cases.

The big exception in Gosnell's simulations was Cincinnati, 1937, when transfers made the outcome different from what it would have been with open lists. This election came amidst the reform coalition's first breakdown, two repeal initiatives, and what was, in retrospect, a halting alternation from Charter to Republican control of city council. At this election, the Charter and Republican slates each bled more than 20 percent of votes to opposing-party winners. The subsequent majority roll rate approached 10 percent of votes, a high up to that point. Based on the account of repeal proposed here, there would not have been such efforts under OLPR.

There are a few objections to OLPR. First, it does not work with formally non-partisan elections. In this case, reformers may want to consider limited or cumulative voting (Bowler et al. 2003). But if we are going to reform elec-tions at higher levels, non-partisan elections do not seem likely.[42] Second, one might say, OLPR does not work for one seat. This is not true, as the party with the most votes would be entitled to the seat, which would go to the candidate with the most votes within that party. Some might even prefer this to same-party runoffs (such as now occur under California "top-two"). A third objection concerns descriptive representation. By letting voters set list order, it is possible that they will "bury" groups for whom representation is a priority. This is especially likely if, given a large number of candidates, voters make decisions based on inferred candidate race and/or gender (Crowder-Meyer et al. 2019). But this can be remedied via quotas.[43]

Clearly, OLPR is hard on independents, who would not be able to seek transfers from major-party candidates. One solution is for independents to

---

[41] Again, Lien (1925: 265) made these arguments fourteen years earlier, having seen four STV elections in Boulder (CO). Gove (1894: 47) made them thirty-one years before Lien.

[42] Any turnout-minded reform package would restore (or retain) partisan elections anyway (Garlick 2015).

[43] The problem also exists in STV. Generally, it is solved by changing the "supply" of candidates (Dhima et al. 2021).

form their own party. Another is for the lone independent to earn so many votes that they win a quota outright. A third is to combine the system with "top-X" preliminary rounds (or what some reformers call a "non-partisan primary"). One such proposal retains single-seat "nomination districts."[44]

One last reason to consider open lists—or any form of list PR, including MMP—is that STV may not "work" in a two-party system. Australian and Irish colleagues sometimes tell me that their countries are "more-or-less" two-party. This is not the same as a strictly two-party system. When there are just two parties, as in two cases dissected here, realignment can get messy.[45] Transfers cross the aisle, and coalitions become scrambled. While these patterns have yet to be established for other U.S. cases, the ones in this book do give pause.

8.4.2 STV with more parties

A second solution is for there to be more parties. Such parties might give structure to voters' rankings, as in Ireland and Scottish local elections (Bennie and Clark 2008; Clark 2020). These parties could work out coalition deals, then get voters to go along with those deals (Sharman et al. 2002). This would mitigate both problems of vote leakage: cross-aisle bargaining and threats to nominal control of government.

Multiple parties also offer defense against repeal activity. In the 1936 initiative discussed above, Progressive Republicans in Cincinnati's Charter Party joined forces with the regular Republican Party. What remained of Charter was able to defeat the measure with help from a third party: Bigelow's Progressive Democrats (see appendix). If reforms are to outlast the coalitions that impose them, other groups must see value in the reforms.[46]

Obviously, it is difficult to "just have" more parties, but Disch (2002: 59–82) gives one point of departure. She argues that political science has helped to discourage new-party entry by insisting on the irrationality of third-party voting. Lowi (1983) makes a similar point, also worth considering. Those

---

[44] Matthew S. Shugart, "Emergency electoral reform: OLPR for the US House," *Fruits & Votes* (blog), January 19, 2021. Online at https://fruitsandvotes.wordpress.com/2021/01/19/emergency-electoral-reform-olpr-for-the-us-house/. Accessed October 13, 2021.

[45] In the third case (New York City), a multiparty system collapsed into a congeries of party-labeled independents.

[46] In New York City, third-party support was insufficient to offset Republicans' departure from the reform coalition. See Appendix A.

who now brand themselves "independent" may be logical seeds for new-party formation. Another option is to support parties that already exist. Meanwhile, it would be up to those parties to show they would be good coalition partners.

8.4.3 STV with less voter choice

Another class of solutions would diminish voter choice. These include allocating seats based on first-choice vote totals, rendering the legislature unimportant, finding some way to control voters' rankings, and/or limiting nominations. All might force dissenters into their own parties.

The Maltese solution, as we have seen, is to award a seat majority to the party with a plurality of first-choice votes. This means that ballot exhaustion and/or vote leakage cannot reverse control of an assembly. It also reduces opportunities for cross-aisle bargaining, by reducing the number of seats winnable in that way. Dissenters seeking to overcome these barriers would benefit from their own party, in order to get sufficient first-choice support.

The Northern Ireland solution is to produce "grand" coalitions directly from election returns. Portfolio allocation in cabinet is based automatically on legislative seat shares. This removes legislative bargaining from the process of forming governments, rendering independents politically unimportant.

The Australian solution is compulsory ranking, whereby a ballot is invalid if it does not contain some minimum number of rankings. For AV elections to the lower chamber, this rule preserved a coalition of right-leaning parties into the 1980s, and it now bolsters a deal between the Greens and Labor (at least as of this writing). Recent elections have seen alternation between these coalitions. In Senate elections, where STV is used, compulsory ranking always has been at work. Up to 1984, the voter had to rank all candidates. Since 1984, the voter has been able to vote "above the line," ratifying some party or "group-ticket" rank-ordering. Recent reforms have relaxed the rule that all candidates be ranked, but voters still must rank at least twelve candidates (below the line) or six group slates (above the line). According to Sharman et al. (2002) and Reilly (2021), "preference-swapping" deals in House elections tend to reappear in these STV races. Voters and candidates who would defy these deals face steep information costs, which is why more than 90 percent of voters cast "above the line" ballots in Senate races (Australian Electoral Commission 2016: 3–4). Partisanship structures rankings by law.

A final solution is the one discovered in Cambridge: restricting nominations to only as many candidates as are needed to win a seat majority. Candidates not able to enter the slate would need to run as very strong independents, otherwise form a new party.

None of these options will sit well with reformers who want freedom from party politics. Their plan is for STV to work the old way. Each party's slate would comprise all factions, and votes would flow freely among them. Coalitions would vary from issue to issue, in a less polarized legislature. History shows that this world without parties is not likely to last long.

8.4.4 General considerations

Instability brings an opportunity to make American democracy work better. This book has argued that reform is common in periods of realignment. Also, it has shown how not to "do" electoral reform—unless the goal is to shrink legislatures and hide candidates' party labels. Those were the old movement's lasting gifts. For readers with other goals, two options are apparent.

One is just to leave the party system to itself. Maybe realignment is a myth. Maybe it should be allowed to play out uninterrupted. There could be merit in either view, assuming reform activity will stop.

The other is to design reforms for competition *among parties*. One good way to get there is a *multiparty reform coalition*.

Repeal Coalitions and Candidate Entry

Chapter 7 documented conditions producing *polarizing* repeal in Cincinnati (1957), New York City (1947), and Worcester (1960). Earlier efforts did not succeed because (a) repeal proponents could not raid reform coalitions or (b) reform coalitions could offset such defections. This appendix uses the best available data to show when reform coalitions could and could not offset defections. A background condition is low candidate entry, which reflects weak demand for "multiparty" institutions. I am not the first to note this demand problem. Johnston and Koene (2000) point to similar patterns in Canadian STV cases.[1]

I will not spend time with failed initiatives in New York City (1938 statewide, 1940 local) nor Worcester (1959). In both cases, repeal proponents did not attract support within reform coalitions. To recap, in New York City, Republican Party leaders withheld support until October 1947 (Zeller and Bone 1948: 1127). The 1959 effort in Worcester failed because it attacked council-manager government, not just the STV system. In turn, it drew no support from CEA ranks (Binstock 1960: VI-16; Southwick 2017).[2]

This appendix proceeds by city. For each, it documents a similar pattern of candidate entry: many at the first STV election, followed by sharp and immediate decline. An exception is Cincinnati in the mid-1930s, when three third parties emerged. Then I use the best available data to analyze composition of STV retention coalitions. Cincinnati's third parties helped to defeat repeal. In New York City, they were neither large nor cohesive enough.

A.1 Cincinnati

For Cincinnati, the best available data are ward-level returns, printed in the *Cincinnati Enquirer*. The sample size (26) is not sufficient for ecological inference. Instead, I estimated all possible least-squares models of the raw repeal "no" vote as a function of voting at the most recent election. This approach is known as a grid search. Data were not available for the 1954 referendum.

---

[1] They write: "... apathy was the more important problem. The adoption of PR did not solve it, especially when it came to attracting better candidates. Indeed, there was a continuing problem of attracting any candidates for municipal offices at all. Where elections were needed, they featured only one or two more candidates than the number of positions to be filled ... " (222). Further, they write: "In short, PR was simply not needed in these places. Its logic and vote transfer procedure also baffled many voters. Although there were few calls for its abandonment, neither were people very supportive. For the local politicians who had adopted it, PR was also an unneeded complication, so it is not surprising they dropped it without feeling the need to consult the citizenry in a plebiscite" (223).

[2] Elsewhere, I have compared precinct-level referendum voting to CEA's first-choice total at the same election. These data are consistent with observer accounts and available on request.

Covariates in the grid search are Charter's first-choice vote total, then first-choice votes for one or two more candidates.[3] Each table below reports four models: one that minimizes statistical significance of the intercept (Min x0*), one that minimizes the absolute value of the estimated intercept (Min abs(x0)), and two that maximize overall model fit (Max RSq, or maximize R-squared, and Min AIC, or minimize the Akaike information criterion). The goal is to see if different types of evidence point in the same direction.

Expectations for the models derive from the logic of a polarizing repeal episode. First, the coefficient on Charter's vote should be substantially less than one (except in 1947, when repeal was meant to be insulating). This is because a polarizing episode involves defection from the reform coalition. Second, the grid search should find anti-repeal votes in groups later incorporated by the reform coalition, otherwise from a third party (or both).

Candidate entry

To start the discussion, note that candidate entry in Cincinnati declined rapidly, surged with third-party entry in the 1930s, and then declined again by 1955–57 (Figure A.1). Two rates are reported: the nominal and effective numbers of candidates. The effective number of candidates equals one over the sum of squared vote proportions (first-choice votes). A dotted line shows how many candidates there would be if just two full slates entered.

In passing, note how the effective number hovers in the low teens, or just about two slates of six. This reflects the parties' vote-management efforts, noted toward the end of Chapter 6. To recap, the party would run as many strong candidates as it needed to win a majority, then "pad" its collective vote with transfers from trailing nominees. Remarkably, six is what the Republican Party nominated in 1925, what Charter may have considered at the same election (Bentley 1926: 466–67), what the CCA settled on in Cambridge (Chapter 7), and what some modern-day slates in Cambridge have contained (Santucci 2019).

Repeal results

Table A.1 reports grid-search results for the 1957 repeal initiative.[4] All four models suggest roughly one-quarter of Charter's 1955 electorate not voting "no" on repeal (i.e., voting "yes" or abstaining). Two models suggest no out-of-party support for keeping STV. Two more suggest support from about two-thirds of Walton H. Bachrach's (R) voters. Bachrach knew Ted Berry from their work as prosecutors, and both had been allies on Fair Employment Practices (Straetz 1958: 49, 106). If these estimates are good, two-thirds of Bachrach's 6,878 votes (just about 4,400) would not have offset Charter's defection (about 10,300 or 14,000 votes, depending on which estimate). Recall that the measure won by over 11,000 votes. Also recall the morning-of newspaper report: "Republicans have attracted the support of the United Steel Workers, numbering about 15,000 Cincinnatians, which previously backed PR."

Table A.2 models the 1936 repeal vote as a function of the 1935 election. This referendum lost by just 759 votes, or 1.1 percentage points. Consistent with Kolesar (1995) on

---

[3] Another option is to look at repeal from the Republican perspective, modeling the "yes" vote instead. These results are available on request.

[4] For ward-level repeal totals, see the *Cincinnati Enquirer* for October 5, 1957, p. 10. For 1955 vote totals, see the *Cincinnati Enquirer* for November 13, 1955, p. 6.

Candidate entry: Cincinnati

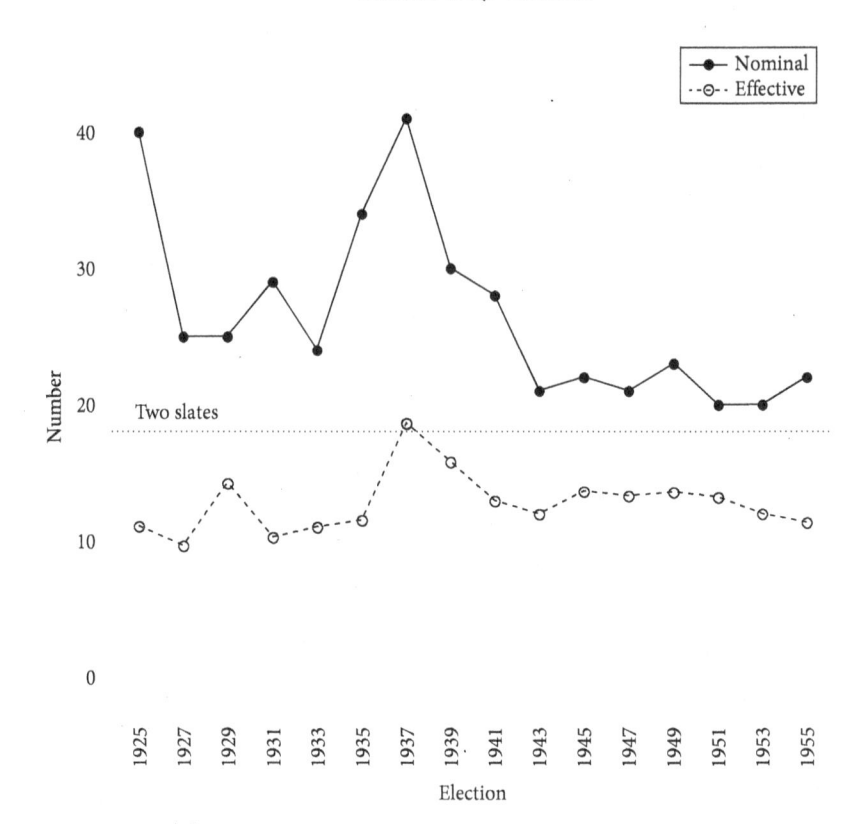

Fig. A.1 Candidate entry in Cincinnati, 1925–55.

many Progressive Republicans returning to the regular party, Charter only contributed half of its vote to STV's retention. Then, depending on the model, it shored this up with votes from Nick Klein (R) or Herb Bigelow (Progressive Democrat). In practice, their coalitions overlapped. Straetz (1958: 65) writes: "Bigelow did have friends on both sides of the fence. Republican Nick Klein announced that he would always be ready to second a Bigelow proposal . . . "

Table A.3 models the 1939 referendum as a function of the 1937 election. This referendum failed by 820 votes, or 0.8 percentage points. Charter only contributed two thirds of its coalition to STV's retention. Based on these models, other support came from Roosevelt Democrats, partly a faction of the local Democratic Party. Straetz (1958: 128–29) reports that this group, with Klein and Bigelow, was part of a push by organized labor to get more power in city council. Further, "Klein also tangled with Congressman Bigelow, who accused Klein of welshing on his promise 'to hook up' only temporarily with the Republicans . . . " In the data, this Roosevelt Democratic support turns up in three

Table A.1 Modeling the Cincinnati 1957 retention vote as a function of 1955 election results.

	Min x0*	Min abs(x0)	Max RSq	Min AIC
Intercept	34.70	34.70	136.77	136.77
	(193.07)	(193.07)	(115.87)	(115.87)
Charter	0.83***	0.83***	0.77***	0.77***
	(0.07)	(0.07)	(0.05)	(0.05)
Rich	0.12	0.12		
	(0.11)	(0.11)		
Bachrach			0.65***	0.65***
			(0.12)	(0.12)
R^2	0.87	0.87	0.94	0.94
Adj. R^2	0.86	0.86	0.93	0.93
Num. obs.	26	26	26	26

*** $p < 0.001$; ** $p < 0.01$; * $p < 0.05$

Table A.2 Modeling the Cincinnati 1936 retention vote as a function of 1935 election results. P = Progressive Democrat, R = Republican.

	Min x0*	Min abs(x0)	Max RSq	Min AIC
Intercept	196.34	196.34	231.32	231.32
	(165.22)	(165.22)	(112.05)	(112.05)
Charter	0.49***	0.49***	0.42***	0.42***
	(0.05)	(0.05)	(0.04)	(0.04)
Klein (R)	0.68*	0.68*		
	(0.31)	(0.31)		
Bigelow (P)			0.36**	0.36**
			(0.11)	(0.11)
R^2	0.84	0.84	0.88	0.88
Adj. R^2	0.83	0.83	0.86	0.86
Num. obs.	26	26	26	26

*** $p < 0.001$; ** $p < 0.01$; * $p < 0.05$

models with coefficients for Arthur Shott, spokesman for the Roosevelt Democrats.[5] After this effort, Charter went into minority status and began courting labor more aggressively.[6]

Finally, Table A.4 models the 1947 referendum as a function of the simultaneous election. Recall that this was not an initiative. Rather, the Republican Party used a six-seat

---

[5] "Factions Analyzed by Shott," *Cincinnati Enquirer*, November 27, 1937, p. 12.

[6] Edward Imbus, a Charter-Democratic incumbent, was sympathetic to this strategy as early as 1935 (Straetz 1958: 65).

Table A.3 Modeling the Cincinnati 1939 retention vote as a function of 1937 election results. R = Republican, RD = Roosevelt Democrat.

	Min x0*	Min abs(x0)	Max RSq	Min AIC
Intercept	629.35**	449.23***	449.23***	449.23***
	(177.37)	(106.68)	(106.68)	(106.68)
Charter	0.64***	0.64***	0.64***	0.64***
	(0.05)	(0.04)	(0.04)	(0.04)
Klein (R)	−0.10			
	(0.27)			
Shott (RD)		12.80*	12.80*	12.80*
		(5.33)	(5.33)	(5.33)
R^2	0.89	0.91	0.91	0.91
Adj. R^2	0.88	0.91	0.91	0.91
Num. obs.	26	26	26	26

***$p < 0.001$; **$p < 0.01$; *$p < 0.05$

Table A.4 Modeling the Cincinnati 1947 retention vote as a function of the simultaneous election. I = Independent, R = Republican.

	Min x0*	Min abs(x0)	Max RSq	Min AIC
Intercept	−419.98	−419.98	−356.71	−356.71
	(531.50)	(531.50)	(451.14)	(451.14)
Charter	1.10***	1.10***	1.09***	1.09***
	(0.15)	(0.15)	(0.13)	(0.13)
Locker (R)	0.64**	0.64**		
	(0.17)	(0.17)		
Berry (I)			1.12***	1.12***
			(0.26)	(0.26)
R^2	0.73	0.73	0.77	0.77
Adj. R^2	0.71	0.71	0.75	0.75
Num. obs.	26	26	26	26

***$p < 0.001$; **$p < 0.01$; *$p < 0.05$

majority (which it got by appointing one of its own to a Charter vacancy) to put repeal on the ballot. All signs suggest it hoped to break an emerging alliance between Charter and Civil Rights leaders. The referendum went badly, losing by 7,592 votes (5.0 points). Council control then swung back to Charter for the first time in a decade. The data are consistent with all of this. First, we see that Charter voters opposed repeal unanimously. Then we see that help came from either of the city's two main Black politicians: Jesse D. Locker (R) or Theodore Berry (I). Berry then ran as a Charter Republican in 1949.

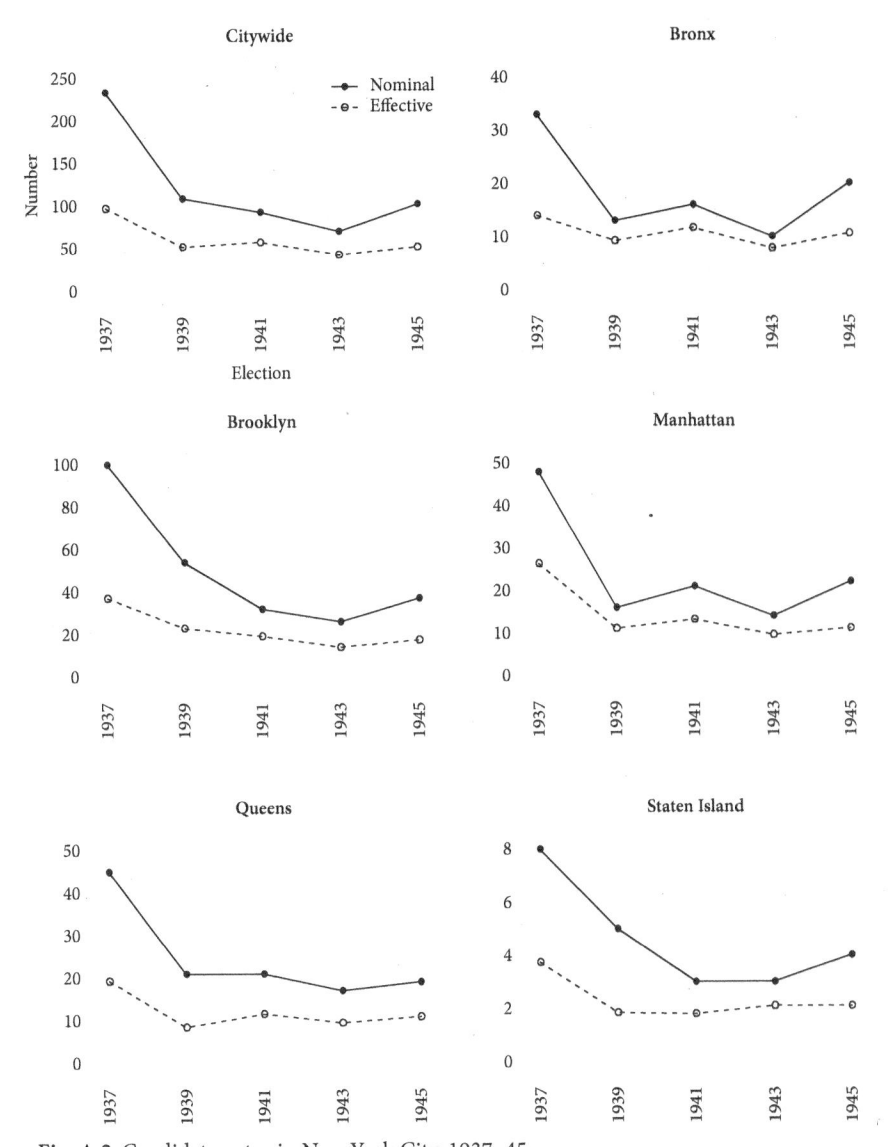

Fig. A.2 Candidate entry in New York City, 1937–45.

A.2 New York City

As in Cincinnati, candidate entry fell sharply after the first election. Figure A.2 plots the nominal and effective numbers of candidates in each borough and citywide.[7] There is

---

[7] Data are from the *Annual Report of the Board of Elections in the City of New York*, on file at the Municipal Library, for odd years 1937–45.

no way to say what these numbers would be in the presence of strong coordination, as district magnitude changed with turnout.

Further, votes for third parties and independents also fell sharply after the first election. According to data from Zeller and Bone (1948: 1132), the percentages of votes (final-round count) going to the major parties at each election were: 55.5 (1937), 73.5 (1939), 70.5 (1941), 75 (1943), and 74 (1945).[8]

On November 4, 1947, Propositon Four replaced STV with single-seat plurality in state assembly districts. The overall breakdown was: 42 percent "yes" (886,258), 29 percent "no" (610,822), and 29 percent "blank" (610,076). Of votes that counted toward the final outcome, 59.2 percent voted "yes," and 40.8 percent voted "no." The raw margin was 275,436 in favor.

Table A.5 gives precinct-level ecological–inference estimates of Proposition Four voting by party registration.[9] Cell entries are the percentage of each party's registrants voting any of four ways: not at all, "yes" to repeal, "no" to repeal, and leaving that part of the ballot blank.[10] Brackets reflect 95-percent credible intervals. A final column gives the citywide number of voters registered with each party. "War voters" were those in active military service.

There are several things to note in the table. First is overall major-party strength. Democrats constituted 61.3 percent of registered voters, Republicans constituted 19.9 percent, and just 18.7 percent fell into other categories. Second is that most pro-repeal votes came from the major parties: a majority of registered Republicans, then roughly 40 percent of Democrats. If we focus on just "yes" and "no" votes, 62 percent of Democrats and 79 percent of Republicans are estimated to have said "yes."

Opposition concentrated in American Labor (nearly 50 percent voting "no," or 84 percent of consequential votes), but even this group faced defections. This is not surprising, as Council President Vincent Impellitteri (D-ALP) called on his voters to support the measure.[11] Ways to defeat the bipartisan repeal coalition might have involved every ALP and Liberal voter (302,582 votes) or every ALP and unaffiliated voter (342,406 votes). Even a coalition of all Liberal and unaffiliated voters could not have prevailed (237,458 votes).

A.3 Worcester

As in the other cities, candidate entry fell sharply after the first election. Table A.3 gives the nominal and effective numbers of candidates, as well as a dotted two-slates line segment. Again, the effective number hovers below this line, reflecting the parties' vote management.

---

[8] American Labor alone fell from 21 percent in 1937 to 11.5 percent in 1939, ending with 10 percent in 1945. Fusion ceased to exist in 1943. Some of its candidates (e.g., Minority Leader Genevieve Earle) went on to run as Republicans who cross-filed as "Citizens' Non-Partisan."

[9] Data are from *Annual Report of the Board of Elections in the City of New York* for 1947, on file at the Municipal Library. Estimates are from the same type of Bayesian multinomial-Dirichlet model used in Chapter 4 (Lau et al. 2007): 25,000 iterations with a burn-in of 1,000 and thinning interval of 200.

[10] "Not voting" is inferred from the total number of registrants in each precinct, minus the sum of yes/no/blank votes.

[11] "Impellitteri Asks Voters to Kill PR," *New York Times*, p. 2, October 30, 1947.

Table A.5 Ecological–inference estimates: percent of party's registered voters voting each way on STV repeal, New York City, November 1947. Ranges in brackets are 95 percent credible intervals.

Party	Not voting	Yes	No	Blank	Registrants
Democratic	1.8 [0.7, 3.9]	40.5 [36.3, 45.1]	24.8 [20.8, 28.7]	32.9 [27.5, 36.5]	1,449,118
Republican	24.1 [18, 29.5]	50.9 [37.8, 62.8]	13.4 [5.5, 22.5]	11.6 [3.8, 22.8]	471,668
American Labor	21.1 [8.5, 34.6]	9.3 [3.2, 19.4]	49.7 [29.8, 67.1]	19.9 [7.1, 39]	203,765
Liberal	32.8 [11.5, 56.9]	13.8 [4.3, 29]	38.1 [14.4, 63.4]	15.3 [4.7, 31.9]	98,817
Unaffiliated	28.7 [10.4, 50.8]	19 [5.8, 38.5]	35.6 [14.3, 58.7]	16.8 [5.2, 34]	138,641
War voters	25.3 [8, 48.5]	25 [7.9, 48]	24.8 [7.4, 48.3]	24.9 [8, 47.9]	685

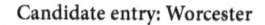

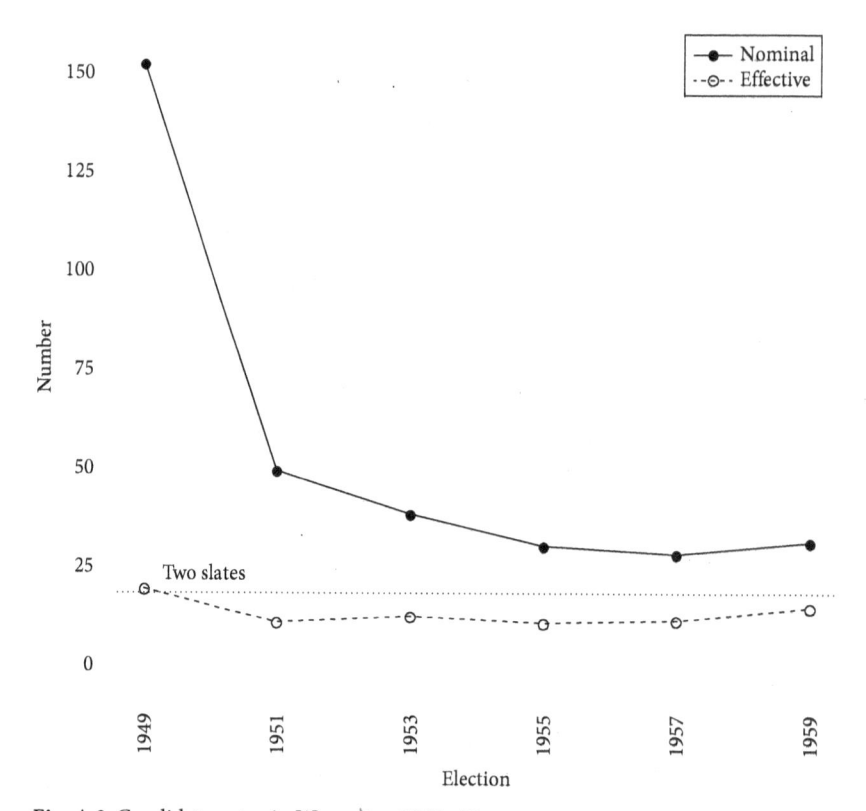

Fig. A.3 Candidate entry in Worcester, 1949–59.

Worcester voters repealed STV on November 8, 1960, alongside the regular election. Question Two replaced STV with non-partisan two-round elections at-large, billed as "ordinary plurality voting." A September "preliminary" would winnow the field to eighteen. This measure won with 51.4 percent voting "yes" (46,982 votes), 33.5 percent "no" (30,593 votes), and 15.1 percent blank (13,787 votes). Of votes that counted toward the final outcome, 60.6 percent voted "yes," and 39.4 percent "no." The raw margin for repeal was 16,389 votes.[12]

Table A.6 gives ecological–inference estimates of support for Question Two by voting in the simultaneous gubernatorial election.[13] Brackets again reflect 95-percent credible intervals. An alternative would be to use the presidential election among John F. Kennedy (D), Richard M. Nixon (R), and others. The gubernatorial results are more plausibly connected to the local party system, especially because Worcester needed state-legislative

[12]   Data are precinct-level and available from the Worcester Election Commission: http://www.worcesterma.gov/election-results/1960-1969/19601108.pdf.

[13]   Again, estimates are based on a Bayesian multinomial-Dirichlet model (Lau et al. 2007): 25,000 iterations with a burn-in of 1,000 and thinning interval of 200.

Table A.6 Ecological–inference estimates: percent for each gubernatorial candidate voting each way on STV repeal, Worcester (MA), November 1960. Ranges in brackets are 95 percent credible intervals. R = Republican, D = Democratic, SLP = Socialist Labor, P = Prohibition.

Candidate	Yes	No	Blank	Total vote
Volpe (R)	24.9 [19.8, 30.2]	67.4 [63.8, 70.5]	7.7 [3.5, 12.1]	39,215
Ward (D)	74.4 [69.8, 78.7]	6.5 [3.8, 9.5]	19.1 [15.3, 22.8]	48,831
Blomen (SLP)	32.8 [10.6, 61.1]	33.3 [10.7, 60.8]	34 [10.8, 61.8]	312
Williams (P)	32.1 [10.6, 59.7]	32.6 [10.4, 60.3]	35.3 [12, 63.5]	649
Blank	25.1 [8.2, 50.3]	29.6 [9.8, 56.1]	45.3 [17.9, 72]	2,355

permission to hold this referendum. There were four candidates: John A. Volpe (R), Joseph D. Ward (D), Henning A. Blomen (Socialist Labor), and Guy S. Williams (Prohibition). Ward carried the city with 53.4 percent, and 96.4 percent voted for major-party candidates.

Patterns in the table are consistent with the repeal politics: a divided Democratic Party (74 percent voting "yes"), then non-negligible Republican support (24.9 percent). Republican "yes" votes were not critical to the margin (estimated at 9,765 of the total 16,389), but they are remarkable anyway. Recall that Republican operatives, from 1959–60, quietly turned against STV: Councilman "Bud" Lane, attorney for the *Worcester Telegram*, and then the *Telegram* itself.

Bibliography

Ahmed, Amel. 2012. *Democracy and the Politics of Electoral System Choice: Engineering Electoral Dominance.* New York: Cambridge University Press.

Aidt, T. S., Jayasri Dutta, and Elena Loukoianova. 2006. "Democracy Comes to Europe: Franchise Extension and Fiscal Outcomes, 1830–1938." *European Economic Review* 50 (2): 249–83.

Aldrich, John H. 1995. *Why Parties? The Origin and Transformation of Party Politics in America.* Chicago: University of Chicago Press.

Alexander, Gerard. 2004. "France: Reform-Mongering between Majority Runoff and Proportionality." Chap. 10 in *Handbook of Electoral System Choice,* edited by Josep M. Colomer, 209–21. New York: Palgrave Macmillan.

Alvarez, R. Michael, Thad E. Hall, and Ines Levin. 2018. "Low-Information Voting: Evidence from Instant-Runoff Elections." *American Politics Research* 46 (6): 1012–38.

Alvarez, R. Michael, and J. Andrew Sinclair. 2011. *Nonpartisan Primary Election Reform: Mitigating Mischief.* New York: Cambridge University Press.

Amorim Neto, Octavio, Gary W. Cox, and Mathew D. McCubbins. 2003. "Agenda Power in Brazil's Camara Dos Deputados, 1989–98." *World Politics* 55 (4): 550–78.

Amy, Douglas J. 2002. *Real Choices / New Voices: How Proportional Representation Elections Could Revitalize American Democracy.* 2nd ed. New York: Columbia University Press.

Anderson, Dennis. 1995. "PR in Toledo: The Neglected Stepchild of Municipal Reform." Chap. 8 in *Proportional Representation and Election Reform in Ohio,* edited by Kathleen L. Barber, 241–81. Ohio State University Press.

Andrews, Josephine T., and Robert W. Jackman. 2005. "Strategic Fools: Electoral Rule Choice under Extreme Uncertainty." *Electoral Studies* 24: 65–84.

Anthony, Joseph, Amy Fried, Robert Glover, and David C. Kimball. 2021. "Ranked Choice Voting in Maine from the Perspective of Local Election Officials." *Election Law Journal* 20 (3): 254–71.

Anzia, Sarah F. 2012. "Partisan Power Play: The Origins of Local Election Timing as an American Political Institution." *Studies in American Political Development* 26 (1): 24–49.

Anzia, Sarah F. 2014. *Timing and Turnout: How Off-Cycle Elections Favor Organized Groups.* Chicago: University of Chicago Press.

APSA Committee on Political Parties. 1950. *Toward a More Responsible Two-Party System.*

Archer, Robin. 2010. *Why Is There No Labor Party in the United States?* Princeton: Princeton University Press.

Argersinger, Peter H. 1980. "'A Place on the Ballot': Fusion Politics and Antifusion Laws." *The American Historical Review* 85 (2): 287–306.

Australian Electoral Commission. 2016. *Above the Line and Below the Line Voting.* Senate Ballot Paper Study. Australian Electoral Commission.

Azari, Julia, and Marc J. Hetherington. 2016. "Back to the Future? What the Politics of the Late Nineteenth Century Can Tell Us about the 2016 Election." *Annals of the American Academy of Political and Social Science* 667 (1): 92–109.

Ball, Howard. 1986. "Racial Vote Dilution: Impact of the Reagan DOJ and the Burger Court on the Voting Rights Act." *Publius* 16 (4): 29–48.

Banducci, Susan A., Todd Donovan, and Jeffrey A. Karp. 1999. "Proportional Representation and Attitudes about Politics: Results from New Zealand." *Electoral Studies* 18: 533–55.

Banducci, Susan A., and Jeffrey A. Karp. 1999. "Perceptions of Fairness and Support for Proportional Representation." *Political Behavior* 21 (3): 217–38.

Banfield, Edward C., and James Q. Wilson. 1963. *City Politics.* Cambridge, MA: Harvard University Press / The MIT Press.

Barber, Kathleen L. 1995a. "Commonalities and Contrasts: Five PR Cities in Retrospect." Chap. 9 in *Proportional Representation and Election Reform in Ohio,* edited by Kathleen L. Barber, 282–309. Ohio State University Press.

Barber, Kathleen L. 1995b. "PR and Boss Rule: The Case of Cleveland." Chap. 5 in *Proportional Representation and Election Reform in Ohio,* edited by Kathleen L. Barber, 116–59. Ohio State University Press.

Barber, Kathleen L. 1995c. "PR as a Progressive Cause." Chap. 2 in *Proportional Representation and Election Reform in Ohio,* edited by Kathleen L. Barber, 38–66. Columbus: Ohio State University Press.

Barber, Kathleen L. ed. 1995d. *Proportional Representation and Election Reform in Ohio.* Columbus: Ohio State University Press.

Barreyre, Nicolas. 2011. "The Politics of Economic Crises: The Panic of 1873, the End of Reconstruction, and the Realignment of American Politics." *Journal of the Gilded Age and Progressive Era* 10 (4): 403–23.

Bawn, Kathleen. 1993. "The Logic of Institutional Preferences: German Electoral Law as a Social Choice Outcome." *American Journal of Political Science* 37 (4): 965–89.

Bawn, Kathleen, Marty Cohen, David Karol, Seth Masket, Hans Noel, and John Zaller. 2012. "A Theory of Political Parties: Groups, Policy Demands, and Nominations in American Politics." *Perspectives on Politics* 10 (3): 571–97.

Bawn, Kathleen, and Frances Rosenbluth. 2006. "Short versus Long Coalitions: Electoral Accountability and the Size of the Public Sector." *American Journal of Political Science* 50 (2): 251–65. https://doi.org/10.1111/j.1540-5907.2006.00182.x.

Bennie, Lynn, and Alistair Clark. 2008. "The Transformation of Local Politics? STV and the 2007 Scottish Local Government Elections." *Representation* 44 (3): 225–38.

Benoit, Kenneth. 2004. "Models of Electoral System Change." *Electoral Studies* 23: 363–89.

Bentley, Henry. 1926. "Cincinnati's Right About Face in Government." *National Municipal Review* (August): 465–73.

Bermeo, Nancy. 1992. "Democracy and the Lessons of Dictatorship." *Comparative Political Studies* 24 (3): 273–91.

Binstock, Robert H. 1960. *A Report on Politics in Worcester, Massachusetts.* Technical report. Cambridge, MA: Joint Center for Urban Studies of the Massachusetts Institute of Technology and Harvard University.

Blais, André, Agnieska Dobrzynska, and Indridi H. Indridason. 2005. "To Adopt or Not to Adopt Proportional Representation: The Politics of Institutional Choice." *British Journal of Political Science* 35 (1): 182–90.

Blais, André, Carolina Plescia, and Semra Sevi. 2021. "Choosing to Vote as Ususal." Unpublished manuscript. February. https://doi.org/10.2139/ssrn.3784822.

Bloomfield, Charles Alpheus. 1926. "Ashtabula's Experience with Proportional Representation." Master's thesis, Columbia University.

Boix, Carles. 1999. "Setting the Rules of the Game: The Choice of Electoral Systems in Advanced Democracies." *American Political Science Review* 93 (3): 609–24.

Bol, Damien. 2016. "Electoral Reform, Values, and Party Self-Interest." *Party Politics* 22 (1): 93–104. https://doi.org/0.1177/1354068813511590.

Bol, Damien, Jean-Benoit Pilet, and Pedro Riera. 2015. "The International Diffusion of Electoral Systems: The Spread of Mechanisms Tempering Proportional Representation across Europe." *European Journal of Political Research* 54: 384–410. https://doi.org/10.1111/1475-6765.12091.

Bowen, Daniel. 2021. "Constituency Size and Evalutions of Government." *Legislative Studies Quarterly.* https://doi.org/10.1111/lsq.12358.

Bowler, Shaun, and David Denemark. 1993. "Split Ticket Voting in Australia: Dealignment and Inconsistent Votes Reconsidered." *Australian Journal of Political Science* 28 (1): 19–37.

Bowler, Shaun, and Todd Donovan. 2008. "Election Reform and (the Lack of) Electoral System Change in the USA." Chap. 3 in *To Keep or To Change First Past The Post? The Politics of Electoral Reform,* edited by André Blais, 90–111. Cambridge: Oxford University Press.

Bowler, Shaun, and Todd Donovan. 2013. *The Limts of Electoral Reform.* Oxford: Oxford University Press.

Bowler, Shaun, Todd Donovan, and David Brockington. 2003. *Electoral Reform and Minority Representation: Local Experiments with Alternative Elections.* Columbus: Ohio State University Press.

Bowler, Shaun, and David M. Farrell. 1991. "Voter Behavior under STV-PR: Solving the Puzzle of the Irish Party System." *Political Behavior* 13 (4): 303–20.

Brady, David W., and Charles S. Bullock. 1980. "Is There a Conservative Coalition in the House?" *Journal of Politics* 42 (2): 549–59.

Bridges, Amy. 1997. *Morning Glories: Municipal Reform in the Southwest.* Princeton: Princeton University Press.

Bridges, Amy, and Thad Kousser. 2011. "Where Politicians Gave Power to the People: Adoption of the Citizen Initiative in the U.S. States." *State Politics and Policy Quarterly* 11 (2): 167–97.

Bridges, Amy, and Richard Kronick. 1999. "Writing the Rules to Win the Game: The Middle-Class Regimes of Municipal Reformers." *Urban Affairs Review* 34 (5): 691–706.

Brooks, David. 2018. "One Reform to Save America." *New York Times* (May 31).

Bucchianeri, Peter. 2020. "Party Competition and Coalitional Stability: Evidence from American Local Government." *American Political Science Review* 114 (4): 1055–70.

Bucklin, James W. 1911. "The Grand Junction Plan of City Government and Its Results." *Annals of the American Academy of Political and Social Science* 38 (3): 87–102.

Buisseret, Peter, and Carlo Prato. 2021. "Strategic Truncation and Instant Runoff." Unpublished manuscript. June.

Burnett, Craig M. 2017. "Parties as an Organizational Force on Nonpartisan City Councils." Early online version. *Party Politics,* https://doi.org/10.1177 /135406881 7737996.

Burnett, Craig M., and Vladimir Kogan. 2015. "Ballot (and Voter) 'Exhaustion' under Instant Runoff Voting: An Examination of Four Ranked-Choice Elections." *Electoral Studies* 37: 41–49. https://doi.org/10.1016/j.electstud.2014.11.006.

Burnham, Robert A. 1990. "Pulling Together for Pluralism: Politics, Planning, and Government in Cincinnati, 1924–1959." PhD diss., University of Cincinnati.

Burnham, Robert A. 1997. "Reform, Politics, and Race in Cincinnati: Proportional Representation and the City Charter Committee, 1924–1959." *Journal of Urban History* 23 (2): 131–63.

Burnham, Robert A. 2013. "Women and Reform in Cincinnati: Responsible Citizenship and the Politics of 'Good Government,' 1924–1955." *Ohio Valley History* 13 (2): 48–69.

Burnham, Walter Dean. 1999. *United States Historical Election Returns, 1824–1968. ICPSR00001-v3.* Inter-university Consortium for Political/Social Research.

Busch, Ronald J. 1995. "Ashtabula: The Pioneer Community." Chap. 4 in *Proportional Representation and Election Reform in Ohio,* edited by Kathleen L. Barber, 83–115. Columbus: Ohio State University Press.

Calabrese, Stephen. 2000. "Multimember District Congressional Elections." *Legislative Studies Quarterly* 25 (4): 611–43.

Calabrese, Stephen. 2006. "An Explanation of the Continuing Federal Government Mandate of Single-member Congressional Districts." *Public Choice* 130 (January): 23–40.

Calvo, Ernesto. 2009. "The Competitive Road to Proportional Representation: Partisan Biases and Electoral Regime Change under Increasing Party Competition." *World Politics* 61 (2): 254–95.

Campbell, Angus, Philip Converse, Warren E. Miller, and Donald E. Stokes. 1960. *The American Voter.* New York: John Wiley & Sons.

Capeci, Doninic J. 1977. "From Different Liberal Perspectives: Fiorello H. La Guardia, Adam Clayton Powell, Jr., and Civil Rights in New York City, 1941–1943." *Journal of Negro History* 62 (2): 160–73.

Carey, John M., and Simon Hix. 2011. "The Electoral Sweet Spot: Low-Magnitude Proportional Electoral Systems." *American Journal of Political Science* 55 (2): 383–97.

Carey, John M., and Matthew S. Shugart. 1995. "Incentives to Cultivate a Personal Vote: A Rank Ordering of Electoral Formulas." *Electoral Studies* 14 (4): 417–39.

Carr, Jered B. 2015. "What Have We Learned about the Performance of Council-Manager Government? A Review and Synthesis of the Research." *Public Administration Review* 75 (5): 673–89.

Carty, R. Kenneth. 1981. *Party and Parish Pump: Electoral Politics in Ireland.* Waterloo: Wilfred Laurier University Press.

Catalinac, Amy, and Lucia Montoya. 2021. "Why Geographically-Targeted Spending under Closed-List Proportional Representation Favors Marginal Districts." *Electoral Studies* 71: 1–10. https://doi.org/10.1016/j.electstud.2021.102329.

Cerrone, Joseph, and Cynthia McClintock. 2021. "Ranked-Choice Voting, Runoff, and Democracy: Insights from Maine and Other U.S. States." Unpublished manuscript. March. https://doi.org/10.2139/ssrn.3769409.

Charles, Guy-Uriel E. 2003. "Racial Identity, Electoral Structures, and the First Amendment Right of Association." *California Law Review* 91 (5): 1209–80.

Chen, Jowei, and Jonathan A. Rodden. 2013. "Unintentional Gerrymandering: Political Geography and Electoral Bias in Legislatures." *Quarterly Journal of Political Science* 8: 239–69.

Childs, Richard S. 1949. "We Must Keep Ballot Short." *National Municipal Review* (July): 328–34.

Childs, Richard S. 1965. *The First Fifty Years of the Council-Manager Plan of Municipal Government.* New York: National Municipal League.

Choi, Cheon Geun, Jungah Bae, and Richard C. Feiock. 2013. "The Adoption and Abandonment of Council-Manager Government." *Public Administration Review* 73 (5): 727–36. https://doi.org/10.1111/puar.12097.

Clark, Alistair. 2012. "Party Organization and Concurrent Multi-level Local Campaigning: The 2007 Scottish Elections under MMP and STV." *Party Politics* 18 (4): 603–22.

Clark, Alistair. 2020. "The Effects of Electoral Reform on Party Campaigns, Voters and Party Systems at the Local Level: From Single Member Plurality to the Single Transferable Vote in Scotland." *Local Government Studies* 47 (1): 79–99.

Clyburn, James. 2020. "Runoff Elections Suppress Black Representation. Relegate Them to the Past." *Washington Post* (December 22). https://wapo.st/3p2eySK.

Cohen, Marty, David Karol, Hans Noel, and John Zaller. 2008. *The Party Decides: Presidential Nominations before and after Reform.* Chicago: University of Chicago Press.

Coll, Joseph A. 2021. "Demographic Disparities Using Ranked-Choice Voting? Ranking Difficulty, Under-Voting, and the 2020 Democratic Primary." *Politics and Governance* 9 (2): 293–305. https://doi.org/10.17645/pag.v9i2.3913.

Collett, Wallace T. 2002. *McCarthyism in Cincinnati: The Bettman-Collett Affair.* Rosemont, PA: Self-published.

Colomer, Josep M. 2005. "It's Parties That Choose Electoral Systems (or, Duverger's Laws Upside Down)." *Political Studies* 53: 1–21.

Colomer, Josep M. 2007. "On the Origins of Electoral Systems and Political Parties: The Role of Elections in Multi-member Districts." *Electoral Studies* 26: 262–73.

Colomer, Josep M., ed. 2011. "Personal Representation: The Neglected Dimension of Electoral Systems." Essex: ECPR Press.

Colomer, Josep M. 2017. "Party System Effects on Electoral Rules." In *Oxford Handbook of Electoral Systems,* edited by Erik Herron, Robert Pekkanen, and Matthew S. Shugart. London: Oxford University Press.

Commons, John R. 1893. "Proportional Representation." *Proportional Representation Review* 1 (1): 7–11.

Commons, John R. 1896. *Proportional Representation.* New York and Boston: Thomas Y. Crowell & Company.

Converse, Philip. 1964. "The Nature of Belief Systems in Mass Publics." In *Ideology and Discontent,* edited by David E. Apter, 206–61. New York: Free Press of Glencoe.

Cooley, Stoughton. 1893. "The Proportional Representation Congress." *Annals of the American Academy of Political and Social Science* 4 (November): 112–17.

Cossolotto, Matthew. 1993. "Forward." Chap. 1 in *Voting and Democracy Report,* edited by Robert Richie. Washington, DC: Center for Voting & Democracy.

Cox, Gary W. 1987. *The Efficient Secret: The Cabinet and the Development of Political Parties in Victorian England.* Cambridge: Cambridge University Press.

Cox, Gary W. 1997. *Making Votes Count: Strategic Coordination in the World's Electoral Systems.* Cambridge: Cambridge University Press.

Cox, Gary W., Jon H. Fiva, and Daniel M. Smith. 2019. "Parties, Legislators, and the Origins of Proportional Representation." *Comparative Political Studies* 51 (1): 102–33.

Cox, Gary W., and Jonathan N. Katz. 2002. *Elbridge Gerry's Salamander: The Electoral Consequences of the Reapportionment Revolution.* New York: Cambridge University Press.

Cox, Gary W., and Mathew D. McCubbins. 1993. *Legislative Leviathan: Party Government in the House*. Berkeley: University of California Press.

Cox, Gary W., and Mathew D. McCubbins. 2005. *Setting the Agenda: Responsible Party Government in the U.S. House of Representatives*. New York: Cambridge University Press.

Cross, William, and Jean-Benoit Pilet, eds. 2015. *The Politics of Party Leadership: A Cross-National Perspective*. Oxford: Oxford University Press.

Crowder-Meyer, Melody, Shana Kushner Gadarian, and Jessica Trounstine. 2019. "Voting Can Be Hard, Information Helps." *Urban Affairs Review* (February). 56 (1): 124–53. https://doi.org/10.1177/1078087419831074.

Cusack, Thomas R., Torben Iversen, and David Soskice. 2007. "Economic Interests and the Origins of Electoral Systems." *American Political Science Review* 101 (3): 373–91.

Dalton, Russell J. 2018. *Political Realignment: Economics, Culture, and Electoral Change*. New York: Oxford University Press.

Debnam, Geoffrey. 1994. "The Adversary Politics Thesis Revisited." *Parliamentary Affairs* 47 (3): 420.

DeCanio, Samuel. 2007. "Religion and Nineteenth-Century Voting Behavior: A New Look at Some Old Data." *Journal of Politics* 69 (2): 339–50.

DeLeon, Richard, Steven Hill, and Lisel Blash. 1998. "The Campaign for Proposition H and Preference Voting in San Francisco, 1996." *Representation* 35 (4): 265–74.

Dewan, Torun, Jaakko Meriläinen, and Janne Tukiainen. 2019. "Victorian Voting: The Origins of Party Orientation and Class Alignment." *American Journal of Political Science* 64 (4): 869–86.

Dhima, Kostanca, Sona N. Golder, Laura B. Stephenson, and Karine Van der Straeten. 2021. "Permissive Electoral Systems and Descriptive Representation." *Electoral Studies* 73.

Diamond, Larry. 2018. "A Victory for Democratic Reform." *The American Interest*. https://www.the-american-interest.com/2018/06/15/a-victory-for-democratic-reform/.

Disch, Lisa Jane. 2002. *The Tyranny of the Two-Party System*. New York: Columbia University Press.

Dobrusin, H. Manuel. 1955. "Proportional Representation in Massachusetts." PhD diss., Boston University.

Dominguez, Casey B. K. 2011. "Does the Party Matter? Endorsements in Congressional Primaries." *Political Research Quarterly* 64 (3): 534–44. https://doi.org/10.1177/1065912910376389.

Drutman, Lee. 2020. *Breaking the Two-Party Doom Loop: The Case for Multiparty Democracy in America*. New York: Oxford University Press.

Drutman, Lee, William A. Galston, and Tod Lindberg. 2018. *Spoiler Alert: Why Americans' Desires for a Third Party Are Unlikely to Come True*. White paper. Democracy Fund Voter Study Group.

Duverger, Maurice. 1954. *Political Parties: Their Organization and Activity in the Modern State*. New York: Wiley.

Dyck, Joshua J., and Mark Baldassare. 2009. "Process Preferences and Voting in Direct Democratic Elections." *Public Opinion Quarterly* 73 (3): 551–65.

Dyck, Joshua J., Shanna Pearson-Merkowitz, and Michael Coates. 2018. "Primary Distrust: Political Distrust and Support for the Insurgent Candidacies of Donald Trump and Bernie Sanders in the 2016 Primary." *PS: Political Science & Politics* 51 (2): 351–57. https://doi.org/10.1017/S1049096517002505.

Edwards, C. William. 1972. "The History of the Citizens' Plan E Association." Unpublished manuscript. January.

Eisenthal, David. 1983. "The Origins of Charter Reform in Worcester: With Particular Attention to Plan E." Honors thesis, Clark University.

Emmenegger, Patrick, and André Walter. 2019. "When Dominant Parties Adopt Proportional Representation: The Mysterious Case of Belgium." First view. *European Political Science Review.* https://doi.org/10.1017/S1755773919000225.

Engler, Irvin. 1921. "Sacramento's New Charter: Proportional Representation and the City Manager Plan Adopted by the Capital of California." *The American City* 24 (January): 4–5.

Engstrom, Erik J. 2004. "The United States: the Past—Moving from Diversity to Uniform Single-Member Districts." Chap. 7 in *Handbook of Electoral System Choice,* edited by Josep M. Colomer, 155–62. New York: Palgrave Macmillan.

Engstrom, Richard L. 1990. "Cincinnati's 1988 Proportional Representation Initiative." *Electoral Studies* 9 (3): 217–25.

Engstrom, Richard L. 2010. "Cumulative and Limited Voting: Minority Electoral Opportunities and More and More." *Saint Louis University Public Law Review* 1 (45): 97–138.

Ergun, Selim Jürgen. 2010. "From Plurality Rule to Proportional Representation." *Economics of Governance* 11 (4): 373–408.

Erie, Steven P. 1988. *Rainbow's End: Irish-Americans and the Dilemmas of Urban Machine Politics, 1840–1985.* Berkeley and Los Angeles, CA: University of California Press.

Evci, Uğurcan, and Marek Kaminski. 2020. "Shot in the Foot: Unintended Political Consequences of Electoral Engineering in the Turkish Parliamentary Elections in 2018." *Turkish Studies* 22 (3): 481–94. https://doi.org/10.1080/14683849.2020.1843443.

Fain, Howard. 1991. "District and Ethnic Loyalties under Proportional Representation in Worcester, 1949–1959." Typescript. https://jacksantucci.com/docs/prlibrary/fain_ethnic_worcester.pdf.

Fain, Howard. 2021. *Race, Runoffs, and Majority Requirements in Winner-Take-All Elections.* Online. https://www.prvoting.com/table-of-contents.

Farrell, Brian. 1985. "Ireland: From Friends and Neighbours to Clients and Partisans." In *Representatives of the People? Parliamentarians and Constituents in Western Democracies,* edited by Vernon Bogdanor, 237–64. London: Gower.

Farrell, David M., and Richard S. Katz. 2014. "Assessing the Proportionality of the Single Transferable Vote." *Representation* 50 (1): 13–26.

Farrell, David M., Malcolm Mackerras, and Ian McAllister. 1996. "Designing Electoral Institutions: STV Systems and their Consequences." *Political Studies* 44 (1): 24–43.

Farrell, David M., and Ian McAllister. 2005. "1902 and the Origins of Preferential Electoral Systems in Australia." *Australian Journal of Politics and History* 51 (2): 155–67.

Farrell, David M., and Ian McAllister. 2006. *The Australian Electoral System: Origins, Variations, and Consequences.* Sydney: University of New South Wales Press.

Feinstein, Michael. 2020. "Why California Should Learn from Maine and Not Alaska on Electoral Reform". *Independent Voter Network,* December. https://ivn.us/posts/why-california-should-learn-from-maine-and-not-alaska-on-electoral-reform.

Finer, Herman. 1924. *The Case against Proportional Representation.* Fabian Tract 211. London: Fabian Society.

Finer, Samuel E. 1975. *Adversary Politics and Electoral Reform.* London: Anthony Wigram.

Fiorina, Morris P. 1977. "An Outline for a Model of Party Choice." *American Journal of Political Science* 21 (3): 601–25.

Fiorina, Morris P. 1981. *Retrospective Voting in American Elections.* New Haven: Yale University Press.

Fiva, Jon H., and Askill H. Halse. 2016. "Local Favoritism in At-Large Proportional Representation Systems." *Journal of Public Economics* 143: 15–26. https://doi.org/10.1016/j.jpubeco.2016.08.002.

Flores, Nicolas. 1993. "A History of One-Winner Districts for Congress." Undergraduate thesis, Stanford University.

Fortunato, David. 2019. "The Electoral Implications of Coalition Policy Making." *British Journal of Political Science* 49 (1): 59–80.

Foulke, William Dudley. 1893. "Proportional Representation as a Remedy for Present Political Evils." *Proportional Representation Review* 1 (2): 37–51.

Francis, Megan Ming. 2019. "The Price of Civil Rights: Black Lives, White Funding, and Movement Capture." *Law & Society Review* 53 (1): 275–309.

Frazier, Erica. 2020. "The Single Transferable Vote Then and Now: Lowell, Massachusetts." Paper presented at the 2020 Annual Meeting of the Southern Political Science Association, January.

Frederickson, H. George, Gary A. Johnson, and Curtis H. Wood. 2004. *The Adapted City: Institutional Dynamics and Structural Change.* London: M.E. Sharpe.

Gallagher, Michael. 1978. "Party Solidarity, Exclusivity, and Inter-Party Relationships in Ireland, 1922–1977: The Evidence of Transfers." *Economic and Social Review* 10 (1): 1–22.

Gallup, Christopher M. 1921. "The First P.R. Election in New England." *National Municipal Review* (July): 357–58.

Gamm, Gerald H. 1989. *The Making of New Deal Democrats: Voting Behavior and Realignment in Boston, 1920–1940.* Chicago: University of Chicago Press.

Gamson, William. 1990. *Strategy of Social Protest.* 2nd e. Belmont: Wadsworth.

Garlick, Alex. 2015. "The Letter after Your Name: Party Labels on Virginia Ballots." *State Politics and Policy Quarterly* 15 (2): 147–70.

Geddes, Barbara. 1990. "How the Cases You Choose Affect the Answers You Get: Selection Bias in Comparative Politics." *Political Analysis* 2 (1): 131–50.

Gehl, Katherine M., and Michael E. Porter. 2018. "H.R.1 is a start, but we must do more for nonpartisan electoral reform." *The Hill* (December). https://thehill.com/blogs/congress-blog/politics/422344-hr1-is-a-start-but-we-must-do-more-for-nonpartisan-electoral.

Gehl, Katherine M., and Michael E. Porter. 2020. *The Politics Industry: How Political Innovation Can Break Partisan Gridlock and Save Our Democracy.* Cambridge, MA: Harvard Business Review Press.

Gilpin, Thomas. 1844. *On the Representation of Minorities of Electors to Act with the Majority in Elected Assemblies.* Philadelphia: John C. Clark.

Gimpel, James. 1996. *National Elections and the Autonomy of American State Party Systems.* Pittsburgh: University of Pittsburgh Press.

Gosnell, Harold F. 1930. "Motives for Voting as Shown by the Cincinnati P.R. Election of 1929." *National Municipal Review* (July): 471–76.

Gosnell, Harold F. 1939. "A List System with Single Candidate Preference." *American Political Science Review* 33 (4): 645–50. https://doi.org/10.2307/1949496.

Gove, William H. 1893. "The Gove System." *Proportional Representation Review* 1 (1): 20–23.

Gove, William H. 1894. "The Relation of the Gove System to Other Methods of Proportional Representation." *Proportional Representation Review* 2 (6): 41–47.

Graham, B. D. 1962. "The Choice of Voting Methods in Federal Poliitcs: 1902–1918." *Australian Journal of Politics and History* 8 (2): 164–181.

Gray, Kenneth E. 1959. *A Report on Politics in Cincinnati.* Technical report. Cambridge, MA: Joint Center for Urban Studies of the Massachusetts Institute of Technology and Harvard University.

Green, Donald, Bradley Palmquist, and Eric Schickler. 2002. *Partisan Hearts and Minds: Political Parties and the Social Identities of Voters.* New Haven and London: Yale University Press.

Grossmann, Matt, and David A. Hopkins. 2016. *Asymmetric Politics: Ideological Republicans and Group Interest Democrats.* New York: Oxford University Press.

Guinier, Lani. 1992. "The Representation of Minority Interests: The Question of Single-Member Districts." *Cardozo Law Review* 14: 1135–74.

Guinier, Lani, and Gerald Torres. 2003. *The Miner's Canary: Enlisting Race, Resisting Power, Transforming Democracy.* Cambridge, MA: Harvard University Press.

Hajnal, Zoltan. 2009. *America's Uneven Democracy: Turnout, Race, and Representation in City Politics.* New York: Cambridge University Press.

Hallett, George Hervey. 1935. "Wheeling Adopts P.R. and Manager." *National Municipal Review* (May): 276–77.

Hallett, George Hervey. 1937. "Hearne of Wheeling Added to P.R. Council." *National Municipal Review* (May): 263.

Hallett, George Hervey. 1941. "Approaching P.R. Elections, An Answer to Dr. Hermens, P.R. Meeting in St. Louis." *National Municipal Review* (October): 609–10.

Hallett, George Hervey. 1944. "Lowell's First P.R. Election." *National Municipal Review* (January): 45–49.

Hallett, George Hervey. 1945. "The First P.R. Election in Long Beach, NY." *National Municipal Review* (December): 581–2.

Hallett, George Hervey, and William Redin Woodward. 1947. "Coos Bay's First P.R. Election." *National Municipal Review* (January): 47.

Hallett, George Hervey, and William Redin Woodward. 1948a. "Hopkins, Minn., Conducts Its First P.R. Election." *National Municipal Review* (January): 396–97.

Hallett, George Hervey, and William Redin Woodward. 1948b. "Saugus, Mass., Holds First P.R. Election." *National Municipal Review* (April): 224–25.

Hallett, George Hervey, and William Redin Woodward. 1949. "P.R. League Loses Two Council Members." *National Municipal Review* (September): 412.

Hallett, George Hervey, and William Redin Woodward. 1950. "Atomic Town Uses P.R." *National Municipal Review* (January): 47–48.

Hare, Christopher, Tzu-Ping Liu, and Robert N. Lupton. 2018. "What Ordered Optimal Classification Reveals about Ideological Structure, Cleavages, and Polarization in the American Mass Public." Early online version. *Public Choice.*

Hare, Thomas. 1859. *A Treatise on the Election of Representatives, Parliamentary and Municipal.* London: Longman, Green, Longman, Roberts.

Harris, Joseph P. 1930. "The Practical Workings of Proportional Representation in the United States and Canada." *National Municipal Review* (May): 3–50.

Harris, Joseph P. 1934. "City Government in the United States. By Charles M. Kneier. (New York: Harper and Brothers. 1934. Pp. vii, 482.)" *American Political Science Review* 28 (5): 950–51. https://doi.org/10.2307/1947429.

Harris, Joseph P. 1951. *A Model Direct Primary Election System: Report of the Committee on Direct Primary.* New York: National Municipal League.

Hassell, Hans J. G. 2017. *The Party's Primary: Control of Congressional Nominations.* New York: Cambridge University Press.

Hatton, Augustus R. 1916. "The Ashtabula Plan: The Latest Step in Municipal Organization." *National Municipal Review* (January): 56–65.

Hatton, Augustus R. 1918. "Kalamazoo Tries Proportional Representation." *Proportional Representation Review* 47: 79–85.

Haynes, Bruce D. 2001. *Red Lines, Black Spaces: The Politics of Race and Space in a Black Middle-Class Suburb.* New Haven: Yale University Press.

Heckelman, Jac C. 1995. "The Effect of the Secret Ballot on Voter Turnout Rates." *Public Choice* 82 (1–2): 107–24.

Heckelman, Jac C. 2004. "The Secret Ballot Protects the Incumbency Advantage." *The Independent Review* 8 (3): 419–25.

Heisel, W. Donald. 1982. "Abandonment of Proportional Representaton and the Impact of 9-X voting in Cincinnati." Presented at the Annual Meeting of the American Political Science Association.

Heller, Abigail. 2021. "Public Support for Electoral Reform: The Role of Electoral System Experience." *Electoral Studies* 72: 1–10.

Hermens, Ferdinand A. 1936. "Proportional Representation and the Break-down of German Democracy." *Social Research* 3 (4): 411–33.

Hermens, Ferdinand A. 1941. *Democracy or Anarchy? A Study of Proportional Representation.* Vol. 1. South Bend: University of Notre Dame.

Hermens, Ferdinand A. 1943. *P.R., Democracy, and Good Government.* South Bend: The Review of Politics, University of Notre Dame.

Herz, Nathaniel. 2020. "An initiative proposes to overhaul Alaska's elections. But not everyone thinks they're broken." *Alaska Public Media* (September 28).

Hibbing, John R., and Elizabeth Theiss-Morse. 2002. *Stealth Democracy: Americans' Beliefs about How Government Should Work.* Cambridge: Cambridge University Press.

Hirano, Shigeo, and James M. Snyder. 2007. "The Decline of Third-Party Voting in the United States." *Journal of Politics* 69 (1): 1–16.

Hirczy de Miño, Wolfgang, and John C. Lane. 1996. "STV in Malta: Some Surprises." *Representation* 34 (1): 21–28. https://doi.org/10.1080/00344899608522982.

Hirczy de Miño, Wolfgang, and John C. Lane. 2000. "Malta: STV in a Two-Party System." Chap. 9 in *Elections in Australia, Ireland, and Malta under the Single Transferable Vote: Reflections on an Embedded Institution,* edited by Shaun Bowler and Bernard Grofman, 178–204. Ann Arbor: University of Michigan Press.

Hoag, Clarence Gilbert. 1913a. "The 'Representative Council Plan' of City Charter." *Equity* 15 (1): 74–83.

Hoag, Clarence Gilbert. 1913b. "The P. R. Campaign in Los Angeles." *Equity* 15 (2): 137–38.

Hoag, Clarence Gilbert. 1913c. "The P. R. Movement in the United States." *Equity* 15 (2): 138–39.

Hoag, Clarence Gilbert. 1914a. "A Protest." *Equity* 16 (1): 51–52.

Hoag, Clarence Gilbert. 1914b. *Effective Voting: Preferential Voting and Proportional Representation*. Technical report. Washington, DC: United States Government Printing Office, January.

Hoag, Clarence Gilbert. 1914c. "Proportional Representation, Preferential Voting, and Direct Primaries." *National Municipal Review* (January): 49–56.

Hoag, Clarence Gilbert. 1914d. "The P.R. Review: An Announcement." *Proportional Representation Review* 3 (32): 2.

Hoag, Clarence Gilbert, and George Hervey Hallett. 1926. *Proportional Representation*. New York: Macmillan.

Hoag, Clarence Gilbert, and George Hervey Hallett. 1932. "Consolidation of the P.R. League and the National Municipal League." *Proportional Representation Review* 3 (102): 1.

Holcomb, Horace Glenwood. 1929. "A Study of Proportional Representation in American Cities." PhD diss., University of Chicago.

Homeshaw, Judith. 2001. "Inventing Hare-Clark: The model arithmetocracy." Chap. 6 in *Elections: Full, Free and Fair*, edited by Marian Sawer, 96–114. Sydney: Federation Press.

Hout, Eliora van der, and Anthony J. McGann. 2009. "Liberal Political Equality Implies Proportional Representation." *Social Choice and Welfare* 33: 617–27.

Hull, Reginald Mott. 1912. "Preferential Voting and How it Works." *National Municipal Review* (July): 386–400.

Humphreys, John H. 1911. *Proportional Representation: A Study in Methods of Election*. London: Methuen.

Isaacs, Edith S. 1967. *Love Affair with a City: The Story of Stanley M. Isaacs*. New York: Random House.

Jacobs, Kristof, and Monique Leyenaar. 2011. "A Conceptual Framework for Major, Minor, and Technical Electoral Reform." *West European Politics* 34 (3): 495–513. https://doi.org/10.1080/01402382.2011.555977.

Jacobs, Kristof, and Simon Otjes. 2015. "Explaining the Size of Assemblies: A Longitudinal Analysis of the Design and Reform of Assembly Sizes in Democracies Around the World." *Electoral Studies* 40: 280–92.

James, Edmund T. 1896. "An Early Essay on Proportional Representation." *The Annals of the American Academy of Political and Social Science* 7 (March): 61–80.

Jenkins, Jeffery A., and Michael C. Munger. 2003. "Investigating the Incidence of Killer Amendments in Congress." *Journal of Politics* 65 (2): 498–517.

Jimenez, Benedict S. 2020. "Municipal Government Form and Budget Outcomes: Political Responsiveness, Bureaucratic Insulation, and the Budgetary Solvency of Cities." *Journal of Public Administration Research and Theory* 30 (1): 161–77.

Johnson, Douglas. 2014. *City Council Election Systems*. Technical report. Turlock, CA: National Demographics Corporation, March.

Johnson, Lewis Jerome. 1914. "Preferential Voting: Its Progress, with Comments and Warnings." *National Municipal Review* (January): 83–92.

Johnston, J. Paul, and Miriam Koene. 2000. "Learning History's Lessons Anew: The Use of STV in Canadian Municipal Eletions." Chap. 10 in *Elections in Australia, Ireland, and Malta under the Single Transferable Vote: Reflections on an Embedded Institution*, edited by Shaun Bowler and Bernard Grofman, 205–48. Ann Arbor: University of Michigan Press.

Jones-D'Agostino, Steven. 2004. "Whither Worcester? Some Look to a Change in Government for a Change in the City's Fortunes." *CommonWealth Magazine* (December 1). https://commonwealthmagazine.org/politics/whither-worcester/.

Karol, David. 2009. *Party Position Change in American Politics: Coalition Management.* Cambridge: Cambridge University Press.

Katz, Richard S. 2003. "Reforming the Italian Electoral Law, 1993." Chap. 5 in *Mixed-Member Electoral Systems: The Best of Both Worlds?*, edited by Matthew S. Shugart and Martin P. Wattenberg, 96–122. Cambridge: Oxford University Press.

Katznelson, Ira. 2013. *Fear Itself: The New Deal and the Origins of Our Time.* New York: W. W. Norton.

Katznelson, Ira, and Quinn Mulroy. 2012. "Was the South Pivotal? Situated Partisanship and Policy Coalitions during the New Deal and Fair Deal." *Journal of Politics* 74 (2): 604–20. https://doi.org/10.1017/S0022381611001940.

Keena, Alex, Michael Latner, Anthony J. McGann, and Charles Anthony Smith. 2021. *Gerrymandering the States: Partisanship, Race, and the Transformation of American Federalism.* New York: Cambridge University Press.

Keyssar, Alexander. 2000. *The Right to Vote: The Contested History of Democracy in the United States.* 1st ed. New York: Basic Books.

Kilgour, D. Marc, Jean-Charles Grégoire, and Angèle M. Foley. 2020. "The Prevalence and Consequences of Ballot Truncation in Ranked-Choice Elections." *Public Choice* 184: 197–218.

Kinder, Donald R., and Nathan P. Kalmoe. 2017. *Neither Liberal nor Conservative: Ideological Innocence in the American Public.* Chicago: University of Chicago Press.

Kingdon, John W. 1984. *Agendas, Alternatives, and Public Policies.* Boston: Little, Brown Co.

Kirkland, Justin H. 2014. "Chamber Size Effects on the Collaborative Structure of Legislatures." *Legislative Studies Quarterly* 39 (2): 169–98. https://doi.org/10.1111/lsq.12041.

Klüver, Heike, and Jae-Jae Spoon. 2019. "Helping or Hurting? How Governing as a Junior Coalition Partner Influences Electoral Outcomes." *Journal of Politics* 82 (4): 1231–42.

Kneier, Charles M. 1957. *City Government in the United States.* 3rd ed. New York: Harper.

Knight, Robert D. 2018. "Strategic Coalitions and Agenda-Setting in Fragmented Congresses: How the PRI Sets the Legislative Agenda in Mexico." *Brazilian Political Science Review* 12 (2): 1–33. https://doi.org/10.1590/1981-3821201800020001.

Koger, Gregory, Seth Masket, and Hans Noel. 2010. "Cooperative Party Factions in American Politics." *American Politics Research* 38 (1): 33–53. https://doi.org/10.1177/1532673X09353509.

Kolesar, Robert J. 1995. "PR in Cincinnati: From 'Good Government' to the Politics of Inclusion?" Chap. 6 in *Proportional Representation and Election Reform in Ohio*, edited by Kathleen L. Barber, 160–208. Columbus: Ohio State University Press.

Kolesar, Robert J. 1996. "Communism, Race, and the Defeat of Proportional Representation in Cold War America." Presented at the New England Historical Association Conference, Amherst College. April.

Kousser, Thad, Scott Lucas, Seth Masket, and Eric McGhee. 2015. "Kingmakers or Cheerleaders? Party Power and the Causal Effects of Endorsements." *Political Research Quarterly* 68 (3): 443–56. https://doi.org/10.1177/1065912915595882.

Kreuzer, Marcus. 2004. "Germany: Partisan Engineering of Personalized Proportional Representation." Chap. 11 in *Handbook of Electoral System Choice*, edited by Josep M. Colomer, 222–236. New York: Palgrave Macmillan.

Kreuzer, Marcus. 2010. "Historical Knowledge and Quantitative Analysis: The Case of the Origins of Proportional Representation." *American Political Science Review* 104 (2): 369–92.

Kuo, Didi, and Jan Teorell. 2017. "Illicit Tactics as Substitutes: Election Fraud, Ballot Reform, and Contested Congressional Elections in the United States, 1860–1930." *Comparative Political Studies* 50 (5): 665–696.

Laakso, Markku, and Rein Taagepera. 1979. "'Effective' Number of Parties: A Measure with Application to West Europe." *Comparative Political Studies* 12 (1): 3–27.

Latner, Michael, and Anthony McGann. 2005. "Geographical Representation under Proportional Representation: The Cases of Israel and the Netherlands." *Electoral Studies* 24: 709–34. https://doi.org/10.1016/j.electstud.2005.02.007.

Latner, Michael, Jack Santucci, and Matthew S. Shugart. 2021. "Multiseat Districts and Larger Assemblies Produce More Diverse Racial Representation." Unpublished manuscript. August. https://doi.org/10.2139/ssrn.3911532.

Lau, Olivia, Ryan T. Moore, and Michael Kellermann. 2007. "eiPack: $R \times C$ Ecological Inference and Higher-Dimension Data Management." *R News* 7 (2): 43–47.

Laver, Michael. 2000. "STV and the Politics of Coalition." Chap. 7 in *Elections in Australia, Ireland, and Malta under the Single Transferable Vote: Reflections on an Embedded Institution*, edited by Shaun Bowler and Bernard Grofman, 135–52. Ann Arbor: University of Michigan Press.

Leduc, Lawrence. 2002. "Opinion Change and Voting Behaviour in Referendums." *European Journal of Political Research* 41: 711–32.

Lee, Frances E. 2016. "Patronage, Logrolls, and 'Polarization': Congressional Parties of the Gilded Age, 1876–1896." *Studies in American Political Development* 30 (2): 116–27.

Leonard, Thomas C. 2016. *Illiberal Reformers: Race, Eugenics, and American Economics in the Progressive Era*. Princeton: Princeton University Press.

Leyenaar, Monique, and Reuven Y. Hazan. 2011. "Reconceptualising Electoral Reform." *West European Politics* 34 (3): 437–455.

Li, Yuhui. 2019. *Dividing the Rulers: How Majority Cycling Saves Democracy*. Ann Arbor: University of Michigan Press.

Lieberman, Evan. 2005. "Nested Analysis as a Mixed-Method Strategy for Comparative Research." *American Political Science Review* 99 (3): 435–52.

Lien, Arnold J. 1925. "Eight Years of Proportional Representaton in Boulder, Colorado." *Washington University Studies* 13 (October): 247–66.

Lijphart, Arend. 1977. *Democracy in Plural Societies: A Comparative Exploration*. New Haven: Yale University Press.

Lijphart, Arend. 1999. *Patterns of Democracy: Government Forms and Performance in Thirty-Six Countries*. New Haven: Yale University Press.

Lippmann, Walter. 1922. *Public Opinion*. New York: Harcourt, Brace & Co.

Lippmann, Walter. 1913 [1975]. "On Municipal Socialism." In *Socialism and the Cities*, edited by Bruce M. Stave, 184–97. New York: Kennikat Press.

Lipset, Seymour Martin. 1959. "Democracy and Working-Class Authoritarianism." *American Sociological Review* 24 (4): 482–501.

Lipset, Seymour Martin, and Stein Rokkan. 1967. *Party Systems and Voter Alignments: Cross-National Perspectives*. New York: Free Press.

Lipson, Leslie. 1948. *The Politics of Equality: New Zealand's Adventures in Democracy*. Chicago: University of Chicago Press.

Lockard, Duane. 1959. *New England State Politics*. Princeton: Princeton University Press.

Lodge, Henry Cabot. 1891. "Parliamentary Obstruction in the United States." *The Nineteenth Century* 29 (3): 423–28.

Lowi, Theodore J. 1983. "Toward a More Responsible Three-Party System: The Mythology of the Two-Party System and the Prospects for Reform." *PS* 16 (4): 699–706.

Lucas, Jack. 2019. "Reaction or Reform? Subnational Evidence on P.R. Adoption from Canadian Cities." *Representation* 56 (1): 89–109.

Lutz, Georg. 2004. "Switzerland: Introducing Proportional Representation from Below." Chap. 15 in *Handbook of Electoral System Choice*, edited by Josep M. Colomer, 279–93. New York: Palgrave Macmillan.

Maloy, J. S. 2019. *Smarter Ballots: Electoral Realism and Reform*. Cham, Switzerland: Palgrave Macmillan.

Marschall, Melissa, Paru Shah, and Anirudh Ruhil. 2011. "Editors' Introduction: A Looking Glass into the Future." *PS: Political Science & Politics* 44 (1): 97–100.

Marsh, Michael. 2000. "Candidate Centered but Party Wrapped: Campaigning in Ireland under STV." Chap. 6 in *Elections in Australia, Ireland, and Malta under the Single Transferable Vote: Reflections on an Embedded Institution*, edited by Shaun Bowler and Bernard Grofman, 114–30. Ann Arbor: University of Michigan Press.

Martin, Shane. 2014. "Why Electoral Systems Don't Always Matter: The Impact of 'Mega-seats' on Legislative Behaviour in Ireland." *Party Politics* 20 (3): 467–79. https://doi.org/10.1177/1354068811436061.

Masket, Seth. 2009. *No Middle Ground: How Informal Party Organizations Control Nominations and Polarize Legislatures*. Ann Arbor: University of Michigan Press.

Masket, Seth. 2016. *The Inevitable Party: Why Attempts to Kill the Party System Fail and How They Weaken Democracy*. New York: Oxford University Press.

Masket, Seth, and Boris Shor. 2014. "Polarization without Parties: Term Limits and Legislative Partisanship in Nebraska's Unicameral Legislature." *State Politics & Policy Quarterly* 15 (1): 67–90. https://doi.org/10.1177/1532440014564984.

Maxey, Chester Collins. 1922. "The Cleveland Election and the New Charter." *American Political Science Review* 16 (1): 83–86.

McBain, Howard Lee. 1922. "Proportional Representation in American Cities." *Political Science Quarterly* 37 (2): 281–98.

McCaffrey, George H. 1938. "New York's 1937 Election and Its Results." *National Municipal Review* (January): 39–45.

McCaffrey, George H. 1939. "Proportional Representation in New York City." *American Political Science Review* 33 (5): 841–52.

McCarthy, Devin, and Jack Santucci. 2021. "Ranked-Choice Voting as a Generational Issue in Modern American Politics." *Politics and Policy* 49 (1): 33–60.

McCarthy, John D., and Mayer N. Zald. 1977. "Resource Mobilization and Social Movements: A Partial Theory." *American Journal of Sociology* 82 (6): 1212–41.

McCarty, Nolan, and Eric Schickler. 2018. "On the Theory of Parties." *Annual Review of Political Science* 21: 175–93. https://doi.org/10.1146/annurev-polisci-061915-123020.

McClintock, Cynthia. 2018. *Electoral Rules and Democracy in Latin America*. New York: Oxford University Press.

McConnaughy, Corrine M. 2013. *The Woman Suffrage Movement in America: A Reassessment*. New York: Cambridge University Press.

McCrackan, W. D. 1893. "Ticino as an Object Lesson." *Proportional Representation Review* 1 (1): 11–15.

McDaniel, Jason A. 2018. "Does More Choice Lead to Reduced Racially Polarized Voting? Assessing the Impact of Ranked-Choice Voting in Mayoral Elections." *California Journal of Politics and Policy* 10 (2): 1–24.

McGann, Anthony J., and Michael Latner. 2012. "The Calculus of Consensus Democracy: Rethinking *Patterns of Democracy* without Veto-Players." *Comparative Political Studies* 46 (7): 823–50. https://doi.org/10.1177/0010414012463883.

McGann, Anthony J., Charles Anthony Smith, Michael Latner, and Alex Keena. 2016. *Gerrymandering in America: The House of Representatives, the Supreme Court, and the Future of Popular Sovereignty.* New York: Cambridge University Press.

McGarry, John, and Brendan O'Leary. 2006. "Consociational Theory, Northern Ireland's Conflict, and its Agreement. Part 1: What Consociationalists Can Learn from Northern Ireland." *Government & Opposition* 41 (1): 43–63.

McGhee, Eric, and Boris Shor. 2017. "Has the Top Two Primary Elected More Moderates?" *Perspectives on Politics* 15 (4): 1053–66. https://doi.org/10.1017/S1537592 717002158.

Michelson, Melissa R., and Scott J. Susin. 2004. "What's in a Name: The Power of Fusion Politics in a Local Election." *Polity* 36 (2): 301–21. https://doi.org/10.1086/POLv36n2ms3235483.

Mill, John Stuart. 1861. *Considerations on Representative Government.* London: Parker, Son, & Bourn.

Millard, Walter J. 1923. "City Manager and P. R. Charter Sustained in Boulder." *National Municipal Review* (September): 532–35.

Millard, Walter J. 1924. "Why a New Government was Proposed for Cincinnati." *National Municipal Review* (November): 601–605.

Millard, Walter J. 1943. "How Important Is a Label?" *National Municipal Review* (May): 250–51.

Miller, Gary, and Norman Schofield. 2003. "Activists and Partian Realignment in the United States." *American Political Science Review* 97 (2): 245–60.

Miller, Gary, and Norman Schofield. 2008. "The Transformation of the Republican and Democratic Party Coalitions in the U.S." *Perspectives on Politics* 6 (3): 433–450.

Miller, Michael A. 2007. "The Littlest District." *Anton News* (May).

Miller, Zane L., and Bruce Tucker. 1990. "The New Urban Politics: Planning and Development in Cincinnati, 1954–1988." Chap. 5 in *Snowbelt Cities: Metropolitan Politics in the Northeast and Midwest since World War II,* edited by Richard M. Bernard, 91–108. Bloomington and Indianapolis: Indiana University Press.

Mitchell, Paul. 2014. "The Single Transferable Vote and Ethnic Conflict: The Evidence from Northern Ireland." *Electoral Studies* 33: 246–57.

Monti, William A. 2011. *Publisher vs. Politician: A Clash of Local Titans.* Waterbury, CT: Lulu Press.

Moskowitz, Daniel J., and Jon C. Rogowski. 2019. "Democracy Thrives in Secret? Ballot Reform and Representation in the United States." Working paper, April.

Mott, Rodney L. 1926. "Invalid Ballots under the Hare System of Proportional Representation." *American Political Science Review* 20 (4): 874–82. https://doi.org/10.1017/S0003055400110536.

Mudde, Cas, and Cristobal Rovira Kaltwasser. 2017. *Populism: A Very Short Introduction.* New York: Oxford University Press.

Nagel, Jack H. 1993. "Populism, Heresthetics and Political Stability: Richard Seddon and the Art of Majority Rule." *British Journal of Political Science* 23 (2): 139–74.

Nagel, Jack H. 1996. "Constitutional Reform and Social Difference in New Zealand." *Cardozo Journal of International and Comparative Law* 4 (2): 373–94.

Nagel, Jack H. 1998. "Social Choice in a Pluralitarian Democracy: The Politics of Market Liberalization in New Zealand." *British Journal of Political Science* 28 (2): 223–67.

Nagel, Jack H. 2006. "Occam No, Archimedes Yes." Chap. 7 in *Democratic Politics and Party Competition: Essays in Honour of Ian Budge,* edited by Judith Bara and Albert Weale, 143–57. London: Routledge.

Nagel, Jack H. 2007. "The Burr Dilemma in Approval Voting." *Journal of Politics* 69 (1): 43–58. https://doi.org/10.1111/j.1468-2508.2007.00493.x.

Nanson, Edward J. 1882. "Methods of Election." *Transactions and Proceedings of the Royal Society of Victoria* 18: 197–240.

National Municipal League. 1921. *Progress Report on a Model State Constitution.* New York: National Municipal League.

National Municipal League. 1924. *A Model State Constitution.* New York: National Municipal League.

Natoli, Salvatore J. 1971. "Zoning and the Development of Urban Land Use Patterns." *Economic Geography* 47 (2): 171–84.

Neely, Francis, and Corey Cook. 2008. "Whose Votes Count? Undervotes, Overvotes, and Ranking in San Francisco's Instant-Runoff Elections." *American Politics Research* 36 (4): 530–54.

Neely, Francis, and Jason A. McDaniel. 2015. "Overvoting and the Equality of Voice under Instant-Runoff Voting in San Francisco." *California Journal of Politics & Policy* 7 (4): 1–27. https://doi.org/10.5070/P2cjpp7428929.

Noel, Hans. 2013. *Political Parties and Political Ideologies in America.* New York: Cambridge University Press.

Nohlen, Dieter. 1984. "Changes and Choices in Electoral Systems." Chap. 21 in *Choosing an Electoral System: Issues and Alternatives,* edited by Arend Lijphart and Bernard Grofman, 217–24. New York: Praeger.

None. 1956. "The Powell Amendment." *The Harvard Crimson* (March).

None. 1963. "Powell's Amendments." *The Harvard Crimson* (May).

Orren, Karen, and Stephen Skowronek. 2004. *The Search for American Political Development.* Cambridge: Cambridge University Press.

Penadés, Alberto. 2008. "Choosing Rules for Government: The Institutional Preferences of Early Socialist Parties." Chap. 7 in *Controlling Governments: Voters, Institutions, and Accountability,* edited by José Maria Maravall and Ignacio Sánches-Cuenca, 202–46. New York: Cambridge University Press.

Persson, Torsten, Gerard Roland, and Guido Tabellini. 2007. "Electoral Rules and Government Spending in Parliamentary Democracies." *Quarterly Journal of Economics* 2 (2): 155–188. https://doi.org/10.1561/100.00006019.

Pilet, Jean-Benoit, and Damien Bol. 2011. "Party Preferences and Electoral Reform: How Time in Government Affects the Likelihood of Supporting Electoral Change." *West European Politics* 34 (3): 568–86. https://doi.org/10.1080/01402382.2011.555984.

Pilon, Dennis. 2006. "Explaining Voting System Reform in Canada, 1874 to 1960." *Journal of Canadian Studies* 40 (3): 135–61.

Pilon, Dennis. 2013. *Wrestling with Democracy: Voting Systems as Politics in the Twentieth-Century West.* Toronto: University of Toronto Press.

Plescia, Carolina, André Blais, and John Högstrom. 2020. "Do People Want a 'Fairer' Electoral System? An Experimental Study in Four Countries." *European Journal of Political Research* 59: 753–51. https://doi.org/10.1111/1475-6765.12372.

Poole, Keith T. 2000. "Nonparametric Unfolding of Binary Choice Data." *Political Analysis* 8 (3): 211–37.

Poole, Keith T. 2005. *Spatial Models of Parliamentary Voting.* New York: Cambridge University Press.

Poole, Keith T., and Howard Rosenthal. 1988. *Political Realignment in American History: Results from a Spatial Scaling of the Congressional Roll Call Record.* Technical report. Carnegie Mellon University.

Poole, Keith T., and Howard Rosenthal. 1997. *Congress: A Political-Economic History of Roll Call Voting.* New York: Oxford University Press.

Porter, Melvin P. 1914. "Preferential Voting and the Rule of the Majority." *National Municipal Review* (July): 581–85.

Powell, Jr., Adam Clayton. 1971. *Adam by Adam: The Autobiography of Adam Clayton Powell, Jr.* New York: Dial Press.

Powell, G. Bingham. 2000. *Elections as Instruments of Democracy: Majoritarian and Proportional Visions.* New Haven: Yale University Press.

Prosterman, Daniel O. 2013. *Defining Democracy: Electoral Reform and the Struggle for Power in New York City.* New York: Oxford University Press.

Quade, Quentin. 1991. "PR and Democratic Statecraft." *Journal of Democracy* 2 (3): 36–41.

Rae, Douglas W. 1967. *The Political Consequences of Electoral Laws.* New Haven: Yale University Press.

Rae, Douglas W. 1968. "A Note on the Fractionalization of Some European Party Systems." *Comparative Political Studies* 1 (3): 413–18.

Ranney, Austin. 1968. "The Representativeness of Primary Electorates." *Midwest Journal of Political Science* 12 (2): 224–38.

Reed, Thomas H., Doris D. Reed, and Ralph A. Straetz. 1957. *Has PR Worked for the Good of Cincinnati? An Appraisal of Cincinnati's Method of Electing Council, 1925–1956.* Cincinnati: Stephen H. Wilder Foundation.

Reilly, Benjamin. 2001. *Democracy in Divided Societies: Electoral Engineering for Conflict Management.* Cambridge: Cambridge University Press.

Reilly, Benjamin. 2021. "Ranked Choice Voting in Australia and America: Do Voters Follow Party Cues?" *Politics and Governance* 9 (2): 271–79.

Reilly, Benjamin, and Michael Maley. 2000. "The Single Transferable Vote and Alternative Vote Compared." Chap. 3 in *Elections in Australia, Ireland, and Malta under the Single Transferable Vote: Reflections on an Embedded Institution,* edited by Shaun Bowler and Bernard Grofman, 37–58. Ann Arbor: University of Michigan Press.

Reilly, Benjamin, and Jack Santucci. 2021. "Are 'Come-from-Behind' RCV Winners Different? A Comparative Analysis." Paper presented at the 2021 Annual Meeting of the American Political Science Association, September.

Reilly, Benjamin, and Jack Stewart. 2021. "Compulsory Preferential Voting, Social Media and 'Come-from-Behind' Electoral Victories in Australia." *Australian Journal of Political Science* 56 (1): 99–112.

Renwick, Alan. 2010. *The Politics of Electoral Reform: Changing the Rules of Democracy.* Cambridge: Cambridge University Press.

Renwick, Alan, and Jean-Benoit Pilet. 2016. *Faces on the Ballot: The Personalization of Electoral Systems in Europe.* Oxford and New York: Oxford University Press.

Rice, Bradley Robert. 1977. *Progressive Cities: The Commission Government Movement in America, 1901–1920.* Austin: University of Texas Press.

Richie, Robert. 2004. "Instant Runoff Voting: What Mexico (and Others) Could Learn." *Election Law Journal* 3 (3): 501–12.

Riker, William H. 1962. *The Theory of Political Coalitions.* New Haven: Yale University Press.

Riker, William H. 1980. "Implications from the Disequillbrium of Majority Rule for the Study of Institutions." *American Political Science Review* 74 (2): 432–46.

Riker, William H. 1982. "The Two-Party System and Duverger's Law: An Essay on the History of Political Science." *American Political Science Review* 76 (4): 753–66.

Rodden, Jonathan A. 2019. *Why Cities Lose: The Deep Roots of the Urban-Rural Political Divide.* New York: Basic Books.

Roher, Miriam. 1939. "A Taft in City Hall." *National Municipal Review* (October): 694–748.

Rokkan, Stein. 1970. *Citizens, Elections, Parties: Approaches to the Comparative Study of the Processes of Development.* Oslo: Universitet-forlaget.

Rosenfeld, Sam. 2020. "It Takes Three (or More)." *Boston Review* (March 17). Online at http://bostonreview.net/politics/sam-rosenfeld-it-takes-three-or-more.

Rosenthal, Howard, and Erik Voeten. 2004. "Analyzing Roll Calls with Perfect Spatial Voting: France 1946–1958." *American Journal of Political Science* 48 (3): 620–32.

Samuels, David J., and Matthew S. Shugart. 2010. *Presidents, Parties, and Prime Ministers: How the Separation of Powers Affects Party Organization and Behavior.* New York: Cambridge University Press.

Sanders, William. 2011. "Alice's Unrepresentative Council: Cause for Intervention?" *Australian Journal of Political Science* 46 (4): 699–706.

Santucci, Jack. 2017. "Party Splits, Not Progressives: The Origins of Proportional Representation in American Local Government." *American Politics Research* 45 (3): 494–526. https://doi.org/10.1177/1532673X16674774.

Santucci, Jack. 2018a. "Evidence of a Winning-Cohesion Tradeoff under Multiwinner Ranked-Choice Voting." *Electoral Studies* 52: 128–38. https://doi.org/10.1016/j.electstud.2017.11.003.

Santucci, Jack. 2018b. "Maine Ranked-Choice Voting as a Case of Electoral-System Change." *Representation* 54 (3): 297–311. https://doi.org/10.1080/00344893.2018.1502208.

Santucci, Jack. 2019. "Factional Voting in Local Elections: The Case of Cambridge, MA." *Urban Affairs Forum* (February 7). Online at https://urbanaffairsreview.com/2019/02/07/factional-voting-in-local-elections-the-case-of-cambridge-ma/.

Santucci, Jack. 2021. "Variants of Ranked-Choice Voting from a Strategic Perspective." *Politics and Governance* 9 (2): 344–53. https://doi.org/10.17645/pag.v9i2.3955.

Santucci, Jack, and Larry Diamond. 2018. "How Ranked-Choice Voting Could Empower Independents and Make American Elections More Inclusive." Key Findings Brief. Scholars Strategy Network, February.

Sarasohn, David. 1989. *The Party of Reform: Democrats in the Progressive Era.* Jackson: University Press of Mississippi.

Schaffner, Brian F., Matthew J. Streb, and Gerald C. Wright. 2001. "Teams without Uniforms: The Nonpartisan Ballot in State and Local Elections." *Political Research Quarterly* 54 (1): 7–30. https://doi.org/10.1177/106591290105400101.

Schaffner, Brian F., Matthew J. Streb, and Gerald C. Wright. 2007. "A New Look at the Republican Advantage in Nonpartisan Elections." *Political Research Quarterly* 60 (2): 240–49.

Schattschneider, Elmer E. 2004 [1942]. *Party Government*. New Brunswick, NJ: Transaction.

Schiesl, Martin J. 1975. "Progressive Reform in Los Angeles under Mayor Alexander, 1909–1913." *California Historical Quarterly* 54 (1): 37–56.

Schlozman, Daniel. 2015. *When Movements Anchor Parties: Electoral Alignments in American History*. Princeton: Princeton University Press.

Schulze, Markus. 2011. "Free Riding and Vote Management under Proportional Representation by the Single Transferable Vote." Typescript, March.

Schwartz, Joel. 1993. *The New York Approach: Robert Moses, Urban Liberals, and Redevelopment of the Inner City*. Columbus: Ohio State University Press.

Schwartz, Thomas. 1989. "Why Parties?" Typescript, UCLA.

Schwartz, Thomas. 2021. "Parties." *Constitutional Political Economy*. https://doi.org/10.1007/s10602-021-09326-w.

Seasongood, Murray L. 1933. *Local Government in the United States: A Challenge and an Opportunity*. Cambridge, MA: Harvard University Press.

Sharman, Campbell, Anthony M. Sayers, and Narelle Miragliotta. 2002. "Trading Party Preferences: The Australian Experience of Preferential Voting." *Electoral Studies* 21 (4): 543–60. https://doi.org/10.1016/S0261-3794(01)00012-9.

Shaw, Frederick. 1954. *The History of the New York City Legislature*. New York: Columbia University Press.

Shefter, Martin. 1986. "Political Incorporation and the Extrusion of the Left: Party Politics and Social Forces in New York City." *Studies in American Political Development* 1 (March): 50–90.

Shor, Boris, and Nolan McCarty. 2011. "The Ideological Mapping of American State Legislatures." *American Political Science Review* 105 (3): 530–51.

Shugart, Matthew S. 2003. "'Extreme' Electoral Systems and the Appeal of the Mixed-Member Alternative." Chap. 2 in *Mixed-Member Electoral Systems: The Best of Both Worlds?*, edited by Matthew S. Shugart and Martin P. Wattenberg, 25–54. Oxford: Oxford University Press.

Shugart, Matthew S. 2008. "Inherent and Contingent Factors in Reform Initiation in Plurality Systems." Chap. 1 in *To Keep or to Change First Past the Post? the Politics of Electoral Reform*, edited by André Blais, 7–60. Oxford: Oxford University Press.

Shugart, Matthew S., and Rein Taagepera. 2017. *Votes from Seats: Logical Models of Electoral Systems*. Cambridge and New York: Cambridge University Press. https://doi.org/10.1017/9781108261128.

Shugart, Matthew S., and Martin P. Wattenberg. 2003. *Mixed-Member Electoral Systems: The Best of Both Worlds?* New York: Oxford University Press.

Sides, John, Chris Tausanovitch, Lynn Vavreck, and Christopher Warshaw. 2018. "On the Representativeness of Primary Electorates." Online. *British Journal of Political Science*. https://doi.org/10.1017/S000712341700062X.

Sigafoos, Robert Alan. 1955. *The Municipal Income Tax: Its History and Problems*. Chicago: Public Information Service.

Silbernagel, Bob. 2021a. "First Grand Junction City Charter Led Nation in Innovation." *The Daily Sentinel* (April). https://www.gjsentinel.com/news/western_colorado/first-grand-junction-city-charter-led-nation-in-innovation/article_b986db5e-93e6-11eb-91d5-d35c7f51c0ec.html.

Silbernagel, Bob. 2021b. "Socialism Had a Brief Run in Grand Junction's Political Realm." *The Daily Sentinel* (April). https://www.gjsentinel.com/news/western_colorado/

socialism-had-a-brief-run-in-grand-junction-s-political-realm/article_8247ff0e-9e47-11eb-bc46-139a70889f1f.html.

Sitton, Tom. 1995. "Proportional Representation and the Decline of Progressive Reform in Los Angeles." *Southern California Quarterly* 77 (4): 347–64.

Smith, Daniel A., and Dustin Fridkin. 2008. "Delegating Direct Democracy: Interparty Legislative Competition and the Adoption of the Initiative in the American States." *American Political Science Review* 102 (3): 333–50. https://doi.org/10.1017/S0003055408080258.

Sorens, Jason. 2016. "The False Promise of Instant Runoff Voting." Cato Institute. https://www.cato-unbound.org/2016/12/09/jason-sorens/false-promise-instant-runoff-voting.

Southwick, Al. 2017. "Proportional Representation for National Elections?" *Telegram.com* (January). https://www.telegram.com/opinion/20170112/al-southwick-proportional-representation-for-national-elections.

Sowers, Don C. 1934. "Sixteen Years of P. R. in Boulder." *National Municipal Review* (January): 27–30.

Spalding, Eliot. 1987a. "How City's Plan E System Came to Be." *Cambridge Chronicle* (November).

Spalding, Eliot. 1987b. "Plan E Debate Split the City in 1938." *Cambridge Chronicle* (October).

Spence, Catherine H. 1893. "Effective Voting." *Proportional Representation Review* 1 (1): 15–20.

Spoon, Jae-Jae, and Heike Klüver. 2019. "Party Convergence and Vote Switching: Explaining Mainstream Party Decline across Europe." *European Journal of Political Research* 58 (4): 1021–42. https://doi.org/10.1111/1475-6765.12331.

Stephenson, Charles M. 1938. "Norris, Tennessee, Uses P.R." *National Municipal Review* (March): 173.

Stevens, Mark H. 2003. "The Los Angeles Municipal Conference of 1913: Stemming the Neo-Conservative Tide." *Southern California Quarterly* 85 (1): 29–82.

Stoll, Heather. 2013. *Changing Societies, Changing Party Systems*. New York: Cambridge University Press.

Straetz, Ralph A. 1958. *PR Politics in Cincinnati: Thirty-Two Years of City Government through Proportional Representation*. New York: New York University Press.

Strøm, Kaare. 1990. *Minority Government and Majority Rule*. Cambridge: Cambridge University Press.

Sugrue, Thomas. 2014. *The Origins of the Urban Crisis: Race and Inequality in Postwar Detroit*. Princeton: Princeton University Press.

Taagepera, Rein, and Matthew S. Shugart. 1989. *Seats & Votes: The Effects and Determinants of Electoral Systems*. New Haven: Yale University Press.

Taft, Charles Phelps. 1971 [1933]. *City Management: The Cincinnati Experience*. Port Washington, NY: Kennikat Press.

Tamas, Bernard Ivan. 2006. "A Divided Political Elite: Why Congress Banned Multimember Districts in 1842." *New Political Science* 28 (1): 24–44.

Tanzer, Laurence Arnold. 1936. "The Proposed New York City Charter." *National Municipal Review* (September): 535–52.

Tanzer, Laurence Arnold. 1937. *The New York City Charter*. New York: Clark Boardman Co.

Taylor, C. F. 1913. "The Preferential Ballot for Insuring Election by a Majority." *Equity* 15 (1): 59–61.

Taylor, Steven L., Matthew S. Shugart, Arend Lijphart, and Bernard Grofman. 2014. *A Different Democracy: American Government in a Thirty-One-Country Perspective.* New Haven: Yale University Press.

Taylor, William S. 1948. "Three Methods of Voting." *The Scientific Monthly* 67 (7): 297–301.

The Editors. 1913a. "How to Mark Your Ballot Tomorrow—Sample Ballot—Recommendations of The Citizen's Committee of One Thousand." *Los Angeles Times* (March): 101.

The Editors. 1913b. "Tomorrow's Important Election: The Proposed Charter Amendments Dissected One by One, and Made Understandable—Socialist Designs Exposed." *Los Angeles Times* (March): II-2.

The Editors. 1913c. "Women Take Stump." *Los Angeles Times* (March): II-16.

The Editors. 1915. "Ashtabula Gets Hare System." *Akron Beacon Journal* (August): 7.

The Editors. 1961. "The City Election." *The Harvard Crimson* (November).

The Editors. 2018. "A Congress for Every American." *New York Times* (November).

Thompson, Carl. 1913. "The Vital Points in Charter Making from a Socialist Point of View." *National Municipal Review* (July): 416–426.

Thürk, Maria, and Heike Klüver. 2021. "The Electoral Implications of Minority Cabinets." Paper presented at the 2021 Annual Conference of the European Political Science Association.

Tilly, Charles, and Lesley J. Wood. 2013. *Social Movements, 1768-2012.* Third ed. Boulder and London: Paradigm Publishers.

Trebbi, Francesco, Philippe Aghion, and Alberto Alesina. 2008. "Electoral Rules and Minority Representation in U.S. Cities." *Quarterly Journal of Economics* 123 (1): 325–57.

Treier, Shawn, and D. Sunshine Hillygus. 2009. "The Nature of Political Ideology in the Contemporary Electorate." *Public Opinion Quarterly* 73 (4): 679–703. https://doi.org/10.1093/poq/nfp067.

Trounstine, Jessica. 2008. *Political Monopolies in American Cities: The Rise and Fall of Bosses and Reformers.* Chicago: University of Chicago Press.

Tullock, Gordon. 1970. "A Simple Algebraic Logrolling Model." *American Economic Review* 60 (3): 419–26.

U.S. Dept. of Commerce, Bureau of the Census. 1978. "County and City Data Book [United States] Consolidated File: City Data, 1944-1977." http://doi.org/10.3886/ICPSR07735.v1.

U'Ren, William Simon. 1896. "Direct Legislation. Without Any Constitution Changing—Will Not Do to Wait for That." Edited by Eltweed Pomeroy. *Direct Legislation Record* 3 (2): 16.

Uscinski, Joseph E., Adam M. Enders, Michelle I. Seelig, Casey A. Klofstad, John R. Funchion, Caleb Everett, Stefan Wuchty, Kamal Premaratne, and Manohar N. Murthi. 2021. "American Politics in Two Dimensions: Partisan and Ideological Identities versus Anti-Establishment Orientations." *American Journal of Political Science* 65 (4): 877–95. https://doi.org/10.1111/ajps.12616.

Valelly, Richard M. 2009. "The Reed Rules and Republican Party Building: A New Look." *Studies in American Political Development* 23: 115–42.

Velde, Henk te. 2013. "Parliamentary Obstruction and the 'Crisis' of European Parliamentary Politics around 1900." *Redescriptions: Political Thought, Conceptual History and Feminist Theory* 16 (1): 125–47. https://doi.org/10.7227/R.16.1.7.

Vesely, Joseph P. 1970. "History of the Hopkins City Charter." Online at http://www.hopkinsmn.com/archives/pdf/hopkins-charter.pdf. February.

Vowles, Jack. 1995. "The Politics of Electoral Reform in New Zealand." *International Political Science Review* 16 (1): 95–115.

Vowles, Jack. 2008. "Systemic Failure, Coordination, and Contingencies: Understanding Electoral System Change in New Zealand." Chap. 6 in *To Keep or to Change First Past the Post? The Politics of Electoral Reform*, edited by André Blais. https://doi.org/10.1093/acprof:oso/9780199539390.003.0007.

Vowles, Jack. 2013. "Campaign Claims, Partisan Cues, and Media Effects in the 2011 British Electoral System Referendum." *Electoral Studies* 23: 253–264. https://doi.org/10.1016/j.electstud.2012.10.009.

Walter, André. 2021. "Socialist Threat? Radical Party Entry, Electoral Alliances, and the Introduction of Proportional Representation." *American Political Science Review* 115 (2): 701–8.

Walter, André, and Patrick Emmenegger. 2021. "Disproportional Threat: Redistricting as an Alternative to Proportional Representation." *Journal of Politics* 83 (3): 917.

Walter, André, and Patrick Emmenegger. 2019. "Majority Protection: The Origins of Distorted Proportional Representation." *Electoral Studies* 59: 64–77. https://doi.org/10.1016/j.electstud.2019.02.002.

Ware, William R. 1873. "The Preferential Vote." In *The Election of Representatives, Parliamentary and Municipal, a Treatise Adapting the Proposed Law to the Ballot, with Appendices on the Preferential and the Cumulative Vote*, 4th ed., edited by Thomas Hare, 351–5. London: Longmans, Green, Reader, and Dyer.

Weaver, Leon. 1982. "Two Cheers for Proportional Representation in Cambridge, Massachusetts." Paper presented at the Annual Meeting of the American Political Science Association, September.

Weaver, Leon. 1986. "The Rise, Decline, and Resurrection of Proportional Representation in Local Governments in the United States." Chap. 8 in *Electoral Laws and Their Political Consequences*, edited by Bernard Grofman and Arend Lijphart, 139–53. New York: Agathon Press.

Weaver, Leon, and James L. Blount. 1995. "Hamilton: PR Defeated by Its Own Success." Chap. 7 in *Proportional Representation and Election Reform in Ohio*, edited by Kathleen L. Barber, 209–40. Columbus: Ohio State University Press.

Weaver, R. Kent. 2003. "Electoral Rules and Electoral Reform in Canada." Chap. 24 in *Mixed-Member Electoral Systems: The Best of Both Worlds?*, edited by Matthew S. Shugart and Martin P. Wattenberg, 542–70. Oxford: Oxford University Press.

Weaver, Timothy P. R. 2021. "Trying Out Our Ideas: Enterprise Zones in the United States and the United Kingdom." Chap. 11 in *How Ideas Shape Urban Political Development*, edited by Richardson Dilworth, 156–70. Philadelphia: University of Pennsylvania Press.

Weeks, O. Douglas. 1937. "Summary of the History and Present Status of Preferential Voting in State Direct Primary Systems." *The Southwestern Social Science Quarterly* 18 (1): 64–67.

Werner, Carl G. 1928. *Charter (adopted 1928) and Code of Ordinances (revised June 18, 1928) of the City of Cincinnati*. Cincinnati: Spokesmen.

White, Steven. 2019. *World War II and American Racial Politics: Public Opinion, the Presidency, and Civil Rights Advocacy*. New York: Cambridge University Press.

Wickham-Jones, Mark. 2018. *Whatever Happened to Party Government?: Controversies in American Political Science.* Ann Arbor: University of Michigan Press.

Williams, Oliver P., and Charles R. Adrian. 1959. "The Insulation of Local Politics under the Nonpartisan Ballot." *American Political Science Review* 53 (4): 1052–63.

Wills-Otero, Laura. 2009. "Electoral Systems in Latin America: Explaining the Adoption of Proportional Representation Systems during the Twentieth Century." *Latin American Politics and Society* 51 (3): 33–58.

Wilson, James Q. 1962. *The Amateur Democrat: Club Politics in Three Cities.* Chicago: University of Chicago Press.

Winter, William O. 1982. "The Long, Unhappy Life of the Hare System in Boulder." Paper presented at the Annual Meeting of the American Political Science Association, September.

Wolraich, Michael. 2014. *Unreasonable Men: Theodore Roosevelt and the Republican Rebels Who Created Progressive Politics.* New York: St. Martin's Press.

Zeller, Belle, and Hugh A. Bone. 1948. "The Repeal of PR in New York City: Ten Years in Retrospect." *American Political Science Review* 42 (6): 1127–48.

Zimmerman, Joseph J., Bernard Grofman, Arend Lijphart, and Leon Weaver. 1986. "George H. Hallett, Jr." *PS: Political Science & Politics* 19 (1): 127–28.

Zingher, Joshua N. 2020. "On the Measurement of Social Class and Its Role in Shaping White Vote Choice in the 2016 U.S. Presidential Election." *Electoral Studies* 64: 102–19.

Index